Birding Texas
with Children

Evault "Bosie" Boswell

Republic of Texas Press

Library of Congress Cataloging-in-Publication Data

Boswell, Evault "Bosie"
    Birding Texas with children / Evault "Bosie" Boswell.
        p.   cm.
    Includes bibliographical references (p.).
    ISBN 1-55622-840-6 (pbk.)
    1. Bird watching—Texas—Guidebooks.   2. Texas—Guidebooks.   I. Title.

QL684.T4 B67   2001   2001018161
598'.07'234764—dc21   CIP

Printed in the United States of America

Photos by author except where otherwise noted.

ISBN 1-55622-840-6
10 9 8 7 6 5 4 3 2 1
0105

All inquiries for volume purchases of this book should be addressed to Wordware
Publishing, Inc., at 2320 Los Rios Boulevard, Plano, Texas 75074. Telephone
inquiries may be made by calling:

(972) 423-0090

Contents

How To Use This Guide vii
Acknowledgments ix
Introduction xi
    Getting Started. 1
    Preparation. 1
    Trip Planning. 2
    How to Dress. 3
    Field Guides 3
    Trip Guides. 4
    Travel Information 5
    Dining 6
    Binoculars and Spotting Scopes 6
    First-Aid Kit 7
    Keep a Log/Scrapbook of Your Trip 8
    Code of Birding Ethics 8

Trans-Pecos

Alpine 14
Balmorhea. 16
Big Bend National Park 17
Del Rio 19
El Paso. 21
Fort Davis 25
Marathon 27
Presidio 28

Panhandle

Abilene 32
Amarillo 35
Canyon 35
Big Spring 39
Dalhart 41
Lubbock 44
Monahans 47

Contents

Muleshoe 49
Odessa 51
Pecos 53
Quitaque 55
Quanah 56
San Angelo 58

Edwards Plateau

Austin 62
Boerne 65
Burnet 67
Fredericksburg 70
Johnson City 73
Kerrville 75
Lago Vista 77
Leakey 79

Northern Plains

Brownwood 84
Cleburne 86
Dallas 88
Denton 91
Fairfield 93
Fort Worth 95
Glen Rose 98
Graham 101
Greenville 103
Hillsboro 106
Lewisville 108
McKinney 110
Mineral Wells 112
Plano 114
Sherman 117
Sulphur Springs 119
Waco 121
Wichita Falls 124

Pineywoods Region

Huntsville 128
Jasper 130
Livingston 132
Longview 134

Lufkin 136
Nacogdoches 136
Marshall 141
Tyler 144

Central Plains Region
Austin 148
Eagle Lake 148
Edna 149
Gonzales 151
La Grange 153
Taylor 155

Upper Coast Region
Brazoria County 158
Bay City and Matagorda County 162
Beaumont/Orange/Port Arthur 164
Galveston 167
Bolivar Peninsula. 168
Houston 172
Palacios. 175
Port Lavaca/Calhoun County. 177

Coastal Bend
Aransas Pass 182
Corpus Christi 184
Kingsville. 189
Port Aransas 192
Rockport-Fulton Area 195

Brush Country
Alice 200
Goliad 202
Laredo 204
San Antonio 207
Three Rivers 212

Rio Grande Region
Brownsville. 216
Edinburg 220
Harlingen 221

Contents

McAllen 224
Mission. 225
Weslaco 227
Zapata 230

Appendix A — Bibliography 233
Appendix B — Binoculars and Scopes 235
Appendix C — State Park Camping and Recreational Facilities . . . 237
Appendix D — Trip Planning Form. 240
Appendix E — Bird Clubs and Organizations 242
Appendix F — Rare Bird Alerts 244
Appendix G — The Great Texas Coastal Birding Trail 245

Index of Attractions. 247
Index of Birds. 253

How To Use This Guide

1. **Decide on the area you want to visit.** Your preference may be decided by several factors:
   a. A personal connection to the area (relatives, friends, etc.)
   b. The variety of bird species you wish to see
   c. A particular entertainment, educational, or historical site you want to visit
   d. Budget considerations

2. **Establish a time.** The time of the year for your family birding expedition may depend on:
   a. School schedules
   b. Vacation times
   c. Availability of recreation, educational, and historical sites you may want to visit

   Note: Birding is always better during the spring or fall migration periods.

3. **Determine the length of your trip.**
   a. Full week
   b. Weekend
   c. Extended weekend
   d. One day

4. **Gather information.** Prepare by obtaining the materials recommended in this guide:
   a. Order a copy of the Texas Department of Transportation Travel Guide.
   b. Purchase a copy of *Birding Texas* by Roland Wauer and Mark Elwonger
   c. Decide on one or more field guides and purchase them.
   d. Contact the Chamber of Commerce in the area you plan to visit and request information.

    e. Check the birding hotlines in the area you plan to visit.

5. **Make the necessary motel or camping reservations.**

    a. Call far enough in advance of your trip to insure getting the accommodations you need.

    b. Be certain to inquire as to the services offered. i.e., kids stay free, free breakfast, etc.

    c. Remember that from the time this guide was written to the time you purchased it, it is probable that some phone numbers and even addresses have changed. Where possible, we have listed toll-free phone numbers that are less susceptible to change, as are web sites and e-mail addresses.

6. **Complete the Trip Planning Form in Appendix D of this guide.**

Plans can always be changed if opportunities dictate, but it is best to start with a solid plan and stick to it as much as possible.

Acknowledgments

Many thanks to Roland H. Wauer and Mark A. Elwonger for permission to use their book *Birding Texas* as a guideline. *Birding Texas With Children* is designed to be used in conjunction with their publication. Although many other resources were consulted, *Birding Texas* is the most up-to-date book on the market to be used as a trip guide when birding in the state, and we have outlined this book to correspond to the birding areas as they are listed in that guide. Also thanks to the Texas Department of Transportation (TxDot) and Mike Talley for permission to use information from the *Texas State Travel Guide, 2000* and *Texas Accommodations Guide, 2000* and "Texas Official Travel Map."

Photos from the collection of George Harmon.

Introduction

Birdwatchers have even changed their name, for those who seek out birds to identify and enjoy now prefer to be called "Birders." Gone is the stereotype of a strangely dressed creature, tramping through the woods with a pair of binoculars around its neck. Today, birders come in all sizes and ages.

Birding is the fastest growing pastime in the United States and has blossomed into a multimillion-dollar tourist industry that attracts all ages and genders. More and more vacation spots in Texas are including birding information in their brochures, and although certain areas such as the Gulf Coast and the Rio Grande Valley are prime birding habitats, every part of the state has birding potential.

From young children to senior adults, the pastime varies from expensive tours led by professional birders to those who only observe the winged wonders at their backyard feeders.

Birding can also be a family-oriented vacation, for Texas is the leader of the nation in species to be seen.

To make birding both enjoyable and educational for children, a trip needs to be carefully planned for maximum production. Small children may be only able to bird in wilderness areas for short periods of time. Therefore, this guide is designed to tell parents not only where to bird with their children, but where to go for other family entertainment in the area being visited, such as museums, historical sites, and entertainment centers. No effort has been made to include all of the possible birding locations, but the sites have been chosen that would lend themselves to birding with children. This is also true of the attractions that may be visited, and it is recommended that a copy of the Texas Department of Transportation's *Texas State Travel Guide* be obtained for a more comprehensive list of museums, historical sites, and entertainment centers.

It should also be noted that information is constantly changing, particularly phone numbers and area codes. For this reason, we have included as many toll free numbers as possible as they are less likely to change, and whenever possible, web site and e-mail addresses have been included.

Also included are recommendations for motels and campgrounds that are family oriented, and dining facilities that range from inexpensive, medium priced, and high priced. Again, this list does not include all the accommodations available in a given area, but is representative of the types and price ranges available. Motel prices are also subject to change and particularly in resort areas will vary a great deal according to the season. Picnic locations that can be utilized for lunch breaks in the field are also noted.

Getting Started

Preparation

One of the best ways to interest children in birding is to teach them to care for birds right in their own backyard. Birds need three things: food, water, and habitat. Much of their source for food and water has been curtailed by suburban development around large cities, and the destruction of birding habitat has been enormous.

The National Wildlife Federation has a program for developing backyard habitat for birds, and their address is listed in the resource section of this book.

Teaching children to provide food and water for the birds in their backyard will give them a head start on identification of the species and will help them learn to use binoculars.

Every part of Texas is a birding area, and taking children on short field trips in the area in which they live will build in them a respect for wildlife and a desire to learn more about birds.

Most cities or areas have bird groups such as Audubon clubs which hold meetings with programs about birds and conduct field trips in the local area. Contacting them will not only help you learn where to go locally to bird, but participating in one or more of their trips will expose you to the wonderful pastime of birding. The birding organizations in Texas are listed in Appendix E of this book.

There are a number of videos available on birding. One of the best is David Attenborough's *The Life of Birds*. Although this set of six videos costs about $89 and covers birds of the world, it is very comprehensive and entertaining as it covers subjects such as "The Mastery of Flight," "The Insatiable Appetite," "Fishing for a Living," "Signals and Songs," "Finding Partners," "Demands of the Egg," "The Problems of Parenthood," and "Limits of Endurance."

The Audubon Society's five-tape video set of the *Birds of North America* allows you to hear and identify 505 birds by video and is priced at $29.95.

A number of books are listed in the resource section, but one of the best is *Everything You Never Learned About Birds*, by Rebecca

Rupp, which was published in 1995 by R.R. Donnelley & Sons Company.

Two books, written by Donald and Lillian Stokes, are excellent resource material for young people. *Back Yard Birding* and *The Hummingbird Book* are well written from a depth of knowledge of birding.

The bibliography in Appendix A of this book lists a number of other good books on birding.

Trip Planning

Texas is home, either permanently or temporarily, to three-fourths of all the birds of North America, and birding potential exists in every part of the state. However, birding with your family will be enhanced by a few simple guidelines.

Where you go may be determined by your own personal desires to visit a particular part of the state or experience another adventure apart from birding such as a theme park or a historical site. It may simply be decided because a visit to grandma's house is a part of your plan. Whatever your goal, advance planning of your trip will enhance your children's enjoyment of the adventure.

Once a destination has been chosen and a time to go decided, you can refer to the section of this book that covers the area and learn the birding spots for that particular part of the state, although only selected birding hot spots are listed. In the bibliography section of this book, birder's guide books are listed that expand on the birding possibilities in a particular area. How many you visit will be determined by the time and budget you have allowed for the trip.

When to go may be decided by vacation times, but keep in mind that more birds will probably be seen during the fall and spring migrations, and many areas have special events, such as the hawk migration from South Texas, the Hummingbird Festival in Rockport, and the Migration Celebration in Brazosport. Spring break is not a good time to visit coastal sites.

In Appendix D, you will find a checklist to help you plan your trip.

How to Dress

Clothing to be worn will depend for the most part on the season of the year you plan your trip, but certain rules apply all year. 1. Dress comfortably. If your trip is going to take you into brush or wooded areas, long pants are preferred. 2. Prepare for bad weather. In Texas, temperatures, rainfall, and wind can vary a great deal from day to day. Rain gear is a must. 3. Poor fitting shoes can make hiking on trails a hardship. Most birders prefer tennis shoes or hiking boots, and be sure socks fit properly and are changed daily. 4. A cap or head covering of some sort is recommended.

Field Guides

Field guides are books that list the birds by "family groups," beginning with loons and grebes. They contain pictures of the birds, and identifying marks known as "field marks" are listed along with information of habitat, feeding habits, nesting, and sound identification.

Although a number of field guides are listed in Appendix A, there are four basic guides that are recommended for novice or inexperienced birders. If you have been birding for some time, you may have your own favorite.

Birds of North America: A Golden Guide to Field Identification
Published by Golden Books Publishing Company, this guide is excellent for beginning birders as it contains splendid drawings of the birds, along with habitat, migration, nesting, and sound information. It also contains small maps that indicate the birds' range and migration routes. This book costs about $13.95.

A Field Guide to the Birds of Texas, this is a new edition of the old favorite
Text and illustrations are by Roger Tory Peterson, the guru of all birders. It is published by Houghton Mifflin Company and costs $21.95. This guide specializes in species found in Texas and adjacent states. Peterson includes little marks that highlight field marks on birds.

National Geographic Field Guide to the Birds of North America
   This guide is out in a new edition and the cost is about $19.95.
   Like the Golden book, it has excellent drawings of the birds, with
   a more comprehensive description and maps showing the birds'
   breeding range, winter range, and year-round range. It is an
   excellent guide but larger than the other two and a little bulky to
   carry in the field, but it can be a great reference guide.

The Sibley Guide to Birds (Audubon Society Nature Guides Series)
   This newest guide was prepared by the staff of the Audubon
   Society and is the most comprehensive field guide to date.
   Illustrations are by David Sibley and over 800 birds are included.
   The pictures show the birds in flight as well as perched. The cost
   is about $35 from Amazon.com or it can be purchased at most
   bookstores.

Other field guides are listed in the resource section. Listed below are
beginner's guides for very young children, which have listings of
only the more common or popular birds in the state.

Beginner's Guide to Birds, Eastern and Western, Stokes ($7.95)

All the Backyard Birds, Jack L. Griggs ($7.95)

Peterson First Guides to Birds, Roger Tory Peterson ($5.95)

Trip Guides

Several books have been published that can be used as a guide in
planning your trip.

A Birder's Guide to the Texas Coast
by Harold R. Holt
   The guide covers the entire length of the Texas coast (640 miles)
   from Port Arthur to Brownsville. It includes detailed advice on
   finding birds and lists not only the where to go, but gives exact
   mileage from one birding spot to another and lists the birds that
   might be seen at a particular time of the year. Published in 1993,
   this guide is still pretty well up to date as far as the primary
   birding areas on the coast are concerned.

A Birder's Guide to the Rio Grande Valley of Texas
by Harold R. Holt
> Both of these guides are remakes of the old James A. Lane guides published in 1973. This American Birding Association sponsored guide covers the area from Brownsville, Texas, and follows the route of the Rio Grande River all the way to El Paso. It includes details on where to bird in areas that include the Big Bend National Park and the Davis Mountains, along with the Edwards Plateau.

Birder's Guide to Texas
by Edward A. Kutac
> Unlike the Holt books, this guide covers the entire state of Texas with very good descriptions of birding areas and list of possible birds to be seen in each. However, this book was first published in 1982 and updated in 1989 and is somewhat dated.

Birding Texas
by Roland H. Wauer & Mark A. Elwonger
> This is the most comprehensive and up-to-date guide on the market today. It covers the entire state and goes into detail on not only the major birding areas, but the local hot spots as well. It also includes an appendix on the status and distribution of Texas species. If you are going to buy only one guide, buy this one.
>
> It features 120 well-defined maps of each of the more than 200 sites presented and a 46-page distribution chart that tells when and where birds occur in the state.
>
> A special feature of the book is a gallery of Texas specialties drawn by artist Mimi Hoppe Wolf and sections on pelagic birding and the Great Texas Birding Trail.

Travel Information

Perhaps the best travel guide available is the *Texas State Travel Guide*, which is published each year by the Texas Department of Transportation, Travel and Information Division, 150 E. Riverside Drive, Austin, Texas 78704. A map of Texas, along with general information on travel including airports, information on climate, rest stops, speed limits, insurance, and auto safety with children are included. The cities of Texas are listed with information on tourist sites to be seen in the area.

Another great book is *Exploring Texas With Children*, by Sharry Buckner and published by Republic of Texas Press. Divided into sections, each city that is included has a list of locations such as museums, historical sites, entertainment centers, and special events.

Dining

The best time to start any birding day is early in the morning. Many motels, and particularly those that cater to families, offer a continental breakfast or "children eat free" as part of the room fee. When making reservations, be sure to check on what they serve, as some only have coffee and doughnuts, while others will have cereal and fruit, along with juice and milk.

National chains such as IHOP and Denny's are open 24 hours a day and have children's menus. McDonald's is another potential breakfast location, and their restrooms are always clean.

Lunch can be an inexpensive picnic packed the night before and shared at a picnic location in the field. Of if you prefer, one of the many fast food restaurants can provide a quick and inexpensive meal for everyone in the family.

Most of the locations listed in this book have an abundance of restaurants, from fast food to expensive dining. In each section, some of the restaurants listed are a little different from the ordinary. Some are expensive for families, but splurging on a good meal can be a real treat after ham and cheese sandwiches out of a cooler on a wooden picnic bench.

But the evening meal need not be expensive. For instance, CiCi's Pizza charges $3.99 for all-you-can-eat pizza and salad and $2.29 for children under ten and under four are free. Even upscale restaurants usually have a children's menu.

Binoculars and Spotting Scopes

Binoculars can range from $19.95 to thousands of dollars, but for the beginner, it is best to purchase an inexpensive pair. If a child develops a greater interest in birding, better binoculars can be bought later. Discount stores generally carry inexpensive binoculars. Prices, of course are subject to change. These were found at K-Mart:

Bushnell's Powerview, Jr. 4 x 30 for very small children are priced at $17.99.

Tasco's Compact with rubber armor #165BD are excellent for children at $39.99.

Vanquard's DR 1025, 10 x 25 are very small and have a wide angle for $39.99.

Vanguard's BR 7350, 10 x 25 are full-size glasses and are priced at $49.99.

Bushnell's Power View, 10 x 25 are small, priced at $59.99.

Vanguard's BF 2050, 20 x 50 are high powered for only $69.99.

More expensive binoculars are available from a variety of firms, and many of these can be found on the web:

Bushnell Binoculars: www.bushnell.com

Bird Watchers: birdwatchers.com or call 1-800-981-2473

Optic Mall: e-mail optics@opticmail.com, or call 612-730-9020

An extensive list of binoculars is also included in Appendix B.

Spotting scopes can represent a major investment in equipment. Generally they are more useful in areas such as lakes or a seashore where birds are more likely to stay in one place for a period of time. Taking a scope on a trail can be a burden, and in most cases they are not effective in heavily wooded or brushy birding areas. On the other hand, they can be very helpful in identifying birds that are out of range of binoculars.

First-Aid Kit

Be sure and have a first-aid kit in your vehicle. Along with the normal bandages and ointments, check to be certain you have insect bite ointment, sun-screen lotion, and treatment for poison ivy and poison oak. It is a good idea to be sure each member of the family knows how to recognize poison ivy and poison oak. Texas is home to several species of poisonous snakes, and children need to learn how to protect themselves from being bitten. At least one adult in the group should be aware of procedures to follow in case of snakebite.

The state also has a generous supply, particularly during the summer months, of chiggers and ticks. If anyone in the family is allergic to wasp or bee stings, a treatment kit should be included. In some areas of Texas, mosquitos can be mistaken for birds. A good supply of bottled water in a cooler is also a good idea.

Keep a Log/Scrapbook of Your Trip

Long trips in the car between birding areas can be boring for children. Besides the normal list of birds seen, have the children collect area bird lists; maps of the area; souvenirs from museums, historical sites, and recreational activities; even family snapshots; and paste them in a scrapbook. Another good idea is to keep a journal of the trip, which can be done in the motel or camp in the evening when the day's birding is done.

Code of Birding Ethics

The American Birding Association has established a code of birding ethics. Teaching your children to respect the welfare of the birds, as well as the property of others, is a very important part of birding.

1. Promote the welfare of birds and their environment.

   a. Support the protection of important bird habitat.

   b. To avoid stressing birds or exposing them to danger, exercise restraint and caution during observation, photography, sound recording, or filming. Limit the use of recordings and other methods of attracting birds, and never use such methods in heavily birded areas or for attracting any species that is Threatened, Endangered, or of Special Concern, or is rare in your local area. Keep well back from nests and nesting colonies, roosts, display areas, and important feeding sites. In such sensitive areas, if there is a need for extended observation, photography, filming, or recording, try to use a blind or hide and take advantage of natural cover. Use artificial light sparingly for filming or photography, especially for close-ups.

   c. Before advertising the presence of a rare bird, evaluate the potential for disturbance to the bird, its surroundings, and other people in the area, and proceed only if access can be controlled, disturbance can be minimized, and permission has been obtained from private landowners. The sites of rare nesting birds should be divulged only to the proper conservation authorities.

    d. Stay on roads, trails, and paths where they exist; otherwise keep habitat disturbance to a minimum.

2. Respect the law and the right of others.

    a. Do not enter private property without the owner's explicit permission.

    b. Follow all laws, rules, and regulations governing use of roads and public areas, both at home and abroad.

    c. Practice common courtesy in contacts with other people. Your exemplary behavior will generate goodwill with birders and nonbirders alike.

3. Ensure that feeders, nest structures, and other artificial bird environments are safe.

    a. Keep dispensers, water, and food clean and free of decay or disease. It is important to feed birds continually during harsh weather.

    b. Maintain and clean nest structures regularly.

    c. If you are attracting birds to an area, ensure the birds are not exposed to predation from cats and other domestic animals or dangers posed by artificial hazards.

4. Group birding, whether organized or impromptu, requires special care. Each individual in the group, in addition to the obligations spelled out in Items #1 and #2, has responsibilities as a group member.

    a. Respect the interests, rights, and skills of fellow birders, as well as those of people participating in other legitimate outdoor activities. Freely share your knowledge and experience except where code 1(c) applies. Be especially helpful to beginning birders.

    b. If you witness unethical birding behavior, assess the situation and intervene if you think it is prudent. When interceding, inform the person(s) of the inappropriate action and attempt, within reason, to have it stopped. If the behavior continues, document it and notify the appropriate individuals or organizations.

Group leaders' responsibilities (amateur and professional trips and tour):

c. Be an exemplary ethical role model for the group. Teach through word and example.

d. Keep groups to a size that limits impact on the environment and does not interfere with others using the same area.

e. Ensure everyone in the group knows of and practices the code.

f. Learn and inform the group of any special circumstances applicable to the areas being visited (e.g., no tape recording allowed).

g. Acknowledge that professional tour companies bear a special responsibility to place the welfare of birds and the benefits of public knowledge ahead of the company's commercial interests. Ideally, leaders should keep track of tour sightings, document unusual occurrences, and submit records to appropriate organizations.

The Code of Birding Ethics is a product of the American Birding Association, P.O. Box 6599, Colorado Springs, CO 80934-6599; 800-859-2473 or 719-578-1614; fax 800-246-3329 or 719-578-1480; e-mail, member@aba.org. Reprinted by permission.

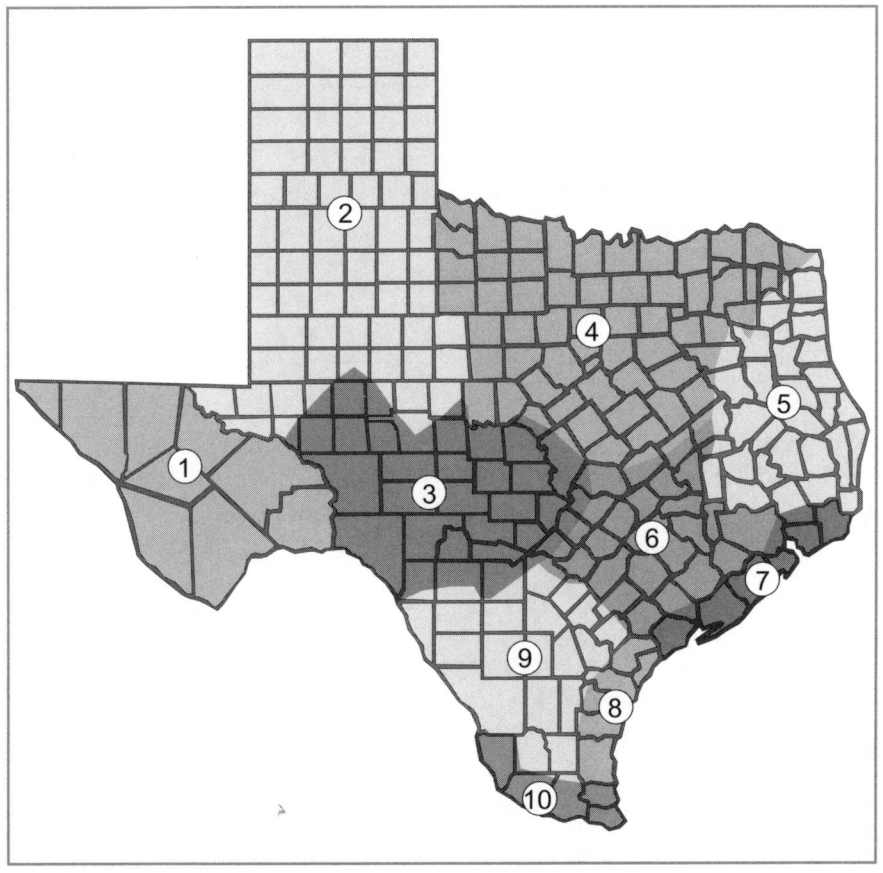

Birding areas of Texas

1. Trans-Pecos
2. Panhandle
3. Edwards Plateau
4. Northern Plains
5. Pineywoods

6. Central Plains
7. Upper Coast
8. Coastal Bend
9. Brush Country
10. Rio Grande Valley

(Source: *Birding Texas*, by Roland H. Wauer
and Mark A. Elwonger)

Trans-Pecos

curve-billed
thrasher

Alpine

Chamber of Commerce
106 N. Third Street
800-561-3735
http://www.alpinetexas.com

This city is the home of Sul Ross University, named for a Civil War general and governor of the state, Lawrence Sullivan Ross. There are not many great birding spots in Alpine, but because of its central location and size, it can be a good home base from which to visit other nearby birding areas.

Birding

Hwy. U.S. 67 & U.S. 90

Alpine is located in the center of the birding areas in the southern Trans-Pecos. Driving along either of these highways in winter, you may see several species of hawks, including Red-tailed, Ferruginous, Rough-legged, and Harris's. The Prairie Falcon is usually seen northwest of Fort Davis on SH 118. Birding along the roadsides may produce Grasshopper, Brewer's, Clay-colored, and Chipping Sparrows, along with Dark-eyed Junco, Lark Bunting, and both McCown's and Chestnut-collared Longspurs. At the rest stop on U.S. 90 about 20 miles from Alpine, summer birds may include Bushtit, Cassin's Kingbird, Vermilion Flycatcher, Black Phoebe, Warbling Vireo, Painted Bunting, and Blue Grosbeak. At Paisano Pass, which is west of Alpine on U.S. 90, several species of swallows may be seen, along with White-throated Swift.

Attractions

Apache Trading Post

A rustic log cabin with a family oriented gift shop features Big Bend collectibles and books on the history and geology of the Big Bend, Mexico, and Indian heritage. Here you can get the lowdown on the mysterious Marfa lights, and the kids will enjoy meeting "Quicksilver Pete," a burro that loves to have his picture made, and Sasha the Wonder Dog.

Woodward Agate Ranch

Let the children pick up their own souvenirs that may include red plume, pom-pom, and a variety of other Texas agates, along with jasper, labradorite, feldspar, calcite, precious opal, and others. There is a fee and you pay by the pound, so be careful, as some of these rocks can get pretty heavy, but it is fun. Located 18 miles south of Alpine on Texas 118.

Festivals

February: Texas Cowboy Poetry Gathering, phone 915-837-2326

Motels

Alpine Inn, 2000 East Hwy. 90, phone 915-837-3417

Best Western Alpine Classic, 2401 East Hwy. 90, phone
915-837-1530

Highland Inn, 1404 East Hwy. 90, phone 915-837-5811

Ramada Limited Alpine, 2800 West Hwy. 90, phone 915-837-1100

Sunday House Motor Inn, 1440 East Hwy. 90, phone
915-837-3363

Dining

Fast food includes, Dairy Queen, McDonald's, Pizza Hut, Sonic,
and Subway

Alpine's Little Mexico, 204 W. Murphy

Frontier Barbeque, 2000 East Hwy. 90

La Casita Restaurant, 1102 E. Ave. I

Longhorn Mesquite Grill, 801 N. 5th

Ponderosa Inn Restaurant, E. Hwy. 90

Twin Peaks Restaurant, 2700 W. Hwy. 90 (201 N. Orange)

Balmorhea

State Park
915-375-2370

Balmorhea is a great place to take a family. It features one of the largest man-made swimming pools fed by springs (22 to 26 million gallons per day). There is room for everyone in the 62,000-square-foot pool, and the state park has motel, camping, restrooms, picnic areas, and playground facilities. Another good place to make your home base while in the area.

Balmorhea Lake

Known as the Oasis of West Texas, this 600-acre spring-fed lake serves as a reservoir for the surrounding agriculture area and is a haven for many water birds. In winter, a scope will be a great help in birding from the north levee and from the dam. Birds you might see are Common Loon; Pied-billed, Eared, Western, and Clark's Grebes; American White Pelican; Great Blue Heron; Green Heron; and Great, Snowy, and Cattle Egrets. The shallow pond on the north side of the levee road will be a good place to see an assortment of shore birds, including American Avocet, Black-necked Stilt, both Greater and Lesser Yellowlegs, and Common Snipe. In the fields around the lake, you can see several migrating grassland birds, including Baird's Sparrow and Smith's Longspur. *Birding Texas* by Roland Wauer and Mark Elwonger states that the "Lillian's" Meadowlark, which is a resident here, may soon by recognized as a species of specific status.

Balmorhea State Park

The biggest feature of the state park is the super-duper swimming pool, but a number of birds can be seen in this relatively small area. The best time to bird here is winter or spring, when you may see such birds as Inca Dove, Black-chinned Hummingbird, Ladder-backed Woodpecker, Scissor-tailed and Vermillion Flycatcher, Curve-billed Thrasher, and Pyrrhuloxia.

Attractions

Balmorhea State Park

The only place to stay, and the kids will love the swimming pool and playground. Plan on preparing your own meals. A great place to relax. Phone 915-375-2370 for reservations.

Big Bend National Park

Park Service Headquarters
P.O. Box 129
915-477-2251

Although one of the premier birding areas in Texas, it would be well to remember that this area can be very hot in the summer, and children should be urged to drink a lot of water and take special precautions against the heat and sun. However, a number of places in the park offer easy, even sit-down birding areas where many birds can be seen with little effort. Depending on the time of year and the age of the children, long and difficult hikes such as the Window Trail should perhaps be avoided. The primary target bird here is the Colima Warbler, but it is usually found at higher altitudes, reached by uphill hiking or horseback.

Birding

This is an expansive park and bird worthy and can hardly be seen in one day, but even a short visit can be productive. Start at Panther Junction at the park headquarters and obtain a map and bird list. Be sure and have your copy of *Birding Texas* handy, for if there ever was an expert on the Big Bend, it is Roland Wauer, who has written several books on the subject. Wauer wrote an earlier book *Birds of the Big Bend National Park and Vicinity*, which is available at the park headquarters at Panther Junction.

Rio Grande Village: A tremendous place for family birding! Within a short distance of each other, you will find several prime birding habitats. In the southeastern corner of the campgrounds, you will find a nature trail where spring migrants can be found, and in the morning you may see the fastest bird in the world, the

Peregrine Falcon, along the river. After dark, several owls can be found including the tiny Elf Owl. Perhaps the brightest of all birds, the Vermillion Flycatcher is common at the park. This is also a good place for a picnic lunch, and there is a store for those things you might have forgotten to bring.

Daniel Ranch and Cottonwood Grove: From the camp-grounds, you can drive to the west end of the area and bird the Daniel Ranch. Several water birds can be seen along the river, and nesting birds include Black Phoebe and Northern Rough-winged Swallow. In the summer, Cliff and Cave Swallows will be present. Look overhead among the cottonwoods for Gray Hawks, and Black Hawks have been seen here. The kids will love the clownish Acorn Woodpecker and their acorn-filled tree trunks.

Dugout Wells: On the way back to Panther Junction from the campgrounds, stop at Dugout Wells, an oasis in the middle of cactus and brush. The water attracts a great number of birds. This is a place where birding is easy.

Boot Springs: A spring or summer hike up to Boot Springs, elevation 6,300 feet, will probably get you a look at the Colima Warbler, but it is a strenuous trip, particularly for small children.

Window Trail: A great place to see birds, including Band-tailed Pigeon, and the trip is all downhill on the way in, but uphill on the way out. There are better places to take children to bird, but the trail can be very rewarding

Sam Nails Ranch: An excellent spot to sit down in the cool shade and wait for the birds to come to you. There are even benches to sit on across from the spring, and sooner or later such species as Scott's Oriole, Pyrrhuloxia, Curve-billed Thrasher, Blue Grosbeak, and Ash-throated Flycatcher may appear. In winter you can see the Green-tailed Towhee, and Varied Bunting has been seen here. The park checklist includes 37 warbler species.

Motels

Within the park there is lodge, restaurant, and gift shop in the Chisos Basin. Reservations are a must. Contact the park for more information. See Appendix C for campgrounds and RV facilities.

Big Bend Motor Inn, Hwy. 118 and FM 170, phone
  1-800-848-BEND (very good and clean)
Chisos Mountains Lodge, Big Bend National Park, phone
  915-477-2291
Lajitas on the Rio Grande Motel, Terlinqua, phone 1-800-944-9907

Dining

Best to take a picnic lunch to the park, or buy what you need at the grocery store in the campground area. The dining room at the lodge has delicious and reasonable meals. If you stay in Study Butte, a trip to the Starlight Theatre in the evening is a must. Located in Terlinqua in an old theater, the food is great and the place is birder friendly. The Big Bend Motor Inn in Study Butte has a restaurant next door that serves a great breakfast. The Roadrunner Deli on Hwy. 118 can fix a sandwich to go.

Del Rio
Chamber of Commerce
1915 Ave. F
830-775-3551
800-889-8149
http://www.drchamber.com

If you want to visit across the border in old Mexico, Del Rio makes a great place to start with local transportation making regular crossings to Ciudad Acuña, where you will find the usual assortment of gift shops selling wrought iron, jewelry, leather craft, pottery, and souvenirs.

Birding

Amistad National Recreation Area

This vast recreational area is a popular site for fishing and boating on the 67,000-acre reservoir that has 850 miles of shoreline. Probably the best birding area for children will be found at sites in the side canyons on Spur 406, where there is a campground, and such species as Brown-crested Flycatcher, Long-billed Thrasher, Olive Sparrow, Scaled Quail, Golden-fronted Woodpecker, and Orchard and Bullock's Orioles may be seen in the spring and summer. The winter is a good time to see water birds, including a number of species of ducks.

Seminole Canyon State Park

Located 9 miles west of Comstock, this may be the best place to bird with children because there is easy access to areas where canyon and desert birds can be found. In the spring and summer, a hike up the canyon can produce White-throated Swift, both Cliff and Cave Swallows, and both Cactus and Canyon Wrens.

Moore Park

A great place for an early morning bird walk, except on weekends, when it can be extremely crowded in this park that lies on San Felipe Creek, off of U.S. 90. Green Kingfisher, Black Phoebe, Vermilion Flycatcher, and Great Kiskadee Flycatcher are a few of the birds you might see.

Attractions

Whitehead Memorial Museum

Depicts the life and legends of the southwest and includes an old trading post of the period and is the burial site of Judge Roy Bean. The museum and exhibits will take about two hours to see. 1308 S. Main St. For information, phone 830-774-7568.

Seminole Canyon Indian Pictographs

Tours of ancient pictographs and archeological sites include a picture of a mountain lion believed to be more than 4,000 years old. Contact the Seminole State Park for information on the tours.

Motels

Amistad Lodge, Hwy. 90 W., phone 830-775-8591

Best Western Inn of Del Rio, 810 Ave. F., phone 800-336-3537

Days Inn, 3808 Hwy. 90 W., phone 800-325-2525

Holiday Inn Express, 3616 Ave. F., phone 830-775-2933

Motel 6, 2115 Ave. F., phone 830-774-2115

Super 8 Motel, 3811 Hwy. 90 W., phone 830-775-7414

Dining

Fast food includes Dairy Queen, Golden Chick, McDonald's, Pizza Hut, Sonic, Subway, and Burger King

Amistad Lodge, W. Hwy. 90 (in the motel)

CiCi's Pizza, 2205 Ave. F

Flamingo's 50's Hamburgers, 1750 Ave. F

Mr. Gatti's Pizza, 2400 Ave. F

Luby's Cafeteria, Plaza del Sol Mall, 2205 Ave. F

Sirloin Stockade, 2015 Ave. F

El Paso

Convention & Visitors Bureau
One Civic Center Plaza
800-351-6024
http://www.elpasocvb.com

The largest city in Texas on the border of Mexico, El Paso is unique not only in location, but in cultural aspects as well. Located in a mountain pass, the city is surrounded by mile-high peaks. Just across the border is Juarez, Mexico, and if you go west, you are soon in New Mexico. This area can be very hot and dry in the summer, and precautions should be taken with children.

Birding

Franklin Mountains State Park

This is open desert scrub habitat. North Franklin Peak reaches an elevation of 7,192 feet and is the top of the 24,000 acres that make up the park, which is located within the city of El Paso. There are a number of trails totaling 14 miles, but you must remember it can be very hot in the summer. However, the park can be well worth the effort, producing such resident species as Scaled and Gambel's Quail, Say's Phoebe, Verdin, Cactus and Rock Wren, Crissal Thrasher, and Pyrrhuloxia. Canyon Wren will be more often heard than seen, with their descending call ringing through the canyons. There is a picnic area at West Cottonwood Springs, and nesting Black-chinned Hummingbird may be found here, along with

Bewick's Wren. During migration, Whispering Springs Canyon trail can be best for birding, and Indigo Bunting is sometimes there in summer. A number of seedeaters can be found in the canyon bottoms, from Lazuli Bunting to Green-tailed and Spotted Towhees. Chipping, Clay-colored, Brewer's, Vesper, Lark, Lincoln's, and White-crowned Sparrows may also be seen.

Fred Hervey Water Reclamation Ponds

Roland Wauer says in *Birding Texas* that the Fred Hervey Water Reclamation Ponds may be the best birding area in the El Paso area. Heavy growth surrounds the sewage ponds, and with the nearness of the desert, a wide variety of species are drawn to the oasis. During migration, the water birds will be abundant, and 35 species of shore birds have been recorded here. Year-round water birds include Pied-billed Grebe, Mallard, Ruddy Duck, Moorhen, and American Coot.

Hueco Tanks State Park

Located east of El Paso in the Hueco Mountains; take U.S. 62/180 out of El Paso for about twenty-two miles and turn north on Hwy. 2775 for about eight miles to the park. This is rugged country. In the summer the North Mountain area will be the best place to bird for such unusual birds as White-throated Swift, Say's Phoebe, Verdin, and even Barn and Great Horned Owls. There is a picnic area here. Old stock tanks can reveal a number of birds during migration, although no water birds nest here. This 860-acre park derives its name from cliffs that form three natural amphitheaters, which contain water most of the time, thus the name hueco, which means tank in Spanish. Rock climbers love this area and can be abundant on weekends.

Attractions

Border Patrol Museum

Exhibits of equipment, documents, books, and memorabilia explain the work of the U.S. Border Patrol. 4315 Transmountain Rd. (Loop 375). Open Tues.-Sun, 9 A.M. to 5 P.M.

El Paso Saddle Blanket Trading Post

The ladies will delight in this El Paso landmark that has been in operation for twenty-five years and features blankets, rugs, Indian artifacts, and Mexican imports. Located at 601 N. Oregon.

El Paso Zoo

Recent expansion of this zoo has made it the finest in West Texas. It contains over seven hundred animals and is set in eighteen acres of natural habitat. There is an aviary where visitors can enter and observe exotic birds firsthand. 4001 E. Paisano.

El Paso Science Center

Children will love the hands-on activities that involve them in studies of solar power, motion, light, illumination, electricity, space science, computers, energy, and the human body. This is one of those places your children can experience activities that will help them in their school studies for years to come. 505 N. Santa Fe St.

El Paso Museum of History

Contains artifacts and memorabilia of the U.S. Cavalry, with charro costumes and saddles. Displays of Southwestern history from the conquistadors to Pancho Villa can be seen here. Located at 12901 Gateway West.

El Paso/Jaurez Tours

If you are interested in going into old Mexico, the best way is to take one of the air-conditioned rubber-tired trolleys that depart from the Civic Center on the hour, beginning at 9 A.M. to 4 P.M., Nov.-Mar. and 10 A.M.-5 P.M., Apr.-Oct. daily. Fiesta Tours offers trips to Juarez in minicoach buses, and hotel pick-up is available. Rancho Grande Tours have shopping tours, a trip to the Guadalupe Mission, industrial parks, country clubs, and the bullfights in season.

Western Park Museum

This museum features dioramas of ancient Indian tribes of the Southwest and has a nature trail displaying native plants. Located at 3401 Transmountain Rd. (Loop 375).

Tigua Indian Reservation

The Ysleta Del Sur Pueblo Cultural Center is operated by the Tigua Indians, who settled here in 1681. The center has a museum, gift shop, Indian social dancing, and a café.

Festivals

Southwestern International Livestock Show & Rodeo, phone 915-532-1401

Motels

Best Western-Sunland Park Inn, 1045 Sunland Park Dr., phone
  915-587-4900

Motel 6-Central, 4800 Gateway Blvd. E., phone 915-533-7521

Quality Inn, 6201 Gateway Blvd. W., phone 915-778-6611

Days Inn East, 10635 Gateway West, phone 915-595-1913

Super 8 Motels, 450 Raynolds, phone 915-771-8388

Travelodge-La Hacienda, 6400 Montana, phone 915-772-4231

Dining

As in any large city, the dining possiblities are endless, and El Paso has an abundance of fast food restaurants.

Village Inn has four locations and is a favorite for family dining.

Little Diner and Tortilla Factory, located at 7209 7th Street, is a favorite for Mexican food fans.

Avila's Mexican Food has great food in a family atmosphere at two locations.

The State Line Steaks and BBQ, 1222 Sunland Park Drive has fantastic barbecue.

Cattleman's Steakhouse is a dining experience located on a working ranch about five miles north of El Paso. If you want to splurge, this is the place to do it. Also has a children's zoo, movie sets, snake pit, Indian maze, Fort Apache, lake walk, children's playground, longhorn cattle, and buffalo. Phone 915-544-3200 for reservations.

Fort Davis

Chamber of Commerce
Box 378
800-524-3015
http://www.fortdavis.com

Fort Davis was founded in 1854 at the crossroads of the Chihuahua Trail and the route of the Overland Stage. Its dining and lodging facilities are limited, but for a birding expedition, the state park is the best place to stay.

Birding

Limpia Creek and the Davis Mountain Loop

Beginning on Hwy. 118 just north of Fort Davis, you will drive along Limpia Creek, which is lined with huge cottonwood trees. By driving slowly and stopping occasionally, you will discover many brush birds. The Common Black Hawk that has also been reported nesting in this area may be seen about 1.8 miles below the entrance to the state park. Other birds you may see along the creek include Orchard and Bullock's Orioles, House Finch, and Lesser Goldfinch. Continue to drive on Hwy. 118 until you reach the Madera Canyon picnic area. This is a most fertile spot to see birds. Nesting birds include Band-tailed Pigeon, White-throated Swift, Acorn Woodpecker, Violet-green Swallow, Bushtit, Hepatic Tanager, Stellar's Jay, Pygmy Nuthatch, and Plumbeous and Hutton's Vireo. After leaving the picnic area, which is a great place for lunch, turn left on Hwy. 166, which will eventually take you back to Hwy. 17, Fort Davis, and the park. Prairie Falcon and Golden Eagle may be seen soaring over the grasslands. This loop can be one of the most exciting drive-by birding experiences in Texas.

Davis Mountains State Park

The Davis Mountains State Park contains 2,777 acres, and the habitat ranges from pinyon-juniper-oak to grassland. There are a lot of trails, but a great many birds can be seen in the vicinity of Indian Lodge. One of those is the Montezuma Quail, which can be seen in the campground or near the Interpretive Center. Other birds resident in summer are Greater Roadrunner, Common Poorwill, Acorn Woodpecker, Black and Say's Phoebe, Cassin's Kingbird, Scrub Jay, Bushtit, and four species of wrens, Cactus, Bewick's, Canyon, and Rock.

Attractions

Fort Davis National Historic Site

Fort Davis, which is operated by the National Park Service, includes restored ruins of one of the frontier forts that protected the settlers during the movement to the west. The troopers escorted wagon trains and mail carriers through the hostile country of West Texas following the Civil War. The fort was abandoned in 1891. There is a museum that features reconstructed barracks and gives an insight into the rugged life of the era. Sound re-creation of a 19th-century military parade, bugles and hoofbeats, the clank and jangle of mounted troops, and music from bands of 1875 echo across the parade ground.

McDonald Observatory

The newest Hobby-Eberly telescope is the third largest in the world. The observatory was built in 1932 atop the 6,791-foot Mount Locke. The visitor center at the foot of Mount Locke presents daily programs from 9 A.M. to 5 P.M. Once a month visitors can look at the stars through the 107-inch telescope, but reservations must be made well in advance. Phone 915-426-3640 for more information.

Neil Museum

A unique display of toys made in Texas includes hundreds of dolls. Located in the Truehart House, built in 1898, the museum is open June to Labor Day, 10 A.M.-5 P.M.

Overland Trail Museum

Another place to give the children a lesson in the history of the United States, named for the stage trail that once passed its front door, this small museum contains pioneer ranch, trail, and law enforcement artifacts.

Motels

Fort Davis Motor Inn, Hwy. 17 North, phone 800-80-DAVIS

Hotel Limpia, Main Street on the square, phone 800-662-5517. Built in 1912, this is like stepping back in time, with wicker furniture and rocking chairs on the porches and verandas.

Indian Lodge, located at the Davis Mountain State Park, phone 915-426-3254.

Dining

There is a restaurant at Hotel Limpia and also at Indian Lodge in the park.

The Drugstore on Main Street has an old-fashioned soda fountain. They also serve sandwiches and is a great place for breakfast.

Cuevo DeLeon, Hwy. 17. Mexican food.

Desert Rose, Hwy. 17.

Mary Lou's, Hwy. 118.

Marathon
Chamber of Commerce
P.O. Box 163
915-386-4516

A gateway to the Big Bend National Park, this city sits at the cross-roads of U.S. 90 and U.S. 285 and was named by a sea captain because it reminded him of Marathon, Greece.

Birding

The Post

Located about five miles south of Marathon, this area is just south of the railroad tracks, across the highway from the Gage Hotel, and is the best year-round birding spot in the area. It is a spring-fed riparian area where you will see Mexican Duck, Scaled Quail, Golden-fronted Woodpecker, Belted Kingfisher, and both Black and Say's Phoebes. In the spring and fall, migrants can be abundant and the potential list is impressive. Black-tailed Gnatcatcher, Crissal Thrasher, Cactus Wren, and Rufous-crowned and Black-throated

Sparrows can be seen year round. Overhead Swainson's Hawk can be seen and the elusive Chihuahuan Raven is present.

Prairie Dog Colony

North of Marathon on Hwy. 385 is an extensive prairie dog colony that the children will enjoy, and you will see Burrowing Owls in the spring and summer. In the grassland surrounding the colony, you may see Scaled Quail, Killdeer, Mourning Dove, Scissor-tailed Flycatcher, Curve-billed Thrasher, Lark Sparrow, and Lark Bunting. Overhead watch for Ferruginous Hawk.

Attractions

Great Marathon Basin

A geologic area noted for the variety of outcroppings of rocks and minerals. A great place to visit if you are a rock hound.

Motels

The historic Gage Hotel, built in the 1920s, has been restored.

Dining

Traditional and Southwestern food is available in the restaurant in the Gage Hotel.

Presidio

Big Bend Ranch State Park Complex
P.O. Box 2319
915-229-3416

As the old saying goes, this is not the end of the world, but you can see it from here. Hot desert habitat located on the Rio Grande northwest of the Big Bend country supports a great many species of wildlife and birds and a hardy group of humans.

Birding

Fort Leaton State Historic Park

A great place to start, since a permit to enter the Big Bend Ranch State Park's Solitario Viewpoint Road must be obtained here. There are picnic grounds at the entrance to the fort that will reveal some interesting desert birds, such as Scaled Quail, Greater Roadrunner, Cactus Wren, and Say's Phoebe, just to name a few. Driving the Solitario Viewpoint Road you may see Pyrrhuloxia, Red-tailed Hawk overhead, Black-tailed Gnatcatcher, Loggerhead Shrike, and Rufous-crowned and Black-throated Sparrows year round. During wet seasons the stock tanks can be active, and in the surrounding grasslands, especially in the La Posta turnoff area, there will be a number of visiting seedeaters in the winter.

Big Bend Ranch State Park

This sixty-mile-long park extends southward along the Rio Grande from Presidio to Lajitas and contains nearly 300,000 acres. This is hot and arid country, and if birding in the summer, precautions should be taken to protect both children and adults from the heat. Entry to the park is by permit only, which must be obtained at the Warnock Center or Fort Leaton. A drive along Hwy. 170 out of Presido can be rewarding, especially in wet seasons, but the Tanque Lara area is dependable in all but the driest times. The list of possible sightings is extensive and well worth the effort.

Attractions

Fort Leaton State Historic Site

A massive adobe fortress was built by Ben Leaton in 1848 just after the Mexican War. Leaton operated a trade business from the fort with Indians and U.S. Army patrols. Over 40 original rooms, 24 are restored and roofed. Restoration is not complete but when finished will include frontier furnishings and interpretive exhibits of the history and culture of the area.

Motels

Three Palms Inn, phone 915-229-3211

La Siesta, phone 915-229-3611

Dining

El Alamo, North Business 67

El Oasis, located at the Three Palms Inn

El Patio, downtown on O'Reilly Street, buffet and salad bar
Sante Fe, West O'Reilly near downtown
Whistle Stop Sandwich Shop, O'Reilly, downtown

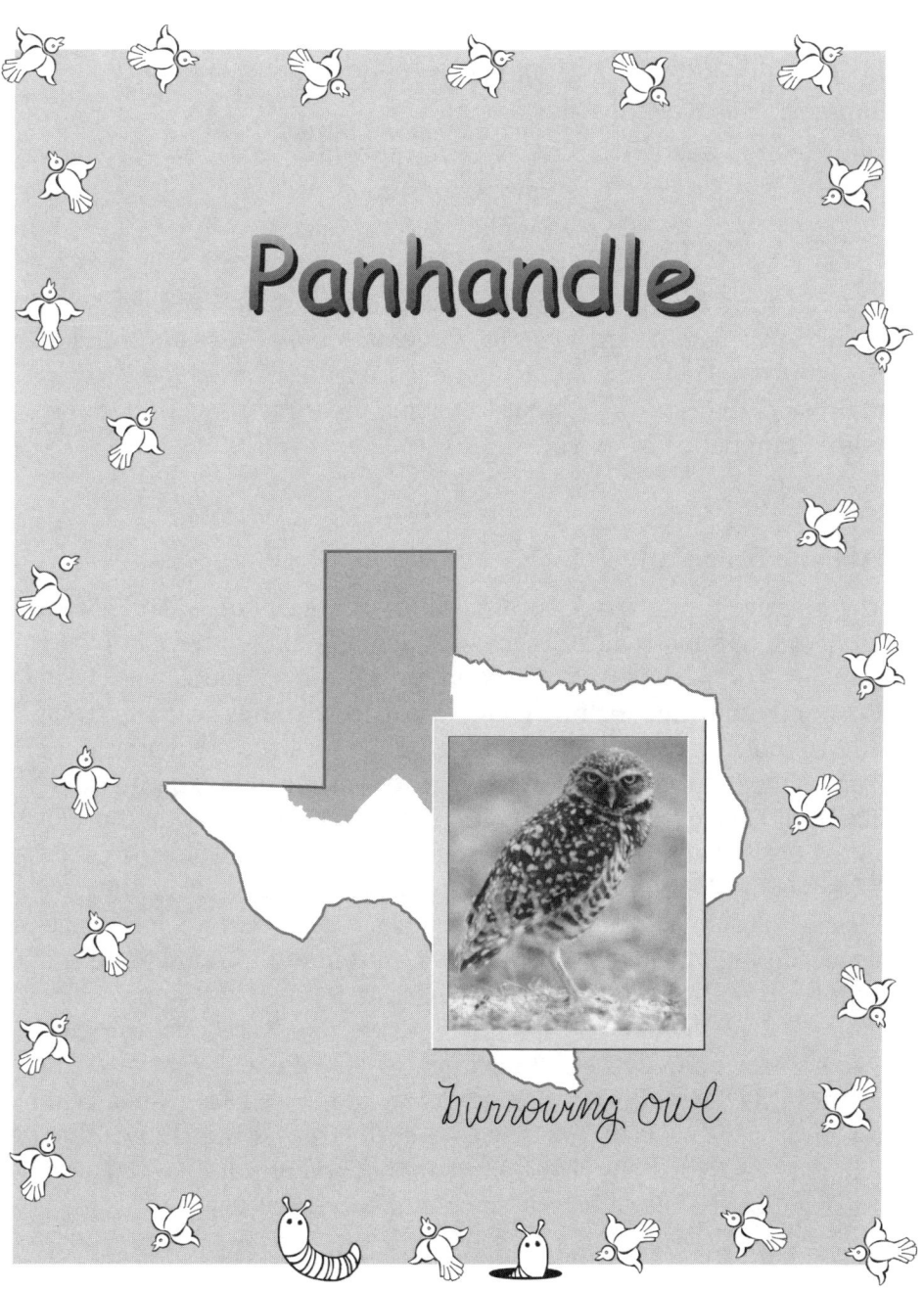

Panhandle

burrowing owl

Abilene

Convention and Visitors Bureau
1101 North 1st
800-727-7704
http://www.abilene.com/visitors
E-mail: visitors@abilene.com

The old song says, "Abilene, Abilene, prettiest town I've ever seen, folks out there don't treat you mean, in Abilene." The historic end of the Chisolm Trail, Abilene actually sits on the edge of West Texas and is a delight to visit, and it has some great places to bird, along with a number of historical sites to see.

Birding

Abilene State Park

This relatively small park, located south of the city of Abilene, has a great mix of habitat including woods, open fields, a creek, and Lake Abilene. The park is 621 acres and has all the attributes necessary for family birding, such as picnic areas, rest rooms with showers, hiking trails, and even a swimming pool. Once the campground of Comanche Indians, there is a large grove of some 4,000 pecan trees. The Elm Creek Nature Trail is the best place to bird, and you will find a great many resident birds such as Inca Doves, Golden-fronted Woodpecker, Ladder-backed Woodpecker, Eastern Phoebe, Blue Jay, Western Scrub-jay, and Tufted Titmouse, just to name a few. Overhead you might see a Cooper's Hawk, and in the evening there is a chance to see, or at least to hear, a Great Horned Owl. In the fields along FM 89, where the habitat is drier, there are Cactus Wren, Pyrrhuloxia, and Northern Bobwhite. On the lake will be a variety of water birds, including Great Blue Heron and Belted Kingfisher. Winter birds may be Pied-billed Grebe, both Green-winged and Blue-winged Teal, Northern Pintail, Bufflehead, and Ruddy Ducks. This is a great place to take a picnic lunch and spend the day.

Kirby Lake

This small lake is located at the junction of U.S. 83 and Loop 322, and about the same birds will be found here as at Lake Abilene. In winter look for American White Pelican, Great, Snowy, and Cattle Egrets, and Ring-billed Gull. In the mud flats will be a number of shore birds, including Greater and Lesser Yellowlegs, Least and White-rumped Sandpipers, Long-billed Dowitcher, and Common Snipe.

Seabee Park

A little farther north of Abilene at the south end of Lake Fort Phantom Hill is Seabee Park, and you can expect to see Sandhill Cranes and even a Barred Owl.

Abilene Waste Water Treatment Plant

Most birders know that a water treatment plant is almost always a good place to find birds, and Abilene is no exception. Located on the north side of the city at the end of CR 309, you can walk the levees with ease and scan the ponds for Cinnamon Teal and Black-bellied and Semipalmated Plovers.

Attractions

Abilene Zoo

One of the largest in the state, the animals here are displayed in areas of natural habitat. Located in Nelson Park, 3 miles east of the city, the Discovery Center houses displays of invertebrates, fish, reptiles, birds, and mammals for the Southwestern United States and Africa. There are picnic areas and a playground in Nelson Park.

Fort Phantom Hill

The ruins of this fort, established in 1851, are a grim reminder of the hardships suffered by the pioneers on the frontier. Built to protect the settlers from Indians, the fort was deserted in 1854 and burned shortly thereafter. A good history lesson for the kids on what the wild West was really like.

Grace Museum

This museum is located in the historic Grace Hotel. Built in 1909, it is really a series of museums, including the Fine Arts, Abilene Historical, and the Children's Museums.

Buffalo Gap Historic Village

Another place for a great lesson in history, this complex has 20 historic buildings, which have all been restored and furnished. A short video in the Old Taylor Courthouse gives the facts about Buffalo Gap Village and West Texas. Exhibits are a country store, railroad depot, blacksmith shop, and woodworking shop. There are also a doctor-dentist office, two-room school, a bank from 1880, buggies and wagons, along with firearms of the era and Indian artifacts.

Paramount Theater

The adults will enjoy this step back into time in the restored theater with drifting clouds and twinkling stars, neon and incandescent cove lighting, and domed turrets. Classic films, plays, and concerts are given year round. Consider a trip here another history lesson for the kids.

Motels

Days Inn, 1702 I-20 East, phone 915-672-6433

Econo Lodge, 1633 W. Stamford, phone 915-673-5424

Hampton Inn, 3917 Ridgemont Dr., phone 915-695-0044

Quality Inn, 505 Pine Street, phone 800-588-0222

Super 8, I-20 & Hwy. 351, phone 800-800-8000

Dining

Fast food restaurants include: Arby's, Burger King, Chick-Fil-A, Golden Chick, McDonald's, Schlotzsky's, Sonic, Subway, Taco Bueno, Wendy's, Whataburger, and Wienerschnitzel

Luby's Cafeteria, 4438 Clack and 1026 N. Judge Ely

El Chico Mexican, Mall of Abilene

Cotton Patch Café, 3302 Clack

Golden Corral, 4100 S. Danville

Green Jeans Salad Bar Plus, 4646 S. 14th

Amarillo
Convention & Visitors Council
1000 S. Polk St.
800-692-1338
http://www.amarillo-cvb.org
E-mail: amarcvb@arn.net
or

Canyon
Convention & Visitors Bureau
1518 5th Avenue
800-999-9481

Canyon is closer to the Buffalo Lake Wildlife Refuge and the Palo Duro Canyon than Amarillo and can be an alternate base for birding and the production of *Texas*. Of course, being a smaller city, the dining and lodging facilities are limited.

Birding

Lake Meredith National Recreation Area

This 45,000 acres is a national recreation area that offers a wide variety of activities, including boating, fishing, hiking, and birding. The best area to bird is Spring Canyon, which is located on the north end of the lake, below the Sanford Dam. The habitat here consists of wooded canyon, open ponds, and marsh. Year-round birds include Pied-billed Grebe, Green-winged Teal, Northern Pintail, Northern Shoveler, Gadwall, and American Wigeon. Virginia Rail may also be seen here, along with Red-winged Blackbirds. You may also spot Horned, Eared, and Western Grebes. In the summer both Blue-winged and Cinnamon Teals can be found, along with a very expansive list of water birds, including both Ring-billed and Herring Gulls. In the open drainage to the north of Spring Canyon, year-round residents include Wild Turkey, Scaled Quail, Northern Flicker, Curve-billed Thrasher, and Rufous-crowned Sparrow. There are several other birding areas, but Spring Canyon, birded fully, can be the most productive. The area is north of Amarillo about 25 miles. Nearer Spring Canyon is Sanford, where food and gas are available, and lodging is available in Fritch or Borger, about 15 miles away, and Dumas, which is 25 miles from the canyon.

Buffalo Lake National Wildlife Refuge

Here you can take a tour drive, starting at the refuge entrance and observation deck site, and make leisurely stops to bird, such as the Cottonwood Canyon Birding Trail, a half-mile loop that is great to bird during spring migration. Yellow-billed Cuckoo, Ash-throated and Scissor-tailed Flycatcher, Blue Grosbeak, and both Orchard and Bullock's Orioles are just a few of the birds you may see here. Take Hwy. 168 south to the prairie dog town and you may see, beyond the camping area, Ring-necked Pheasant, Scaled Quail, Horned Lark, Burrowing Owl, Dickcissel, and Lark Bunting. In the winter, overhead, such hawks as Northern Harrier, Ferruginous, and Rough-legged may be seen soaring. Other possibilities include Golden Eagle, Sandhill Cranes, and even Short-eared Owl. Stewart Marsh, located at the end of the tour drive, has an observation blind. Recent drops in the lake level have reduced the number of water birds that can be seen here, but the resulting mud flats are a haven for many shore birds. There is another prairie dog colony near Canyon, and the field surrounding it can hold longspurs, including McCown's, Lapland, and Chestnut-collared. On rare occasions, even Smith's have been seen here. The city of Canyon is located on the very edge of the refuge and offers both lodging and dining facilities.

Palo Duro Canyon State Park

A visit to Palo Duro Canyon would be worth it, even if there were no birds to see. This is a fantastic sight to see, a huge hole in flat West Texas that was formed by the Prairie Dog Town Fork of the Red River. There are 16,402 acres within the park, and there is a visitors center, hiking and horseback riding trails, and a running trail. Also located here is the Goodnight Trading Post and the Pioneer Amphitheatre where summer performances of musical drama illustrates Texas history. (See Pioneer Amphitheatre below.) Driving the loop road through the canyon will provide the best birding, starting at Hackberry Camp and driving through the Juniper, Cottonwood, and Sunflower areas. Year-round species will include Scaled Quail, Western Scrub-jay, Tufted Titmouse, and Bewick's Wren. In winter

Inca Dove, Downy Woodpecker, Golden-crowned and Ruby-crowned Kinglet, Townsend's Solitaire, Cedar Waxwing, and Dark-eyed Juncos will be present.

Attractions

Amarillo Zoo

A zoo with a western flavor features a herd of buffalo and animals of the high plains. There is a special "Texotic" section. Open Tues.-Sun., 9:30 A.M.-5 P.M.

Amarillo: American Quarter Horse Heritage Center and Museum

If your family interest runs toward horses, you and the kids will love this museum with its hands-on exhibits, video presentations, artifacts, and live demonstrations concerning the quarter horse breed. Includes the Quarter Horse Hall of Fame and has demonstrations of rodeo, ranching, and racing as it concerns quarter horses.

Amarillo: Cadillac Ranch

About 12 miles west from downtown at the Hope exit is the strangest crop grown in West Texas: Ten Cadillacs are buried nose down in a field. Why? As a tribute to the golden years of Cadillac, 1949 to 1963.

Amarillo: Don Harrington Discovery Center

A 51-acre park hosts exhibits concerning physical, earth, and life sciences each summer. Your kids will find over a hundred hands-on projects, and the planetarium will be a real education for the entire family. The Botanical Gardens features outdoor educational exhibits, live plants, and butterflies where children can learn by touch and feel. The Helium Monument is a six-story stainless steel time column that was erected in 1968 to commemorate the natural element that is found here in great quantity.

Amarillo: English Field Air and Space Museum

If the family has any interest at all in aviation history, this is a great place to visit. This 34-acre site was created by the Texas Aviation Historical Society. Learn about the flight of Charles Lindbergh, the *Spruce Goose* of Howard Hughes, and the final flight of Wiley Post and Will Rogers, along with the mystery of the disappearance of Amelia Earhart. Exhibits include: C-7A Caribou, A-7E Corsair II, OV-1B Mohawk, UH-1m (Huey) Iroquois helicopter, a collection of thermo-nuclear weapons, and the Nordon M9B bombsight.

Canyon: Pioneer Amphitheatre

Summer can be very hot and dry in West Texas, but a good reason to go there during the hot months, aside from the great birding opportunities, is to view the spectacular outdoor production of *Texas*, which is presented nightly except Sundays from late June through late August. Located in Palo Duro Canyon, an 800-foot cliff provides the backdrop for the show as actors present the history of Texas in drama, humor, dancing, and music that fills the canyons. There is a barbecue dinner before the show (for a fee), and it is best to make reservations. Call *Texas* Information Office 1514 5th Avenue in Canyon, 806-655-2181.

Canyon: Panhandle-Plains Historical Museum

On the campus of West Texas State A&M University, this museum records the early history of the state through Old West exhibits that include a chuck wagon, gun collection, prehistoric fossils and wildlife, and a collection of Indian cultures. It is really five museums in one with Frank Reaugh Collections showing Southwestern art.

Festivals

May: Funfest (food, games, and music), 806-374-0802

June: Cowboy Roundup Cattle Drive and Rodeo, 806-374-1497

Amarillo Motels

Best Western Inn-Sante Fe, 4600 I-40 East, phone 800-528-1234

Days Inn, East, 1701 I-40 East, phone 800-325-2525

Hampton Inn, 1700 I-40 East, phone 800-HAMPTON

Quality Inn & Suites, 1803 Lakeside, phone 800-847-6556

Red Roof Inn, 1620 I-40 East, phone 800-843-7663

Travelodge East, 3205 I-40 East, phone 800-578-7875

Amarillo Dining

Amarillo is blessed with a wide variety of fast food restaurants.
On the Border, 2401 Soncy Road
La Fiesta, 5807 W. 45th Avenue
Catfish Shack, 3301 Olsen Blvd.
Western Sizzlin Steakhouse, 2921 I-40 West
Furr's Cafeteria, 2640 Wolfin
Luby's Cafeteria, 2101 South Coulter & 4530 Canyon Drive
Doodle's Hamburger Stores, 3908 Eaton Drive

Canyon Motels

Holiday Inn Express, 2901 Fourth Avenue, phone 806-655-4445
Goodnight Inn, Highway 87 South, phone 800-654-7350
Buffalo Inn, U.S. Higway 87 & 217, phone 800-526-9968

Canyon Dining

Fast food options include Dairy Queen, Domino's Pizza, Braum's,
  Burger King, McDonald's, Pizza Hut, and Schlotzsky's
Cope's Coney Island, 2201 4th Avenue
Cattle Call, Westgate Mall
Pepitos Mexican Restaurant, 408 23rd Street
Ranch House Café, 810 23rd Street
Teresa's Diner, 419 16th Street

Big Spring

Chamber of Commerce
215 W. 3rd Street
915-263-7641
http://www.bigspringtx.com

The city was named for the natural spring on Sulphur Draw, today located in the center of the city park. The area was first reached by white men in 1849 and today is a thriving city and home of Howard College, Dorothy Garrett Coliseum, and Southwest Collegiate Institute for the Deaf.

Birding

Big Spring State Park

Though not very large (382 acres), the practically adjacent Comanche Trail Park and the Sandhill Crane Sanctuary make this an
enjoyable, driveable birding expedition. From Big Spring, take Hwy.
87 south to FM 700. Comanche Trail Park can be an excellent place
to see Mississippi Kite, Golden-fronted Woodpecker, Vermilion Flycatcher, Painted Bunting, and both Orchard and Bullock's Orioles in
the summer. It is also a good place to bird during migration, when a
number of songbirds may be seen. Big Spring State Park is located in
pinyon-juniper woodlands and harbors a number of year-round
birds such as Western Scrub-jay, Bewick's Wren, Canyon Towhee,
and both Rufous Crowned and Lark Sparrows. In summer you may
see Ash-throated Flycatchers and Scissor-tailed Flycatchers, along
with Western Kingbird and Painted Bunting. A drive around the
McMahonwrinkle Airport on the perimeter road will take you to a
prairie dog town where you can see Burrowing Owl. From Hwy.
700, take West Third Street, turn right on Jones Street to reach the
Sandhill Crane Sanctuary, and from late October to April, you can
see a multitude of the cranes, along with geese and even a rare
Whooper Crane. Birds that nest here are Snowy Plover, Black-
necked Stilt, and American Avocet.

Attractions

Heritage Museum

This museum displays pioneer and Indian artifacts, art exhibits, and
displays of local history. It has the largest collection of Texas longhorn steer horns and a rare exhibit of phonographs from the late
1800s to 1920, with models made by Edison, Victor, and Columbia.

Potton House

The home of the Joseph Potton family, built around the turn of the
century, has been restored and is listed in the National Register of
Historic Places, with an excellent display of furnishings. Mom will
enjoy, even if the kids don't.

Vietnam Memorial

A tribute to the men who fought in Vietnam, the stone is the same as that used in the National Vietnam Memorial in Washington, D.C. and can be seen on FM 700.

Motels

Econo Lodge, I-20 & U.S. 87, phone 915-263-5200

Best Western, I-20 & U.S. 87, phone 915-267-1601

Great Western, 2900 I-20 East, phone 915-267-4553

Days Inn, 2701 S. Gregg St., phone 915-267-5237

Dining

Fast food options include: Burger King, KFC, McDonald's, Sonic, Gill's Fried Chicken, Dairy Queen, Pizza Inn, Pizza Hut, and Whataburger

La Posada, 206 N.W. 4th St.

Casa Blanca, 1005 Lamesa Hwy.

T-N-T Bar-B-Que, 1611 E. 4th Street

Ponderosa Restaurant, 2703 Gregg

Denny's, 1710 E. 3rd

Furr's Family Dining, 2503 S. Gregg St.

Dalhart

Chamber of Commerce
P.O. Box 967
806-249-5646

Dalhart is not the end of Texas, but you can see it from there. Or almost, for a drive north of about thirty miles will take you to the Oklahoma state line, and drive west thirty miles and you will be in New Mexico. But like its unusual location, it also has some very interesting birding sites and places to visit.

Birding

Lake Rita Blanca State Park

The recently developed Lake Rita Blanca State Park was once part of the XIT Ranch, which contained more than three million acres. Located just southwest of the city of Dalhart, the lake can be seen better with a scope, either from the park or from the dam. Resident birds are Pied-billed Grebe, Great Blue Heron, Mallard, Northern Pintail, Northern Shoveler, Redhead and Ruddy Ducks. Black-crowned and Yellow-crowned Night-Herons may also be seen. The narrow canyons around the edge of the lake are a good place to bird in the spring or fall for migrants, and there are numerous resident birds to be seen.

Rita Blanca National Grassland

Located about 18 miles north of Dalhart, this can be a hot and dusty drive in summer over many unpaved roads, but the birding can be worth it if you watch the groves of trees where nesting species include Swainson's, Red-tailed, and Ferruginous Hawks, along with Kestrels, Prairie Falcons, and even Ring-necked Pheasants. Long-billed Curlew, Burrowing Owl, and Horned Lark may also be seen here, along with a host of other birds.

Cactus Lake

From Lake Rita Blanca State Park, drive east on either U.S. 287 or FM 281 to Cactus Lake. Although not large, the water in the arid area can attract a great many migrants in winter, including thousands of geese such as Snow, Ross's, and Canadian. Both Bald and Golden Eagles may be seen in winter. During spring migration, huge numbers of waterfowl can be seen, and as many as 10,000 Wilson's Phalaropes have been seen on the playa, while thousands of swallows dip into the lake during the late summer. You may also find Ring-necked Pheasant in the surrounding grasslands.

Attractions

Dallam-Hartley Counties XIT Museum

Railroad antiques, Indian artifacts, frontier firearms, cowboy clothing, and saddles are included in this display of Old West history, including a furnished kitchen, parlor, and bedroom from about 1900, and a frontier chapel and pump organ. Open Tues-Sat., 9 A.M. to 5 P.M.

Empty Saddle Monument

Located on U.S. 87 North, a great place to have a family photo session is in front of the monument commemorating the life of a former XIT ranch hand.

Festivals

XIT Rodeo and Reunion. If you and the kids like rodeo, this could be right up your alley. The largest amateur rodeo in the world has been held here for over a half century in August. For more information, call 806-249-5646.

Motels

Best Western-Nursanickel Motel, Hwy. 87 South, phone
806-244-5637

Comfort Inn, U.S. 54 E., phone 806-249-8585

Days Inn of Dalhart, 701 Liberal Street/54 East, phone
800-DAYSINN

Dining

Nursanickel Retaurant, U.S. Hwy. 87 South

Country Heart Bakery, 518 W. 7th Street

Lubbock

Convention & Visitors Bureau
1301 Broadway, Suite 200
800-692-4035
http://www.lubbocklegends.com

Lubbock is the major city of the South Plains. A thriving metropolitan area that once was the heart of the cattle industry, it is now home to several major schools, such as Lubbock Christian University and Texas Tech University, and of course, Buddy Holly.

Birding

Buffalo Springs Lake

The Llano Estacado Audubon Society maintains a 55-acre section of this county-owned recreation area where a 1.7-mile nature trail is available for birding. The trail is not too difficult, except it begins and ends with a series of switchbacks on the face of the canyon cliff and could be strenuous for smaller children. It is particularly good during the spring and fall, when migrants are passing through. Nesting birds include Green Heron, Yellow-billed Cuckoo, Black-chinned Hummingbird, and Blue Grosbeak. Other species to be found along the trail in summer are Inca Doves, Golden-fronted Woodpecker, Ladder-backed Woodpecker, and Ash-throated and Scissor-tailed Flycatchers. Early in the morning or at dusk, you may see the Great Horned Owl floating overhead, or in the summer, a Common Nighthawk or Common Poorwill. Lake Ransom is just downstream from Buffalo Springs Lake and has about the same water birds, including a great number of Canadian Geese in the winter.

Twin Ponds and Boles Lake

Twin Ponds and Boles Lake are back in town. Twin ponds are located on each side of Highway 835, and Boles Lake is in the same area on Boles Road. Both water areas attract a good many birds during migration, and Boles Lake has mud flats that will draw a number of shore birds, including Snowy Plover, Black-necked Stilt, and American Avocet.

Mackenzie Park

There is another one of those prairie dog colonies, and as usual, the Burrowing Owl may be seen here, although they may be hard to find in winter.

Lake Six

Located next to the Lubbock Cemetery, there is a loop road around the lake and several places to stop and observe birds. Year-round birds include Golden-fronted Woodpecker, Carolina Wren, and both Great-tailed and Common Grackles. During migration this can be a real hot spot, and in summer, swallows can be abundant including Northern Rough-winged, Cliff, and Barn. Lubbock Cemetery can be a hot spot for migrating warblers in the spring, and in winter, Cedar Waxwing, Bohemian Waxwing, Evening Grosbeak, Pine Siskin, and Clark's Nutcracker can be seen. Located at MLK Blvd. and 19th Street. Couch's Kingbird has been a recent visitor to the area, and American Robins and Blue Jays abound.

Attractions

American Wind Power Center

With one windmill that dates back to the 1860s, this center preserves the history of windmills on a 28-acre site where more than 50 windmills are displayed in the museum.

Buddy Holly Center

Perhaps a nostalgic visit for mom and dad and a boring time for the kids, who won't know who the famous Lubbock native was (unless they saw the movie), this multiuse cultural arts facility honors the famed rock-n-roller. This not only displays memorabilia of the famed singer but is the home of the Texas Musician's Hall of Fame. The Buddy Holly Statue and Walk of Fame pays tribute to other Texas celebrities such as Mac Davis, Waylon Jennings, Jimmy Dean, Tanya Tucker, Roy Orbison, Bob Wills, the Gatlin Brothers, and other Texans.

Lubbock Memorial Arboretum

This 93-acre park has a lake with ducks, and the Hodges Rose Garden is open daily. On the second Saturday of the month, gardening programs are presented at the Interpretive Center.

Omnimax and Science Spectrum

If the kids got bored at the Buddy Holly Center and the Arboretum, you can make it up to them by taking them to the Omnimax and Science Spectrum where 70mm images are projected on a 58-ft-domed screen. In the Science Spectrum the kids can learn with hands-on exhibits of science, nature, and technology. There is even a "Kidspace" for preschoolers.

Joyland Amusement Park

Still got bored children? Then take them to Mackenzie Park and let them ride some of the twenty-five rides, including a water coaster and roller coaster. Call 806-763-2719 for open times.

Ellen Trout Zoo and Park

Known for their work with breeding programs of West African Crowned Cranes and Louisiana Pine Snakes, this zoo is fully accredited and offers displays of a variety of other animals and birds. Located at 402 Zoo Circle off Loop 287 North.

Motels

Best Western Lubbock Regency, 6624 I-27, phone 806-745-2208
Fairfield Inn, 4007 S. Loop 289, phone 806-795-1288
Lubbock Inn, 3901 19th Street, 800-545-8226
Motel 6, 909 66th Street, phone 806-745-5541

Dining

The Caboose on 50th Street. Good food, lots of games
Home Plate Diner (4 locations)
Pete's Drive-In (4 locations), good hamburgers
Abuelo's Mexican Restaurant, 4401 82nd Street

Orlando's Italian Restaurant, 2402 Avenue Q and 6951
  Indiana

Ray's Drive In Café, 420 Timberland Dr. and 918 S. John Redditt
  Dr.

Monahans
Chamber of Comerce
401 S. Dwight Ave.
915-943-2187
http://www.monahans.org

Established in 1881 as a stop for the Texas and Pacific Railroad, this community is the center of a prosperous cattle and oil business. Oil wells are even drilled some distance from town and slanted to pump oil from beneath city hall, the courthouse, banks, and other business houses.

Birding

Monahans Sandhills State Park

Take I-20 out of Odessa toward Monahans to the entrance of this 3,840-acre park that consists of miles of white sand dunes ranging up to 70 feet in height. Be sure and take plenty of water. The best birding area is the nature trail behind the visitors center where there is a water station that, in this arid country, attracts a lot of birds that can be viewed from the window of the center. This center also contains exhibits of wildlife of the area, history, and archeology. There are a number of picnic areas in the park. Year-round residents include Scaled Quail, Cactus and Bewick's Wrens, Curve-billed Thrasher, Canyon Towhee, and Black-throated Sparrow. Many more species can be found in the sandy grassland in the area of the visitors center. A drive to the far north end of the park will bring you to several willow thickets, accessible at the end of the paved road. Nesting birds here are Mourning Doves, Yellow-billed Cuckoo, Black-chinned Hummingbird, and Western Kingbird, just to name a few. Hawks such as Northern Harrier, Sharp-shinned, and Cooper's Hawks may be seen overhead, as well as Prairie Falcon. Swainson's

Hawk is here in the summer, and in winter you may see Red-tailed Hawk, Ferruginous Hawk, Golden Eagle, and Burrowing Owl.

Attractions

Million Barrel Museum

This museum is located in an oil-storage tank that was built in 1928 and abandoned due to a leak. In 1987 it was converted into a museum featuring the restored Holman House that was the hotel and terminal of the Monahans-Fort Stockton Stage Line. Period furnishings and the first Ward County jail are displayed, along with oil field equipment. Open daily. Located on Hwy. 80 east of the city.

Pyote Museum and Rattlesnake Bomber Base

Home of the 19th (B-17) Bomb Group during World War II, this museum has exhibits of local history and mementos of the base. It is located in the county park and has picnic areas, swimming pool, and a three-hole golf course.

Motels

Colonial/Best Western, 702 SW I-20, phone 915-943-4345

Texan Inn, 806 W. I-20, phone 915-943-7585

Silver Spur, 400 E. Sealy, phone 915-943-5461

Dining

Fast food options include Sonic, McDonald's, Subway, Pizza Hut, and Dairy Queen.

K Bob's Steak House, 901 S. Stockton

Dicky's Mexican Restaurant, 400 N. Main

Leal's Mexican Restaurant, 114 W. Sealy

Muleshoe

Chamber of Commerce
215 S. 1st St.
806-272-4248

Perhaps one of the best-known towns in Texas, primarily because of its unusual name, this city was organized in 1926 and today is the center for marketing and shipping of High Plains agricultural products.

Birding

Muleshoe National Wildlife Refuge

This is the oldest national wildlife refuge in Texas, established in 1935. The 5,809 acres were set aside as a wintering area for migratory waterfowl and particularly the Sandhill Cranes, but the prairie habitat and the lakes make it a great birding spot. As many as 250,000 Sandhill Cranes (1981) have been counted here, but the number has been greatly reduced since. The cranes can be seen on Lower Pauls Lake where they roost at night, flying in and out of the refuge during the day. The lakes will also harbor a number of ducks, including Green-winged Teal, Mallard, Northern Pintail, Northern Shoveler, Gadwall, and American Wigeon. Others are fewer in number but Wood Duck, Canvasback, Redhead, and Ring-necked Duck may also be present. Several species of grebes can be seen such as Horned, Eared, and Western. Geese are present, including the Ross'. In the mud flats around Paul's Lake Harbor in the summer, you will find Black-crowned Night-Herons, Snowy Plover, Black-necked Stilt, and American Avocet. In the prairie grasses look for both Red-winged and Yellow-headed Blackbirds. Soaring overhead you may see several hawks species including Red-tailed, and Northern Bobwhite and Scaled Quail may be seen along the main entrance road. At the refuge headquarters there is a prairie dog colony and as is so often true, Burrowing Owls are here. There is a variety of sparrows in the grasslands, including Cassin's, Lark, and Grasshopper. The mile-long nature trail can be very productive.

Attractions

National Mule Memorial

You might expect a city with the name of Muleshoe to have a memorial to the long-eared beast that helped tame the West, pulling covered wagons and playing a big role in building the railroads, and you will not be disappointed. The monument was unveiled on July 4, 1965, near the intersection of U.S. 70/84 in downtown. Don't miss it, for there is not much else to see in Muleshoe unless you want to be there for the Labor Day mule rodeo. This is a good spot to take pictures.

Festivals

Cranefest. Held in November to welcome the 25,000+ Sandhill Cranes back to the oldest National Wildlife Refuge in the state of Texas. One-day activities include sunrise breakfast, sunset picnic, wildlife tours, and exhibits at the refuge. Sidewalk Art contest for kids K-12 is held in Muleshoe, 21 miles from the refuge, with prizes awarded. Contact: Muleshoe Chamber of Commerce.

Motels

Heritage House Inn, 2301 West American Blvd., phone
    800-253-5896
Economy Inn, 2701 West American Blvd., phone 806-272-4261
Heritage Budget Inn, 1827 West American Blvd., phone
    806-272-4533
Valley Motel, 1515 West American Blvd., phone 806-272-4279

Dining

Leal's Restaurant (good Mexican), 1010 West American Blvd.
McDonald's, 1315 West American Blvd.
Dinner Bell, 2103 West American Blvd.
Tino's Mexican Restaurant, 104 West American Blvd.
Pizza Hut, 1412 West American Blvd.

Odessa

Convention & Visitors Bureau
700 N. Grant, Suite 200
800-780-HOST
http://www.odessachamber.com
E-mail: info@odessacvb.com

Odessa is not particularly a birding area, but you can reach the Red Bluff Lake and Monahans Sandhills State Park areas from there if you prefer to stay in a larger city. It is 36 miles to the city of Monahans, and 26 more to Pecos, which is about 52 miles south of Red Bluff Lake. Staying in Mohahans or Pecos will give you more time to bird, and if you want a further adventure, you can cross the New Mexico state line and take in Carlsbad Caverns.

Attractions

American Airpower Heritage Museum and Confederate Air Force

This museum is dedicated to preserving at least one of each type of the 300,000 aircraft produced during World War II and is the finest collection of flyable WWII combat aircraft. Some twenty of the 137 aircraft of the Confederate Air Force on display are P-40 Warhawk, P-38 Lightning, P-47 Thunderbolt, P-51 Mustang, F4U Corsair, and German Heinkel and Messerschmitts. Others include the famous B-17 Flying Fortress and the B-25 Mitchell. For more information, go to their web site at: www.avdigest.com.

Midland County Historical Museum

History of the area is displayed through photos, pioneer relics, and mementos of the War Between the States, World Wars I & II, and Indian artifacts. Open three days a week. For information, phone 915-688-8947.

Museum of the Southwest Complex

Located in a 1934 mansion that is listed on the National Register of Historic Places, this museum has carved wooden friezes, hand-painted tile, and Italian marble fireplaces. Collections of art are from Texas artists, photographers, and sculptors. Includes the

Fredda Turner Durham Children's Museum and the Marian Blakemore Planetarium. This can be another great learning experience for your family.

Odessa Meteor Crater

Just west of the site of Odessa, some 20,000 years ago, this meteor hit the earth, leaving a hole 500 feet in diameter. Through the years, the winds and sand of West Texas have almost filled the crater. A nature trail winds through the crater today. There is a free brochure available at the Chamber of Commerce that tells the story and gives directions.

Presidential Museum

This unusual museum displays artifacts from presidential political campaigns of the past, with campaign buttons, posters, and even political cartoons. There is also a collection of dolls with replicas of hair styles worn by the first ladies. May not be all that interesting to the kids, but it could help them out in their history studies in school.

Festivals

September: Permian Basin Fair and Expo, phone 915-550-3232

Motels

Best Western, 110 W. Interstate 20, phone 915-337-3006
Days Inn, 3075 E. Business Loop 20, phone 915-335-8000
Delux Inn, 1518 South Grant, phone 915-333-1486
La Quinta Odessa, 5001 E. Hwy. 80, 915-333-2820
Parkway Inn Motel, 3071 E. Business Loop 20, 915-332-4224
Super 8 Motel, 6713 E. Business Loop 20, phone 800-800-8000

Dining

Casa Blanca Restaurant, 523 E. Illinois Ave (Mexican)
CiCi's Pizza, 4400 N. Midland Drive
Luby's Cafeteria, 2510 W. Louisiana Ave.
Murray's Delicatessen, 3211 W. Wadley Ave.
Jorge's Mexican Café, 3323 N. Midland Drive
Price's Barbecue, 700 E. Texas Ave.

Pecos

Chamber of Commerce
111 S. Cedar St.
915-445-2406

Besides the many western tales, including Pecos Bill, the city is well known for having the sweetest cantaloupes in the United States, which are grown in the irrigated fields around the city. Their flavor is believed to come from the alkali soil, the western sun, and the altitude.

Birding

Red Bluff Lake

Red Bluff Lake is located on the Pecos River, 43 miles north of the city of Pecos. The best birding area is on each side of the dam on the south end of the lake, near the little town of Red Bluff. This 11,700-acre reservoir supports a number of water sports and fishing and can also be a great place to bird. The park just northwest of the town of Red Bluff gives you a look at the southwest corner of the lake, and in winter you may see a multitude of waterfowl, including Horned, Eared, Western, and Clark's Grebes. There will also be a number of duck species, from Ruddy to Northern Shoveler to American Wigeon and Gadwall, just to name a few. In this area you may also see American Pipit and several species of sparrows such as Black-throated and Savannahs. On the other side of the dam the water birds will be about the same, but you may also see American White Pelicans, and in the air look for Harrier, Red-tailed, and Rough-legged Hawks, along with American Kestrel. Smaller birds can be seen in the area below the dam where there is a pool with salt cedars. It is a good place to see Verdin, Bewick's Wren, Orange-crowned and Yellow-rumped Warblers, as well as Green-tailed Tohee. In winter the desert habitat is the home of Cactus Wren and both Sage and Crissal Thrashers. This is a rather remote area and has not been birded a great deal, so you may even find some surprises.

Attractions

Maxey Park and Zoo

Pecos is a city of less than 12,000 population, but it has a zoo with buffalo, deer, javelina, mountain lions, and antelope. There is a picnic area and a playground for children.

West-of-the-Pecos Museum and Park

Housed in an old western saloon, this three-story building was once also a hotel, and restored ornate fixtures are from the late 1800s. It is the site of a real western shoot-out, where a quick-draw bartender named Barney Riggs gunned down a couple of outlaws. There are a total of fifty rooms depicting West Texas history.

Festivals

June: Night in Old Pecos/Cantaloupe Festival and Pageant, phone 915-445-2406

Motels

Best Western-Swiss Clock Inn, 900 W. Palmer, 915-447-2215

Motel 6, 3002 S. Cedar Street, 800-4-MOTEL6

Quality Inn, Highway 20, 915-445-5404

Dining

The Swiss Clock Inn serves breakfast, and there is a 24-hour restaurant in the Quality Motel.

Flying J Truck Stop, Highway 20

Town & Country Subs, Highway 20

McDonald's, Highway 20

Quitaque

Chamber of Commerce
Located in City Hall
806-455-1456

Quitaque (pronounced Kit-a-Kway) was the site of a trading post for the Plains Indians and a stagecoach stop in the 1890s. With a population of less than 500, the main attraction in the area is the Caprock Canyons and their beautiful rock formations.

Birding

Caprock Canyon State Park

Roland Wauer (*Birding Texas*) calls this one of the state's most underrated parks, not just for the birding possibilities, but for the abundance of beautiful scenery, with exposed red sandstone and siltstone that are the most colorful found anywhere. With a family, the best place to bird is Lake Theo, a relatively small lake on the south side of the 13,906-acre park, and Dry Creek, which is on the west side of Lake Theo. Both are accessible on a dirt road. Resident birds are Pied-billed Grebe, Mallard, Killdeer, and Ring-billed Gull. In the summer Least Bittern and Spotted Sandpiper have been seen, and winter ducks include Green-winged Teal, Northern Shoveler, Gadwall, American Wigeon, Canvasback, and Bufflehead. Both Hooded and Common Mergansers may also be present. In nearby cottonwoods many migrant songbirds can be seen in fall and spring, and nesting birds are Yellow-billed Cuckoo, Western Kingbird, Scissor-tailed Flycatcher, Yellow Warbler, Blue Grosbeak, and Orchard and Bullock's Orioles. There is an extensive hiking trail (6.5 miles) that is a great place to see the beauty of the landscape, but it may be too rigorous for small children.

Circle Dot Caprock Adventure

From May through October, the Circle Dot Ranch offers a Comanchero Breakfast or a Chuck Wagon Supper for a combined total of 20 people or more. Call the Chamber of Commerce for more information.

Motels

Rails to Trails Lodge, phone 806-455-1344

Quitaque Quail Lodge, phone 806-455-1261

Dale & Donna Smith Ranch (has accommodations), 806-455-1259

Dining

Caprock Café, 201 Main Street

Sportsman Restaurant, 116 Main Street

Quanah

Chamber of Commerce
220 S. Main St.
940-663-2222

If you really want to get away from it all, this is about as far away as you can get. But it can be interesting, both from a birding standpoint and attractions to see. Located just south of the Red River at the intersection of Highways 6 and 287, this can be a pleasant, surprising place to visit.

Birding

Cooper Breaks State Park and Pease River

The 60-acre lake in this 1,933-acre state park may not sound very large, but in this arid land, any water will attract a multitude of birds. There is a visitors center with exhibits of bison and Comanche Indians artifacts. There is also a herd of longhorn cattle. The park has camping and picnicking facilities. The best area to bird with children is the Lake Copper Breaks and the Juniper Ridge Nature Trail, which have easy access. A tremendous assortment of water birds can be found on the lake, including Pied-billed Grebe, Ruddy Duck, and Belted Kingfisher. Yellow Rails are also present. In the winter, birds might include Eared Grebe and both Blue-winged and Cinnamon Teal, along with Bufflehead, Hooded Merganser, and American Wigeon. Around the lake you can see Marsh Wren (learn the sound, they are usually hard to see), Red-winged Blackbirds, and both Song and Swamp Sparrows. North of the lake is an area called Big Pond, but it will produce about the same variety of water birds. West of the lake is the 2-mile-long Bull Canyon Trail, but the Juniper Ridge Trail is shorter and may be better for children. Resident birds in both areas include Northern Bobwhite, Greater Roadrunner, Bewick's Wren, Canyon Towhee, and Rufous-crowned Sparrow, just to name a few. Overhead you should see Red-tailed and American Kestrel Hawks. A different habitat can be found on the Pease River, located south of the park along SH 6 and accessible at the bridge. The riparian habitat, the river, and the mud flats can be a great place to bird during migration.

Attractions

Hardeman County Museum

Located in an old county jail built in 1891, the museum occupies the lower floor with exhibits of Quanah and Hardeman County history and in stark contrast, a Space room furnished by NASA and the Smithsonian Institute. Open daily from 2 P.M. to 6 P.M. 101 Green Street.

Quanah, Acme and Pacific Railway Depot

An extension of the Hardeman Museum, this three-story building was built in 1908 in Spanish Mission style with red Ludowici Serville tile roof. It is listed in the National Register of Historic Places.

Medicine Mounds

There are four mounds that rise to 350 feet above the plains. The Comanche Indians believed the mounds to be the dwelling place of spirits that could cure ills, thus the name. They are on private property but can be seen from Hwy. 287, about 5 miles south.

Motels

Quanah Parker Inn, Hwy. 287, phone 940-663-6365

Casa Royale Motel, Hwy. 287, phone 940-663-6341

Landmark (Bed & Breakfast), phone 940-663-5792

Dining

Medicine Mound Depot Restaurant, built in 1910, moved to site on U.S. 287. Good food if you don't spoil your appetite on the parched peanuts.

Several fast foods are available, including Pizza Hut, Dairy Queen, Subway, TCBY, and Golden Light Café.

Dutch's Café, Hwy. 287 West

Ken's, Hwy. 287 West

Red's Drive In, Hwy. 287 East

Daffodil Express, 204 S. Main (sandwich shop in a gift store)

San Angelo
Chamber of Commerce
500 Rio Concho Drive
915-655-4136
http://www.SanAngelo.com

San Angelo developed around the site of Fort Concho and today is a widely diversified city of industry, medical, and retirement facilities. It is home of Goodfellow Air Force Base and the leading market for wool and mohair. It is also the home of San Angelo State University.

Birding

San Angelo State Park & O. C. Fisher Lake

This relatively new lake and park (established in 1994) covers 12,500 acres of West Texas plains and contains the 5,440-acre O.C. Fisher Lake, which is managed by the Corps of Engineers. It is a popular place to fish, boat, and swim. Birders will also find it rewarding and easy to explore with children. The Isabel Harte camp area, which can be reached by driving out of San Angelo on Hwy. 853 and turning right on 2288, offers a good view of the lake and water birds, including two Blue Heron rookeries. North again on 2288 (or a hike up the Wilderness Trail) will take you to the North Concho area, where you will see a variety of birds, including Yellow-breasted Chat, Bell's Vireo, Blue Grosbeak, Painted Bunting, and both Orchard and Bullock's Orioles. The beautiful Vermilion

Flycatcher can also be seen here, along with Eastern Bluebird. The Wilderness Trail between the River Bend Camping area and the Highland Scenic Lookout can be very productive for grassland birds such as Scaled Quail, Greater Roadrunner, and Groove-billed Ani. Cassin's, Rufous-crowned, Lark, and Black-throated Sparrows may also be present along the trial. In the winter, Rock Wrens can be found on the dam, and a variety of sparrows flit around in the grassy fields. The McCown's and Chestnut-collared Longspurs can also be found.

Hummer House Texas Gems

If you are looking for a real birding getaway, try Dan Brown's Hummer House Texas Gems, located south of San Angelo where hummingbirds consumed 680 pounds of sugar in one season. Hummer House has two bedrooms and two baths, with a kitchen, living area, and large porch for bird watching in comfort. The star of the show is the Black-chinned Hummer, which appears at the feeders in great numbers. The birds nest here, and hundreds of the birds are banded. The observation room is air conditioned and filled with chairs for the comfort of visitors. Deer and wild turkeys are also frequent visitors. This is a very unusual place to bird. A brochure packet on Hummer House is available by contacting Dan or Joann Brown, P.O. Box 555, Christoval, Texas 76935. Phone 915-255-2254 or see their web page at: www.hummerhouse-texasgems.com.

Attractions

San Angelo Children's Art Museum

Located in the Cactus Hotel, built in 1929, the Children's Museum has hands-on activities for kids of all ages to explore and create. For information, phone 915-659-4391. The hotel has a restaurant and coffee shop.

San Angelo Nature Center

There are displays of native wildlife such as reptiles and amphibians, mounted birds, a 200-gallon aquarium, a glass-enclosed beehive, and an ant farm. There are also audiovisual educational programs.

Fort Concho

The most interesting historical spot in the area is Fort Concho, which was established in 1867, and there are 23 original and restored buildings. This is one of the best preserved of the frontier forts that were built to protect settlers and wagon trains headed west after the Civil War. Exhibits tell the story of the fort and the Indian campaigns.

Motels

Motel 6, 311 N. Bryant, phone 800-4-MOTEL6

Econo Lodge, 2502 Loop 306, phone 915-944-4513

Travelodge, 333 Rio Concho Drive, phone 915-659-0749

Super 8, 1601 S. Bryant, phone 915-653-1323

Quality Inn, 4205 S. Bryant, phone 915-653-6966

Days Inn, 413 Jackson, phone 800-325-2525

Dining

Catfish Corner, 313 W. Beauregard and 3415 S. Chadbourne

Fuente's Original Café, 9 E. Avenue K

Charcoal House, 1205 N. Chadbourne St. and 1616 Bryant
    (burgers)

Shakey's Pizza Parlor, 20 Howard St.

Pleasant Village, 23 S. Park St.

Spaghetti Western, 2307 Loop 306

Edwards Plateau

painted bunting

Austin

Convention & Visitors Bureau
201 E. Second St.
800-926-2282
http://www.austintexas.org

The state capital is another of those metropolitan areas where you might not expect to find a lot of good birding areas, but even within the city, there are a number of hot spots. As with any large city, the traffic can be a problem, and a motel on the edge of the Austin or even in nearby smaller cities may be best for a base of operation for your family birding outing. Austin also contains a great number of attractions for family entertainment. We have listed a few, but for an expanded list, see *Exploring Texas With Children* by Sharry Buckner or the Texas Department of Transportation's *Texas State Travel Guide*.

Birding

Austin Northwest

There are three areas within a short drive of each other that can produce a great many birds, even in the hustle and bustle of a large city. The Emma Long Metro Park is located in the bend of Lake Austin and can be reached by taking City Park Road west from Hwy. 2222. The star bird of the area is the endangered Golden-cheeked Warbler, which will appear from the middle of March to July. The birds can be seen along the City Park Road or in the junipers and oaks on Turkey Creek Trail. In the park, which consists of open areas and scattered trees, you may see Northern Bobwhite, Rock (Pigeons) and Inca Doves, Blue Grosbeak, Eastern Meadowlark, and Orchard Oriole in summer. Along the edge of Lake Austin you may also find Red-bellied Woodpecker and Red-eyed Vireo. In winter the fields are home to a number of sparrow species, including Chipping, Song, Lincoln's, White-throated, and White-crowned. The Wild Basin Wilderness Preserve is just off of Loop 360, just north of Bee Caves Road (FM 2244). There is a 1.5-mile trail that leads to Laurel Falls and along Possum Creek that is a great birding area in the summer with the presence of Western Scrub-jay, Carolina Chickadee, Tufted

Titmouse, Bewick's Wren, House Finch, and Lesser Goldfinch. North on 360 you will find the Forest Ridge Preserve just south of Spicewood Springs Road. There is a hiking trail, and most of the birds found at the Wild Basin Wilderness Preserve will also be found here.

Austin Central

This area contains a number of spots and trails that are within the metropolitan area of the city, beginning with the State Capitol grounds and including Eastwoods Metropolitan Park, Zilker Park, the Barton Creek Greenbelt, and Town Lake and Longhorn Dam. All of these areas are particularly excellent for birding during the spring migration when neotropical migrants pass through. Flycatchers, vireos, warblers, tanagers, and orioles are among the more common visitors. Birding in this area can require some walking or driving from one spot to the other. Eastwoods Metropolitan Park, near the University of Texas campus, is a good place to start, and Zilker Metropolitan Park is a large area of lawns and trees with trails along the river that will provide some excellent birding. Perhaps the best place to take a family is along the Barton Creek Greenbelt, which is a popular running trail in Austin. But a walk through the diverse habitat will produce a number of species at any time of year, and from March to July, the Golden-cheeked Warbler will be present from the Gus Fruh Assess Point or at the MoPac Trailhead.

Hornsby Bend Wastewater Treatment Plant

Roland Wauer calls this the best birding year round in the Austin area. It is located in a bend of the Colorado River just off FM 973 and is open daily from dawn to dusk. You can drive or walk along the sewage ponds (counterclockwise), and in summer you should see a great many water birds such as Pied-billed Grebe, Great Egret, Mallard, Ruddy Duck, Yellow-crowned Night-Heron, and both White and White-faced Ibis, along with the snake bird, Anhinga, Wood Stork, and Mottled Duck. Winter will bring a different assortment, including a number of ducks, geese, gulls, and terns. In the fields nearby you may see American Golden-plover and Upland Sandpiper. Walking the road, you may also see a number of songbirds in the spring and a variety of sparrows. Although most of the birds can be seen with binoculars, a spotting scope is a good tool to have here not only to see the birds, but to study them closely.

Attractions

Austin Children's Museum

The themes of this hands-on museum for children are: How different people live, the human body, and everyday science and technology. Kids can touch, play, and climb to learn more about the subjects. Located at W. 2nd St. at Colorado St. Phone 512-472-2499 for information.

Austin Zoo

Designed for the enjoyment of children where they can have hands-on encounters with a number of different animals, along with pony and train rides. There is a picnic area. Call 800-291-1490 for more information or visit their web site at: www.austinzoo.com.

Republic of Texas Museum

This museum contains artifacts and hands-on exhibits pertaining to the history of Texas. Owned and operated by the Daughters of the Republic of Texas since the 1890s, it is located at 510 Anderson Lane. Another opportunity for your kids to get a history lesson that will help them in school for years to come.

George Washington Carver Museum

The exhibits here are constantly changing to show photos, artifacts, folk craft, and art pertaining to black history and culture in Austin. Located at 1165 E. Angelina St. by the Carver Library.

Lyndon B. Johnson Library and Museum

Here is an excellent place for kids to learn about the history of Texas and America. There is a replica of the oval office, as well as a collection of gifts from foreign heads of state given to LBJ, and a moon rock. Exhibits are changed on a regular basis.

Motels

As in other big cities, the housing opportunities are limitless. However, since this is the state capital, it is best to make reservations well in advance because many special events take place here that can eliminate most of the rooms in a hurry. Round Rock and Georgetown are just a couple of the alternate places to call home while you are in the area.

Dining

Again, the possibilities are almost unlimited, with multitudes of fast food outlets and family restaurants. For a list of finer dining places, contact the Chamber of Commerce for a copy of their brochure "Enjoy Austin," which is also available at many motels.

Dan's Hamburgers, 1822 S. Congress Ave. and 5602 Lamar Blvd.

Jason's Deli, 3300 Bee Caves Rd. and 9722 Great Hills Trail

Rosie's Tamale House, 102 E. Oltorf, 13436 Hwy. 71 W. and 13776 Hwy. 183 N.

El Mercado, 1302 S. First St., 1702 Lavaca St., and 7414 Burnet Rd.

Celebration Station, 4525 S. I-35

Spaghetti Warehouse, 117 W. Fourth St.

Boerne

Chamber of Commerce
One Main Plaza
830-249-8000
http://www.boerne.org

Pronounced Burn-ee, this city was established in 1851 and is known for its fishing streams and lakes and hunting opportunities.

Birding

Guadalupe River State Park

The Guadalupe River runs through the center of this 1,900-acre state park, leaving a rugged landscape with huge cypress trees lining the edge of the river. It is used for canoeing and tubing and can be very busy on the weekends and holidays. Another 2,300 acres are located in adjacent Honey Creek State Natural Area, which is open only on Saturday morning for interpretive tours at $5 per family. As with many birding areas on the Edwards Plateau, the primary target for most birders is the endangered Golden-cheeked Warbler, which can be found in the canyons along the river and in the Honey Creek State Natural Area. The best place to bird is at the end of the road at the day use area. This is the beginning place for a 2-mile loop trail that runs upriver where you might see Green and Belted Kingfisher, along with Cliff Swallows, and after dark you may hear a Common Poorwill. In the spring and summer, the habitat along the river will harbor a number of birds, including several species of vireos and warblers. There are a number of nesting birds here and Green Heron, Yellow-billed Cuckoo, Black-chinned Hummingbirds, and Eastern Wood-Pewee can be seen. In the winter the best place to bird is the day use area where you should see the Golden-fronted Woodpecker.

Attractions

Cascade Caverns

First opened to visitors in 1932, these caverns got their name from the 90-foot underground waterfall. Guides conduct one-hour tours along well-lighted walking trails. Lots of cave formations and clear pools. A great place to visit in the summer when you need to cool off.

Cave Without A Name

If your family enjoys visiting caves, this is one you probably never heard of because it has not been exploited commercially as many of the caves in Texas have, but it is a beautiful place to visit and enjoy. It is located six miles north on FM 474; turn right on Kreutzberg Road and follow the signs about five miles to the cave.

Motels

Best Western-Texas Country Inn, 35150 I-10 West, phone
    800-299-9791

Key to the Hills Motel, 1228 S. Main, phone 800-690-5763

Motor Inn At Comfort, Hwy. 878 & I-10, Comfort, TX, phone
    830-995-3822

Roadway Inn Fiesta Park, 19793 I-10 West, phone 800-228-2000

Dining

Back Porch @ Stagecoach Station, 259 S. Main

Boerne Vistro & Country Inn, 911 S. Main

Country Spirit Restaurant, 707 S. Main

Denny's, 435 W. Bandera Road

Peach Tree Country Kitchen, 448 S. Main

Po-Po Family Restaurant, 435 NE I-10 W. Access Rd.

Fast food options include Church's Chicken and Sonic Drive-in

Burnet

Chamber of Commerce
703 Buchanan Drive
512-756-4297
http://www.burnetchamber.org

Before you visit here, be sure you know how to pronounce the name. Locals will correct you if you say bur-net and tell you that it is burn-it and rhymes with durn-it. It has been named the bluebonnet capital of Texas, and in spring the roadsides are alive with wildflowers. A favorite of many tourists for its antique shopping and historic downtown square.

Birding

Vanishing Texas River Cruise Bald Eagle Tours

Well worth the price of admission, this boat tour aboard the *Texas Eagle II*, a three-deck, 200-passenger riverboat, takes you out on the Colorado River above Lake Buchanan. November through mid-March, the possibility of a close look at an eagle or two is very good. This can be a pleasant time to rest and at the same time see not only the eagles but the other water birds along the route. The tour lasts about two and one-half hours. Call 1-800-4RIVER4 for rates and schedules. There are camping and RV hook-ups available at the site.

Canyon of the Eagles

This 900-acre nature park has a 64-room lodge and miles of sandy beaches and a bird and butterfly trail. Eagle Eye Observatory was built in cooperation with the Austin Astronomical Society and has several 22-inch telescopes for public use, as well as pedestals where visitors can set up their own scopes. The emphasis is on star-gazing, but there are a number of birds to look at as well, and this is the departure place for the Vanishing Texas River Cruise.

Inks Lake State Park

Inks Lake is the smallest of a series of six lakes located on the Colorado River, and the 1,200-acre lake dominates the 2,000-acre park that bears its name. It is a popular recreation spot for boating and fishing. The best time to bird is early in the morning and avoid the busy weekends and holidays. However, from July to September the park has canoe trips that put a special emphasis on birding. Very limited dining and lodging facilities are available close to the park, so Burnet is your best bet for a home base, since it is only 13 miles from the lake. The wetlands attract a great many waterfowl, from Great Blue Heron that nest in the sycamore trees, to Pied-billed Grebe, Gadwall, Lesser Scaup, Bufflehead, Red-breasted Merganser, Ring-billed Gull, and Forster's Tern, which may be seen in the winter. Killdeer and Belted Kingfisher are also present, and even Bald Eagles may be seen. A few of the other species to be seen here will be in the grasslands in summer and may include Wild Turkey, Greater Roadrunner, Verdin, and both Cactus and Canyon Wrens. Sparrows include Lark and Black-throated. There are several walking trails that will lead you through a variety of habitat. The best place to bird is the riparian zones along the river at the Inks Dam National Fish Hatchery, which has a picnic area.

Longhorn Caverns State Park

Drive south from the Inks Dam National Fish Hatchery on Park Road 4 and you will come to the small, but potentially productive, park called Longhorn Caverns. This is another one of those spots on the Edwards Plateau where you can easily see the Golden-cheeked Warbler. Also in the summer you may see Yellow-billed Cuckoo, Black-chinned Hummingbird, Ladder-backed Woodpecker, White-eyed

Vireo, Canyon Towhee, and both Rufous-crowned and Lark Sparrows. Around the picnic area look for Inca Dove, Greater Roadrunner, and Golden-fronted Woodpecker. At dusk you may see Common Nighthawk, and Chimney Swift, Purple Martin, and Cliff and Barn Swallows are also present.

Attractions

Highland Lakes CAF Air Museum

Another educational spot has displays by the Hill Country Squadron of the Confederate Air Force, including WWII fighter planes, firearms, and memorabilia. Located at the Burnet Municipal Airport on south U.S. 281.

Hill Country Flyer

Take the kids on a real steam engine excursion train that runs from Cedar Park City Hall near U.S. 183 and R.M. 1431 near Austin to Burnet. The train is pulled by Engine No. 786, a 75-year-old steam locomotive. The ride is two hours long through the Hill Country and runs on weekends. For more information, phone 512-477-8468.

Motels

Howard Johnson, 908 Buchanan, phone 800-1-GO-HOJO (downtown)

Holiday Inn Express, 810 S. Water, phone 512-756-1789

In addition to the motels, there are a number of resorts in the area such as Canyon of the Eagles Lodge and Nature Park, Hwy. 2341, Lake Buchanan, phone 800-977-0081. It is the new home of the Vanishing Texas River Cruise.

Dining

Fast food options include Dairy Queen, Mr. Gatti's Pizza, Pizza Hut, McDonald's, Sonic, and Whataburger.

Burnet County Bar B Que, Hwy. 29 West

Riverwalk Café, 635 Hwy. 29 West

Highlander Restaurant and Steakhouse, 401 Buchanan Dr. #11 (Hwy. 29 West)

Fredericksburg

Convention & Visitors Bureau
106 N. Adams
830-997-6523
http://www.fredericksburg-texas.com

Almost like taking a step back in time, this city was founded in 1846 by German immigrants and still retains a great deal of the Old World flavor in its shops, restaurants, and festivities.

Birding

Enchanted Rock State Natural Area

This is one of the most unusual rock formations in the state of Texas. A dome of pink granite rises 400 feet above the surrounding landscape, and the exposed stone is only the tip of the Enchanted Rock batholith, which covers over 90 square miles and is estimated to be 1 billion years old. The rock itself is worth the trip. Although the dome offers little in bird habitat, the surrounding natural area covers 1,643 acres with over 5 miles of hiking trails. During the summer months, one of the best places to bird is the Sandy Creek flood plain, which is behind the entrance station. Eastern Phoebe, Barn Swallow, Northern Mockingbird, and House Finch can be seen at the entrance, and Bell's Vireo, Blue Grosbeak, Painted Bunting, and Red-winged Blackbirds may be seen in the same area. Both Golden-fronted Woodpecker and Ladder-backed Woodpeckers can also be seen in the brush surrounding the area. A hike on the Loop Trail will produce some of the same species, along with Wild Turkey, Northern Bobwhite, and Greater Roadrunner. And even though you may not see the bird, you may hear the descending call of the Canyon Wren. The four-mile-long trail may be too much for small children, especially in the heat of summer. At Moss Pond you can see Belted Kingfisher, and in winter the fields will contain an assortment of sparrows, including Vesper, Savannah, Fox, Song, Lincoln's, White-throated, White-crowned, and Harris's.

Attractions

Admiral Nimitz Museum and Historical Center

A sure-fire history lesson for the children, this complex contains the restored Nimitz Steamboat Hotel, which houses the history of Admiral Chester Nimitz, naval commander during World War II; the George Bush Gallery of the National Museum of the Pacific War, which has lifelike exhibits from the battles in the Pacific; the Garden of Peace, a gift from the people of Japan; and the History Walk that is lined with vintage aircraft, tanks, and guns. There is also a Memorial Wall, and the Plaza of the Presidents from Franklin Roosevelt to George Bush Sr.

Fredericksburg Butterfly Ranch and Habitat

Watch the process of a butterfly life cycle as butterflies lay eggs on larval plants in the brood cages. This working butterfly ranch specializes in monarch and native butterflies and is an educational experience for children and adults alike. Located at 508 West Main Street in the historic Loeffer-Weber House, built in 1846. A nature shop is stocked with items related to butterflies.

Pioneer Museum Complex

Examples of early German structures and artifacts are centered around an 1849 eight-room pioneer home and store. There is an authentic blacksmith shop, smokehouse and "Sunday Haus," plus a log cabin, wagon shed, and schoolhouse. There is also a fire museum with early Fredericksburg fire fighting equipment.

Lady Bird Johnson Municipal Park

Enjoy the beauty of this 190-acre municipal park named in honor of the former first lady who has done so much to beautify Texas. There are RV sites, an 18-hole golf course, swimming, tennis, volleyball, and badminton. Picnic areas have grills, and a lake is available for boating, fishing, canoes, and paddle boats.

Historic District, Heart of Fredericksburg

This self-guided tour of historic Fredericksburg has over 80 points of interest. You can get a free tour guide map of the district at the visitor center at 106 N. Adams Street.

Festivals

May: Founders Day Festival, phone 830-997-2835

October: Oktoberfest, phone 830-997-4810

Motels

Budget Host Deluxe Inn, phone 830-997-3344

Comfort Inn, phone 830-997-9811

Days Inn Suites, phone 800-320-1830

Econo Lodge Motel, phone 888-919-3830

Dining

Do not visit Fredericksburg without dining in one of several authentic German restaurants. The city has many of the usual fast foods, including McDonald's, Mr. Gatti's, Pizza Hut, Sonic, Dairy Queen, Church's Chicken, and Subway.

Mamacita's Mexican Restaurant, 506 E. Main

Old German Bakery & Restaurant, 225 W. Main

Porky's Hamburger & Onion Rings, 904 W. Main

Sunday House German-American Restaurant, 515 E. Main

The Dog Haus, 155 E. Main

Johnson City
Chamber of Commerce
P.O. Box 485
830-868-7684

Johnson City is best known as the home of Lyndon Baines Johnson and is the site of the LBJ National Historical Park. There are a number of local birding spots not listed in guidebooks, such as the Hills Vineyard and under the bridge on 281. Check with the Chamber of Commerce for more.

Birding

Pedernales Falls State Park

The Pedernales River flows through this 4,860-acre park located about 32 miles west of Austin. It is open for swimming and tubing on the river and can be very busy on weekends. There are more than 20 miles of trails, including the 8.2-mile Wolf Mountain Trail. The area is a favorite for hikers, but birders, even without going on the strenuous hiking trails, can find an abundance of birds, including the much sought after Golden-cheeked Warbler, which can be found in the park from mid-March through June. The bird can be seen just beyond the entrance, along the Wolf Mountain Trail, and along the Hill Country Nature Trail. The Hill Country Nature Trail may be the best birding spot for a family, but a drive up to Duck Pond and Cypress Pool at the north end of the park can give you a look at some interesting birds. On the way, there is a bird blind that can also be productive. At the blind you can see the open fields and brush, and in winter a number of seedeaters can be seen here, including House Wren, Spotted Towhee, and an assortment of sparrows, including Chipping, Field, Vesper, Savannah, Grasshopper, Fox, Song, Lincoln's, White-throated, White-crowned, and Harris's. At Duck Pond, look for the beautiful Wood Duck and the brilliant Vermilion Flycatcher in summer. At Pedernales Falls and Cypress Pool, sightings may be made of both Belted and Green Kingfishers, along with Red-bellied Woodpecker and both Blue and Green Herons in the summer, along with Yellow-throated and Red-eyed Vireos and Summer Tanager. Painted Bunting is also seen in the area.

Attractions

Exotic Resort Zoo

Take a guided tour around this 137 acres of woodland in one of the zoo's vehicles, and you will see greater kudu from Africa, whose horns can grow to five feet in length, or a blue bull from India, an eland, or even an American bison. There is a petting zoo where children can actually feed and pet young animals. For information call 830-868-4357.

Lyndon B. Johnson National Historical Park

Stop at the visitors center for information, to see the exhibits, to see an audiovisual program, or even listen to a ranger talk. See the 100-year-old building where Lyndon Johnson lived, and there are artifacts of the Johnson family including furnishings and period furniture. Tours of the home are conducted every half hour. Also on the grounds is a 1856 dogtrot cabin, 1880 stone farm buildings, and an exhibit area. Open daily and operated by the National Park Service.

Festivals

April: National Park Week, phone 830-868-7128

Motels

Charles' Motel, Hwy. 281 South, phone 830-868-7171

Save Inn Motel, Hwy. 281 and 290, phone 830-868-4044

Dining

Fast food includes Burger King, Dairy Queen, and Hot Stuff Pizza

Cap's Deli, 502 W. Main

Charles', 209 Hwy. 281-290 South

Feed Mill Café, 103 W. Main

Hill Country Cupboard, 101 Hwy. 281-290

Pasquales' Mexican, 608 E. Main

Ronnie's Pit BBQ, 211 Hwy. 281-290 South

Uncle Kunkel's BBQ, 110 Hwy. 281-290 South

Kerrville

Convention & Visitors Bureau
2108 Sidney Baker
800-221-7958
http://www.ktc.net/kerrcvb

It is believed by many that this area has the most healthful climate in the nation. Capt. Charles A. Schreiner, Confederate soldier and Texas Ranger, established a mercantile business here in 1869, and the area has continued to expand. The surrounding area, due to the scenic wonders and climate, is home to a number of dude ranches and religious encampments.

Birding

Kerrville-Schreiner State Park

Although primarily a recreational area, this relatively small state park (517 acres) is situated on the upper Guadalupe River and is located about four miles from Kerrville. The best place to bird is along the river northeast of Hwy. 173. The outer loop road on the other side of the highway is also promising, and during migration, flycatchers, vireos, warblers, tanagers, and orioles may be seen. Resident water birds include Pied-billed Grebe, Great Blue Heron, and Double-crested Cormorant. In winter along the river you may see Eared Grebe, Green-winged Teal, Northern Pintail, Northern Shoveler, Gadwall, and American Wigeon, along with others such as Lesser Scaup and Ruddy Duck. In the summer there are a number of nesting birds such as Yellow-billed Cuckoo, Acadian, Great Crested, and Scissor-tailed Flycatcher. Smaller birds include Blue-gray Gnatcatcher, three species of vireos, Yellow-breasted Chat, and Summer Tanager. Along the river you may see or hear Barred and Eastern Screech-Owls. In the camping area at dusk you could see a Great Horned Owl. Others include Eastern Bluebird and Vermilion Flycatcher. On the outer loop road in the winter, possibilities are good to see Red-breasted Nuthatch, Brown Creeper, and both Golden-crowned and Ruby-crowned Kinglets, along with Hermit Thrush. The fields along the roads provide habitat for a number of sparrows, from Chipping and Vesper to both White-throated and

White-crowned. On the way back to town, if you have time, stop at the Louis Hayes Park just outside Kerrville and walk the nature trail, which can be very good for birding during migration.

Attractions

Cowboy Artists of America Museum

If you are interested in cowboys and art, this museum contains works by some of the best-known artists in the field including Joe Beeler, James Boren, and Melvin Warren. There are permanent displays as well as rotating exhibits and workshops.

Hill Country Museum

Captain Charles A. Schreiner, born in France, was an early settler of the Kerrville area, and this museum showcases artifacts and memorabilia in his home with period furnishings and French crystal chandeliers.

Kerrville Camera Safari

A drive-through park with exotic animals from Texas and around the world. This is a great chance to use your camera, and be sure and take your binoculars along.

Festivals

April: Kerrville Easter Festival and Chili Classic, phone
    830-792-3535
May/June: Kerrville Folk Festival, phone 830-257-3600
May: Kerrville Texas State Arts and Crafts, phone 830-896-5711

Motels

Best Western-Sunday House Inn, 2124 Sidney Baker, phone
    830-896-1313 or 800-677-9477
Budget Inn, 1804 Sidney Baker, phone 800-219-8158
Comfort Inn, 2001 Sidney Baker, phone 830-792-7700
Days Inn of Kerrville, 2000 Sidney Baker, phone 830-896-1000
Econo Lodge and Conference Center, 2145 Sidney Baker, phone
    830-896-1711 or 800-225-1374
Super 8 Motel, 2127 Sidney Baker, phone 800-274-2111

Dining

Choo-Choo's Bar-B-Que, 615 Schreiner St. or 2126 Sidney Baker N.

Hill Country Café—A Texas Legend, 806 Main Street

Acapulco Restaurant, 1718 Sidney Baker N.

Cracker Barrel, 2110 Sidney Baker

Denny's, 209 Sidney Baker S.

Luby's Cafeteria, 1845 Sidney Baker

A wide choice of fast foods include Dairy Queen (3 locations), Church's, Little Caesar's, Mr. Gatti's, Pizza Hut, Taco Bell, and Whataburger.

Lago Vista

Chamber of Commerce
20811 Dawn Drive
888-328-5246
http://www.lagovista.org
E-mail: lagovista@prismnet.com

This lakeside resort development has blossomed into a community and was incorporated in 1984. It is the gateway to the Balcones Canyonlands National Wildlife Refuge.

Birding

Balcones Canyonlands National Wildlife Refuge

This refuge of 46,000 acres was established in 1992 primarily for the protection of the nesting areas of the Golden-cheeked Warbler and the Black-capped Vireo. Only two areas are now open to the public. On the northernmost part of the refuge, the Eckhardt Tract covers about 200 acres and can be the home of as many as 20 pairs of the Black-capped Vireos. There is a viewing platform near the entrance and parking area. In addition to the endangered species, birds that nest here include Mourning Dove, Yellow-billed Cuckoo, Black-chinned Hummingbird, White-eyed Vireo, Yellow Breasted Chat, Summer Tanager, Painted Bunting, and several species of sparrows. A little farther south is the Nagel Tract, a diversified habitat that has a 2-mile loop trail with prairie, creek, and riparian habitat along with oak and juniper woodlands. Year-round residents are Wild Turkey, Northern Bobwhite, Greater Roadrunner, Western Scrub-jay, Tufted Titmouse, and both Carolina and Bewick's Wrens. There are a number of sparrows, and Cooper's and Red-shouldered Hawk may be seen, as well as both Eastern Screech-Owl and Great Horned Owl. Of course, the star of the area is the Golden-cheeked Warbler, which can be seen from mid-March through July. The bird list is rather extensive, with four species of flycatchers, including the Vermilion, and two swallows, Cliff and Barn.

Attractions

Lago Vista Airpower Museum

This museum has a collection of more than 150 model aircraft from both World Wars, Korea, Vietnam, and Desert Storm, including L-4 Grasshopper and RF-4C Phantom Jet. There are also exhibits of uniforms, guns, diaries, medals, photographs, and books from 1914 through Desert Storm. Located at Lago Vista Airport in Hanger 9. Open only on weekends from 1-5.

Festivals

Texas Songbird Festival. Held in May, this festival is at Lago Vista, the gateway to the Balcones Canyonlands National Wildlife Refuge, the home of the Black-capped Vireo and the Golden-cheeked Warbler. Contact: Lago Vista Chamber of Commerce.

Motels

Cow Creek Lodge, FM 1431 at Cow Creek, phone 512-267-3652
Lago Vista Resort, 1900 American Drive, phone 512-267-0900
The Shores at Lake Travis, 1917 American Drive, 800-850-2901

Dining

Critters, 5803 Thunderbird
Shades Café, 18200 Lake Point Cove, Point Ventura
True Grits Texas Grill, 18645 FM 1431, Jonestown
Windjammer, 1918 American Drive

Leakey

Frio County Chamber of Commerce
830-232-5222

This small town (pronounced Lake-E) is the center of some of the best birding areas on the Edward's Plateau, and although the housing and dining facilities are limited, it can be an excellent home base for several prime birding spots in the area. In March many hummingbirds can be seen in the area.

Birding

Garner State Park

This park is one of the gems of the state parks, with 1,420 acres nestled in the hills along the Frio River. It is one of the busiest, with campers and recreational activities filling the weekends and holidays. It is also one of the places the Golden-cheeked Warbler can be found during nesting season. Best place to bird is along the river in the Pecan Grove area on the south side of the park. The camping area is an excellent place to bird during migration, and you may see a wide variety of flycatchers, vireos, warblers, tanagers, and orioles. In the summer Great Blue Heron, Wood Duck, Yellow-billed Cuckoo, Belted Kingfisher, Green Kingfisher, and Golden-fronted Woodpecker should be present, along with Blue-gray Gnatcatcher and several species of vireos such as White-eyed and Red-eyed. At night, several owls may be heard, including the Eastern Screech-Owl and Barred Owl. Overhead you may see both Black and Turkey Vultures, Red-shouldered and Red-tailed Hawks, along with Common Raven. At the Shady Meadows camping area, the Golden-cheeked Warbler will be present from mid-March through July along with Black-chinned Hummingbird, Ladder-backed Woodpecker, Canyon Towhee, and Rufous-crowned Sparrow. You may see the Bewick's Wren, Rock Wren, and hear the descending call of the Canyon Wren. In the early morning or at dusk, listen for the Common Poorwill.

Lost Maples State Park

If you are interested in fall colors, this is a great place to visit from late October to mid-November when the bigtooth maples begin to turn into a brilliant display of red, yellow, and orange. The park can be busy on weekends during this time. In addition to the birds that may be seen, the park offers some beautiful scenery with its canyons and overviews. It is actually closer to the small community of Vanderpool (population 20) than Leakey, but dining and housing are limited. Lost Maples covers 2,208 acres and is another place to see the Golden-cheeked Warbler, usually along the first mile of the East Trail, along Can Creek. The list of birds that can be seen in summer is impressive, with Black-chinned Hummingbirds present, along with Eastern Wood-Pewee, Acadian, Ash-throated, and Scissor-tailed Flycatchers. Western Scrub-jay can also be seen here, as well as Bushtit and three species of wrens: Canyon, Carolina, and Bewick. Other summer visitors include Summer Tanager, Canyon Towhee, and both Rufous-crowned and Chipping Sparrows. In the picnic area there is open space, and overhead you want to watch the floating vultures, as there could be a Zone-tailed Hawk with them. At night you may hear, or even see, both Great Horned Owl and Eastern Screech-Owl, and members of the "goat-sucker" family such as Common Poorwill and Chuck-will's-widow are more likely to be heard than seen. In the fields several species of sparrows such as Chipping, Field, Fox, White-throated, and White-crowned may be present.

Attractions

Real County Historical Museum

This museum contains artifacts depicting the history of Real County area in period rooms. It is located on the courthouse square and is open Friday and Saturday from 10 A.M. to 4 P.M.

Scenic Drives

There are some beautiful wonders of nature to be seen by driving along FM 337, especially during the fall months, but the scenery is spectacular at any time of the year, with wooded steeps and brilliant valleys. FM 187 will take you to Lost Maples, known for its beautiful fall colors, and U.S. 83 skirts the East Frio River, and 12 miles north there is a roadside park with a lovely view for a picnic.

Motels

Frio Canyon Lodge, U.S. Hwy. 83 & FM 337, phone 830-232-6800

River Haven Cabins, P.O. Box 610, phone 830-232-5400

Neal's Lodges, P.O. Box 165, Concan, TX 78838, phone 830-232-6118. Neal's has lodges, camping, horseback riding, hayrides, and tubing. It is also a great place to bird; the Black-capped Vireo has been seen here. Mary Anna and Rodger Roosa are birder friendly.

Dining

Frio Canyon Restaurant, U.S. Hwy. 83 at FM 337

Hill Country BBQ, U.S. Hwy. 83 S.

Mama Chole's, U.S. Hwy. 83 N.

Northern Plains

cedar waxwing

Brownwood

Chamber of Commerce
600A Depot Street
P.O. Box 880
915-646-9535
http://www.brownwood.com

This city is located in the very heart of Texas and once was a major cotton buying center and is home of Howard Payne University.

Birding

Lake Brownwood State Park

Located about 16 miles from Brownwood, this 568-acre park is on the western edge of Lake Brownwood, an 18,000-acre reservoir that gathers water from two tributaries of the Colorado River. There are hiking trails, and it is primarily a recreational lake with boating and fishing.

A number of resident birds can be found just inside the entrance on Texas Oak Trail, which contains a mix of mesquite grassland and oak savannah habitats. Possibilities include Black-chinned Hummingbird, Tufted Titmouse, and three species of wrens: Cactus, Carolina, and Bewick. Eastern Bluebirds are also seen here, along with Canyon Towhee, Rufous-crowned Sparrow, and Eastern Meadowlark. In the summer you may see Mississippi Kite, Common Nighthawk, Western Kingbird, Blue-gray Gnatcatchers, and the beautiful Painted Bunting. Wintertime will produce a new assortment of birds, from Ruby-crowned Kinglet to Cedar Waxwing, and the fields will contain several species of sparrows such as Chipping, Field, Vesper, Song, White-crowned, and Harris's. On the lake itself you can see Great Blue Heron, Pied-billed Grebe, and Mallard Ducks, along with both Horned and Eared Grebes, Northern Pintail, Northern Shoveler, Gadwall, American Wigeon, Redhead, and Ring-necked Duck. Sandhill Cranes sometimes appear in the winter in the fields surrounding the park.

Attractions

Brown County Museum of History

Exhibits include seven rooms in the old castle-like jail, and there is an exhibit that traces the history of communications. Located in the 200 block of N. Broadway. Open Wed. 1 P.M. to 4 P.M. and Sat. 11 A.M. to 4 P.M.

Douglas MacArthur Academy of Freedom

This facility is affiliated with Howard Payne University, and the displays depict history and government in the Western world. Personal memoirs of General Douglas MacArthur are featured, along with replicas of Egyptian tomb statues, and Magna Carta Hall is a replica of an English castle room. The meeting room in Independence Hall is also among the displays. Open when school is in session, phone 915-646-2502 for more information.

Camp Bowie Memorial Park

This small park has displays of military equipment, cannon, and armor and honors the men of the 36th Infantry Division. It is located at Burnett Drive and Travis Road in the Camp Bowie Industrial Area.

Festivals

Pecan Fest, phone 915-646-9535

Motels

Best Western, 410 E. Commerce, phone 800-528-1234

Days Inn, 515 E. Commerce, phone 800-537-8483

Gate I Inn, 4410 Hwy. 377 South, phone 800-400-8300

Luxury Inn, 1008 W. Commerce, phone 915-641-1818

Dining

Golden Corral, 313 E. Commerce

Underwood's Cafeteria, 402 W. Commerce

Red Wagon, 401 E. Main

Skillet's, 500 E. Commerce

Humphrey Pete's, 102 Early Blvd.

Mama's Kitchen, 409 E. Commerce

Fast food choices are: Burger King, Chicken Express, Sonic, Subway, Domino's, and Taco Bell.

Cleburne

Chamber of Commerce
1511 W. Henderson St.
817-645-2455
http://www.cleburne.com
E-mail: nell@cleburnechamber.com

The city was called Camp Henderson until 1867 when it was changed to honor Civil War Confederate General Pat Cleburne. The railroad has played an important role in the growth of the city, and the state's largest railroad construction and repair shops were located here at one time. At Hulen Park the historic locomotive #3417 is being restored.

Birding

Cleburne State Park

Over 500 acres surrounding Cedar Lake, this park has a variety of habitats, but the north end of the lake will produce the most species. Reach the park on U.S. 67, Park Road 21 out of Cleburne about 12 miles south. It would be simple to make this a stopover on your way to the Glen Rose birding area. Good for migrating songbirds, the park also will produce Black-chinned Hummingbird, as well as Red-bellied and Downy Woodpeckers, Great Crested Flycatcher, Carolina Wren, Tufted Titmouse, Summer Tanager, and Red-winged Blackbirds. Although few waterfowl are present in the spring, Great Blue Heron, Little Blue Heron, and Green Heron can be seen in summer, along with Wood Ducks. Hike Coyote Rim Nature Trail from the campground to the spillway and you may see Ladder-backed Woodpecker, Blue-gray Gnatcatcher, and Black and White Warblers, as well as several species of sparrows.

Attractions

Johnson County Courthouse

Built in 1912, this six-story structure is supported by four columns of matched marble and is ornately garnished in old ivory and gold cut plaster. The dome has beautiful stained glass. Located downtown and open during business hours.

Layland Museum

Contains memorabilia of Johnson County history and early Texas. Includes Indian artifacts dating to pre-Columbian cultures, fossils, and genealogy records. Located in Carnegie Library, 201 N. Caddo.

Motels

American Inn, 1836 N. Main, phone 817-641-3451

Best Western-Smithfield Inn, 1707 W. Henderson, phone 817-556-3330

Days Inn, U.S. Hwy. 67 W. at N. Ridgeway, phone 817-645-8836

Five Star Inn, 2701 S. I-35, W. Exit 32, phone 817-645-1271

Western Inn, 1411 E. Henderson, 817-645-4386

Dining

Fast food restaurants include Braum's, Chicken Express, Church's, Dairy Queen, McDonald's, Schlotzsky's, Sonic, and Whataburger.

Catfish Cabin, 408 Hwy. 174 Rio Vista

CiCi's Pizza, 1301 W. Henderson

Golden Corral, 1623 W. Henderson

Jose's Mexican Restaurant, 728 N. Main (this is excellent and reasonable Mexican food)

Peel Country, 1704 N. Main

Susannah's Home Style Cooking, 1514 W. Henderson

Dallas

Convention & Visitors Bureau
1201 Elm Street
800-C-DALLAS
http://www.dallascvb.com

The metroplex is so extensive and contains so many visitor's sites, that only a special few are listed in this book. Dining and motels also are in abundance. It is suggested you obtain a copy of *Exploring Dallas With Children* by Kay McCasland Threadgill or *Exploring Texas With Children* by Sharry Buckner for more information.

Birding

White Rock Lake Park

Located on the northeast side of Dallas, this 1,119-acre lake is a popular boating area (no motorized) and has hiking and walking trails, along with picnicking areas. It is usually very busy on weekends. The spillway is a good place to see shore birds and waders. In the winter, Yellow-bellied Sapsuckers, Northern Flicker, Brown Creepers, Winter Wren, and Golden-crowned and Ruby-crowned Kinglets can be seen. In the spring and summer, with a scope, many waterfowl can be seen from the dam, including Great Blue, Black-crowned, and Yellow-crowned Night-Herons. Great and Snowy Egrets are common, as are Mallard Ducks. A wider variety of water birds can be seen in the winter, including Pied-billed Grebes, Double-crested Cormorant, Green-winged Teal, Mallard, Gadwall, American Wigeon, Ring-necked Duck, Lesser Scaup, and Ruddy Duck. Common Loon, Horned and Eared Grebes are present in lesser numbers. Several species of gulls and terns can be seen, as well as White Pelicans. The wooded areas can also produce many neotropical migrants in spring or fall. Full-time residents include Red-shouldered Hawk, Yellow-billed Cuckoo, Eastern Screech-Owl, Barred Owl, Red-bellied and Downy Woodpeckers, Blue Jays, and American Crows.

Southside Water Treatment Plant

To reach the Southside Water Treatment Plant from I-30, take I-45 south to U.S. 175 and go south until you pass under I-20. Then take the third exit onto Beltline Road West and follow Beltline for about two miles. Visitors are welcome but need to remember this is an operating treatment plant. Go during the week as the gates are sometimes closed on weekends. Summer birds include Black-bellied Whistling Ducks, Common Moorhen, and Black-necked Stilts. An assortment of egrets and herons can be seen in winter, and Wood Ducks, Green-winged Teals, Mallards, and Northern Pintails and Northern Shovelers can also be present. You can drive or walk around the comparatively small area, and resident birds include Pied-billed Grebe, Cattle Egret, Wood Duck, American Coot, Killdeer, Rock Dove, Great-tailed and Common Grackles, and Red-winged Blackbirds. The mud flats attract a number of shore birds such as Lesser Yellowlegs and at least six species of sandpipers.

Cedar Hill State Park and Dallas Nature Center

This is a 1,810-acre state park, located on the northeastern edge of Joe Pool Lake. The cedar-covered hills offer an entirely different habitat than you will find elsewhere in the Dallas area. From I-20, west of Duncanville, take FM 1362 south to the park entrance. This is another great place for a family picnic. Along the trails and roads on the edge of the lake, the possibilities are almost endless.

The Dallas Nature Center is just to the east of the park between FM 1362 and Mountain Creek Road. It is a nonprofit organization designed to foster a greater appreciation and understanding of the natural environment through conservation, education, recreation, and research. There are guided walks and educational programs. Another place for your children to learn about nature.

Attractions

For a comprehensive list of attractions in the Dallas area, refer to *Exploring Dallas With Children* by Kay McCasland Threadgill, Republic of Texas Press. Also consult the Texas Department of Transportation' *Texas State Travel Guide*.

African-American Museum

One of the largest collections of African-American folk art in the country, this museum was founded in 1974 and has a 36,000-square-foot facility dedicated to the preservation and display of African-American artistic, cultural, and historical materials. Located at 3536 Grand Avenue at Fair Park entrance.

Age of Steam Railroad Museum (in Fair Park)

Four steam locomotives, including "Big Boy," the world's largest. This display of railroad equipment includes dining cars, lounge cars, and Pullman sleeping cars. Hold your ears when the whistle demonstration is held during tours.

Dallas Aquarium (in Fair Park)

Featuring a 10,500-gallon, nine-foot-tall Amazon Flooded Forest Exhibit with twenty species of fish from the Amazon River. There is an educational video and over 375 species of aquatic animals, including marine and freshwater fish, reptiles, amphibians, and invertebrates.

Museum of Natural History

Displays of wildlife native to Texas are set in authentic natural habitat. Located in Fair Park. Open 10 A.M. to 5 P.M. every day except Thanksgiving and Christmas. Admission fee.

Dallas Zoo

A trip to the zoo will consume an entire day and cut into your birding time, but this zoo has over 2,000 animals, including many endangered and rare species. A 25-acre Wilds of Africa display features over 90 species of African birds, mammals, and reptiles in a natural setting.

The Sixth Floor

Give your family a lesson in history at the Texas School Book Depository building from which President John F. Kennedy was assassinated. Exhibits feature photographs, artifacts, a 30-minute video, and six films. Located at 411 Elm Street.

Festivals

September: State Fair of Texas, phone 214-565-9931

Motels

The list of accommodations in the Dallas area is very extensive and includes most chain motels. Please refer to the Texas Department of Transportation Accommodations Guide (comes with the Travel Guide). Request information on motels that will allow you to avoid, as much as possible, the Dallas early morning and evening rush hour traffic. If you plan to visit the birding areas listed above, accommodations in Garland or Mesquite would put you nearer the White Rock Lake and the Southside Water Treatment Plant. The Cedar Hill State Park is located south of Interstate 20 near Duncanville. Any motel on LBJ Freeway (Loop 635) will put you in driving distance.

Dining

As with the motel accommodations, the list of Dallas restaurants is too extensive to list here. In such a metroplex, it is safe to say that finding a restaurant will not be a problem, particularly in the areas where motels are located.

Denton

Chamber of Commerce
P.O. Drawer P
414 Parkway
940-382-7895
888-381-1818
http://www.denton-chamber.org
E-mail: cvb@iglobal.net

Located north of Dallas, this growing metropolitan city is situated between two large lakes, Ray Roberts to the north, and Lake Lewisville to the south. Both lakes are greatly used as recreational and fishing areas but can also be of interest to the birder.

Birding

Ray Roberts Lake

This relatively new lake covers 22,745 acres and is owned by the city of Dallas as a reservoir. It is used a great deal for recreational purposes, such as fishing and boating, and can be very busy on weekends. For a list of possible bird species to be seen, consult the listings for Lewisville Lake Park, as they are very similar.

Cross Timbers Park Project

Located along Hickory Creek Road in Denton County, the Cross Timbers Project envisions a 43-acre park connected to a greenbelt extending into a total of 80 acres along the Hickory Creek watershed. Plans call for hiking trails, children's educational programs, and of course birding. The target goal for opening is the summer of 2001. Call 940-349-PARK for more information.

Attractions

Denton County Historical Museum and Texas Heritage Center

Displays depict life at the turn of the century. Rotating exhibits include artifacts and memorabilia. Also has a family and genealogy research center. Located at the Mills Denton Factory Stores.

Denton County Courthouse-on-the-Square Museum

This museum in located in the Denton County Courthouse that was built in 1886 and reviews Denton's history with special displays, including Indian and Denton County pottery, American pressed blue glass, weaponry, and dolls.

Little Chapel in the Woods

Located on the campus of Texas Woman's University, this chapel was designed by O'Neil Ford and completed in 1939. Ten stained glass windows depict the theme of "Woman Ministering to Human Needs." Open during school hours.

Motels

Days Inn, 601 S. I-35 E. Exit 465B, phone 940-566-1990. Children under five free

Excel Inn of Denton, 4211 N. I-35, phone 800-356-8013. Under 18 free

Super 8, 620 S. I-35 E., phone 800-800-8000. Under 12 free

Motel 6, 4125 N. I-35, phone 940-566-4798

Howard Johnson Express, 3116 Bandera, phone 800-444-6835

Holiday Inn, 1500 Dallas Drive, phone 800-465-4329

Dining

Fast food restaurants in Denton include: Arby's, Burger Barn, Burger King, Dairy Queen, Golden Fried Chicken, Grandy's, Taco Bell, Jack-in-the-Box, KFC, Long John Silver's, McDonald's, CiCi's Pizza, Schlotzsky's, Sonic, Subway, Weinerschnitzel, Wendy's, and Whataburger.

Colter's Bar-B-Q, 2229 S. I-35 E.

Good Eats Café, 5812 North I-35 (family style eating at a reasonable price)

Western Sizzlin Steak House, 2000 W. University Drive

Pancho's, 1117 Avenue C. (inexpensive Mexican food)

Tia's Tex Mex, 2416 Lillian Miller Pkwy.

Denton County Independent Hamburger Co., two locations (very good), 113 W. Hickory and 715 Sunset

Fairfield

Chamber of Commerce
820 East Commerce
903-389-5792

Freestone County got its name from the freestone rock in the area, and Fairfield, the county seat, is known as a banking, market, and shipping center. A rock quarry, sawmill, and lignite coal mine, along with oil and gas production, play a big role in the area's economy.

Birding

Fairfield Lake State Park

Perhaps the least known of Texas birding areas, this 1,460-acre park
and the warm waters of the 2,400-acre lake (a result of the operation of the Texas Utilities Big Brown Steam Electric Power plant on
the north shore) are very attractive to a wide variety of bird species.
At the entrance from Hwy. 3285 out of Fairfield, turn right and go to
the bird watching trail, a mile-long hike that passes through
oak-juniper habitat as well as fields and skirts the south tip of the
lake, which has a great many cattails. In the summer you may see
White-breasted Nuthatch, Eastern Bluebird, Painted Bunting in the
fields, and Pied-billed Grebe, Anhinga, Snowy Egrets, Wood Duck,
Least Tern, and even Belted Kingfisher in the marshes. Prothonotary
Warbler has also been seen in the area. Go back to the entrance and
take PR 64 to the picnic area, which sits in the fork of the southern
legs of the lake. Here you will see about the same variety of birds in
the summer, but there are also beaver ponds, and during migration
and in winter, this is an excellent site to bird. In the winter Bald
Eagles are attracted to the warm waters, and tours are offered several times a month from November to February. Contact the park at
901-389-4515. Up to 20 eagles have been seen.

Attractions

Freestone County Museum

Housed in a 100-year-old jail where the gunman John Wesley
Hardin was once incarcerated, this museum features period furni-
ture, historical documents, and a telephone display. There is a
cannon on the courthouse lawn that is a relic of the Civil War
Sibley's Brigade, a Confederate force that fought Federal forces in
New Mexico in 1862.

Festivals

October: Falcon Fest, phone 903-389-4514

Motels

Budget Inn, I-45 and Hwy. 27 West, phone 903-389-5443

Holiday Inn Express, 603 West Commerce (Hwy. 84 W.), phone 1-800-HOL-IDAY

Regency Inn, 903 West Highway 84, phone 903-389-4440

Sam's Motel, I-45 and Highway 84, phone 903-389-2172

Dining

Fast foods are: Burger King, Dairy Queen, Jack-in-the-Box, KFC, Texas Burger, McDonald's, Subway, and Taco Bell.

Dalia's Mexican Restaurant, 1340 W. Hwy. 84

Gilberto's Mexican Restaurant, 300 I-45

Pizza Hut of Fairfield, West Hwy. 84

Ponte's Diner, 680 W. Hwy. 84

Sam's Original Restaurant, 390 E. I-45

Something Different, West Hwy. 84

Fort Worth

Convention & Visitors Bureau
415 Throckmorton in Sundance Square
800-433-5747

A metropolitan area that grew from a military camp established by Gen. Winfield Scott at the end of the Mexican War and named for Gen. William Worth, who took part in that war. Diversified now with industrial plants and a business center, the city was made famous as a major shipping headquarters for Texas cattlemen after the Civil War. The city calls itself the Museum Capital of the Southwest and has numerous attractions. For a complete list, consult the Texas Department of Transportation's *State Travel Guide*. It is the home of Southwestern Baptist Theological Seminary, Tarrant County Junior College, Texas Christian University, University of North Texas Health Science Center, and Texas Wesleyan University.

Birding

Fort Worth Nature Center and Lake Worth

The largest urban refuge in North America, this 3,500-acre sanctuary is located on the northwestern side of Fort Worth just off Loop 820 on Hwy. 199. There are 25 miles of hiking and birding trails, and the variety of habitats are easy to access. Perhaps the best birding, especially for children, can be found on the 900-foot Lotus Marsh Boardwalk, which will give a good view of many of the area's wetland birds such as Pied-billed Grebe, Great Blue Heron, Great Egret, Wood Duck, American Coot, and Belted Kingfisher. In summer the variety of species is expanded to include Snowy Egret, Little Blue and Green Herons, Black-crowned and Yellow-crowned Night-Herons, Anhinga, Least Bittern, Tricolored Heron, White Ibis, Roseate Spoonbill, Wood Stork, Black-bellied Whistling Duck, Purple Gallinule, and Common Moorhen. The bottomland forest along the lakeshore can best be birded from Greer Island and the causeway. In the spring and fall migration periods, this vegetated area will provide habitat for a great many birds, including flycatchers, vireos, warblers, tanagers, and orioles. You may also see Yellow- billed Cuckoo, Red-bellied and Downy Woodpecker, Blue Jay, Carolina Chickadee, Tufted Titmouse, and both White-eyed and Red-eyed Vireos. Lake birds can best be seen from Greer Island, and a scope would come in handy here. Take the Oak Motte Trail, which provides an entirely different environment and variety of birds, including Northern Bobwhite and Wild Turkey. In the winter the prairie sites will contain a great many sparrows, including Field, Vesper, Fox, Song, Lincoln's, Swamp, White-throated, White-crowned, and Harris's. For more information on the nature center, contact: Fort Worth Nature Center, Park and Recreation Department, 9601 Fossil Ridge, Fort Worth, TX 76135, phone 817-237-1111.

Benbrook Lake

Located just southwest of Fort Worth on Hwy. 377, this 3,770-acre lake is managed by the Army Corps of Engineers and can be very busy on weekends and holidays. Summer birds to be found in the area are similar to those at Lake Worth, and it is a magnet for migrating birds during late spring and fall. A scope to scan the shoreline can produce a good look at American Avocet and a number of sandpiper species. Shore bird possibilities include both Greater and Lesser Yellowlegs, Long-billed Dowitcher, Willet, Wilson's Phalarope, and Dunlin. Both Forster's and Least Tern may be seen, along with Marbled Godwit. A look at the sky might reveal a fishing Osprey, and even a Bald Eagle may be seen in the winter.

Attractions

Fort Worth Museum of Science and History

A "hands-on" type museum where young children can learn about science by doing. At KIDSPACE, they can participate in such activities as puppetry, Water Works, and Build-a-house.

Other areas include "People and Their Possessions," "Your Body," "History of Medicine," "Calculators and Computers," "Rocks and Fossils," and "Hands on History." The Omni Theater is a tremendous experience for youngsters and oldsters alike, with shows on the huge curved screen depicting great natural events or man-made adventure such as space discovery. In the Noble Planetarium, young people can enjoy programs on astronomy, and at DinoDig, they can dig for dinosaur bones in the discovery area.

Fort Worth Zoo

Selected as one of the outstanding zoos in the nation, the Fort Worth Zoo features different areas such as Koala Outback, Herpetarium, with its natural exhibits and collection of frogs, crocodiles, and snakes, Asian Falls where visitors walk along a raised boardwalk to see Sumatran tigers and bears, and the World of Primates with species of all the great apes that includes an indoor rain forest for gorillas, monkeys, and free-flying tropical birds, and the Plains exhibit that displays Mexican wolves and other creatures of the Southwest in a natural setting.

Vintage Flying Museum

Located at Meacham Airport, this display may appeal more to Dad than the kids. Restorations of vintage aircraft from World War II, the Korean conflict, and Vietnam, along with a variety of support vehicles are on display on weekends. For a weekday guided tour, reservations must be made. Call 817-624-1935 for more information.

Pate Museum of Transportation

This museum has a fantastic display of antique railroad cars, vintage and classic automobiles, military aircraft, navy minesweeper, and others. Again, this may appeal more to adults than children, but it can also be very educational. Located on U.S. 377 southwest of Fort Worth in the little community of Cresson.

For more information on sights to be visited with children, consult *Exploring Fort Worth With Children* by Michael Bumagin or *Exploring Texas With Children* by Sharry Buckner.

Motels

As with any large city, there is an enormous selection of lodging available. To visit the Fort Worth Nature Center and Lake Worth, or Benbrook Lake, housing should be obtained on the west side of the city, thus avoiding a great deal of traffic. Any place on Loop 820 West would be appropriate.

Dining

There is an endless selection of places to eat in the Fort Worth area. If you stay in the area, it is probable many restaurants will be located in the proximity of your motel.

Glen Rose

Convention and Visitors Bureau
888-346-6282

Glen Rose is a unique part of the state of Texas, worthy of a visit whether you bird or not. The educational opportunities for children are unlimited, from the wildlife park to learning about dinosaurs. The Fossil Rim Wildlife Center is a must visit. Take time to enjoy this magnificent place.

Birding

Dinosaur Valley State Park

Located 4 miles west of Glen Rose on U.S. 67 and FM 205, this 1,523-acre park is a designated National Natural Landmark, primarily to protect the dinosaur tracks exposed in the riverbed of the Paluxy River. Both the Black-capped Vireo and the Golden-cheeked Warbler are found here. The best time to find them is from mid-March to June. Fields along the entrance road can produce a number of birds in the summer, including Northern Bobwhite, Killdeer, Greater Roadrunner, Dickcissel, and Eastern Meadowlark. Along the river you may find in summer Great Blue and Green Herons. Yellow-billed Cuckoo, Belted Kingfisher, White-eyed and Bell's Vireos and Yellow-breasted Chat may also be seen. At dusk you may hear the Common Poorwills. In winter, Mallards, Green-winged Teal, and Gadwall can be spotted, and overhead look for Northern Harrier, Sharp-shinned, and Cooper's Hawks. Also in winter you may see Golden-crowned and Ruby-crowned Kinglets, Hermit Thrush, and Spotted Towhee, along with Vesper, Savannah, LeConte's, Fox, Song, and Lincoln's, White-throated, White-crowned, and Harris's Sparrows. Plan to spend extra time and have a picnic. After birding, visit the dinosaur tracks.

Attractions

The Paluxy River flows over solid rock and contains some of the best preserved dinosaur tracks in Texas. Tracks include the first sauropod tracks found in the world, along with those of duckbilled dinosaurs, which were over thirty feet long. There is an admission charge, and picnic areas are in the park. There is also an interpretive exhibit to give visitors a glimpse of how Texas looked 100 million years ago. The information your children will gain here will be helpful in their school studies for years to come.

Barnard Mill and Art Museum

Built in the 1860s, this museum contains oils, bronzes, and primitive artifacts in the new part of the building built in the 1940s. Listed in the National Register of Historic Places and the Texas Historic Register.

Comanche Peak Information Center

Comanche Peak is a nuclear power site, and tours are available of the control room simulator with an educational film. Open Mon.-Sat. 9 A.M. to 4 P.M. Located on FM 56 North.

Creation Evidences Museum

Fossil displays, Acrocanthosauus bones, dinosaur footprint casts. Tours daily Tues.-Sat. 10 A.M.-4 P.M. Last tour begins at 3 P.M. Four miles west on U.S. 67 to FM 205.

Fossil Rim Wildlife Center

Prepare to be amazed. This wildlife refuge has some of the most endangered species in the world, including white rhino, cheetah, and Grevy's zebra. A total of 60 species in natural habitat. Drive through or spend the day at the Lodge of the Foothills Safari Camp. There is a petting pasture, café, nature store, and picnic area, along with a nature trail and learning center. This can be one of the most exciting experiences your children will have in relation to wildlife and nature. If you do nothing else while in the Glen Rose area, visit this refuge.

The Promise

A re-enactment of the life of Christ is presented in an outdoor amphitheatre with a cast of 80. Performances are given during June through October, usually on Friday and Saturday nights. For exact dates, times, and admission charges, phone 254-897-4341.

Festivals

May: Bluegrass Picnic & Arts and Crafts Festival, phone
    254-897-2321
September: Annual Fall Bluegrass Reunion, phone 254-897-2321

Motels

Glen Rose Motel, 300 SW Big Bend Trail, phone 254-897-2635
Glen Rose Motor Inn, Hwy. 67 & Hwy. 56, phone 254-897-2940
There are several lodges in the area, but most of them are very expensive for families. If you are interested, contact the Chamber of Commerce for information or go to the web site:

http://wwwtexasoutside.com/glenrose/lodging.htm. There are also a number of Bed & Breakfasts listed on the same site, along with several campsites and RV parks.

Dining

Chachi's Mexican Restaurant, E. Hwy. 67

Hammond's BarBQue, E. Hwy. 67

Inn On The River, 205 S.W. Barnard St. (reservations only, may be expensive for a family)

Others include Burger King, Chicken Express, Dairy Queen, Debbie's Home Cooking, Donna K's Catfish, Pojo's Family Restaurant, and Subway.

Graham
Chamber of Commerce
608 Elm St.
940-549-3355

Founded in 1872 along the railroad lines of the Chicago, Rock Island, and Gulf Railroads, this city is now the agriculture center of the area. Located about 80 miles northwest of Fort Worth, its proximity to the massive Possum Kingdom Lake makes it a prime recreational area, as well as a good place to bird.

Birding

Possum Kingdom State Park

Possum Kingdom Lake is 65 miles long, has more than 300 miles of shoreline, and covers 19,800 acres. The state park is located on the southeastern corner of the lake. Primary use of the lake is recreation, and it can be very crowded on weekends and holidays. Entrance is on PR 33, and best birding opportunities are in this area. Two exciting birds to be found here are the Golden-cheeked Warbler from mid-March through July, and the Black-capped Vireo, which is seen outside the park. The Longhorn Trail on the north side of the park runs along a leg of the lake and can be very productive for birding in summer when you can see Yellow-billed Cuckoo, Black-chinned Hummingbird, Ladder-backed Woodpecker, Tufted

Titmouse, Bushtit, Blue-gray Gnatcatcher, White-eyed Vireo, and Field Sparrow. In the mesquite grassland you might encounter Wild Turkey, Northern Bobwhite, Greater Roadrunner, Golden-fronted Woodpecker, and Eastern Phoebe. There is a scenic overlook on the trail, and by scanning the water you may see Great Blue, Little Blue, and Green Herons along the shore. Both Great and Snowy Egrets are present, and in the winter water birds can include Green-winged Teal, Northern Pintail, Gadwall, American Wigeon, Bufflehead, and both Bonaparte's and Ring-billed Gulls. There is also the possibility of seeing an Osprey or a Bald Eagle. In the winter in the grasslands a number of sparrows will be present, including Field, Vesper, Lark, Savannah, Fox, Song, Lincoln's, Swamp, White-crowned, and White-throated. This area is probably the best for family birding, but several other areas of interest are listed in *Birding Texas*.

Attractions

Robert E. Richeson Memorial Museum

Artifacts from World War II include munitions, uniforms, and models of aircraft of the era. Located at the Graham Municipal Airport, U.S. 380 east of the city. Phone 940-549-3355.

Fort Belknap

The site of a fort established in 1851 on the Brazos River that was one of the largest forts in North Texas prior to the Civil War. Its purpose was to protect settlers and travelers from Indians and was a stop on the Butterfield Overland Mail Route. It was abandoned in 1867 after the Civil War and is a county recreational site with museum, archives, and picnic facilities. Located three miles south of Newcastle off of Texas 251.

Motels

Gateway Inn, 1401 Hwy. 16 South, phone 940-549-0222 (has restaurant)

Travelers Inn, 1516 Hwy. 16 South, phone 940-549-0274 (has restaurant)

Roadway Inn, 1919 Hwy. 16 South, phone 940-549-8320

Dining

Fast Foods: Chicken Express, Dairy King, Dairy Queen (2), Golden Chick, KFC, McDonald's, Pizza Hut, Pizza Pro, Sonic, Subway, Taco Bell, and Whataburger.

Golden China, 1104 Cypress

Foy's Steak and Seafood, 400 Elm Street

K Bob's Restaurant, 111 Hwy. 16 South

The Last Pizza Show, 526 Oak Street on the Square

Mi Casa Grande Mexican Restaurant, 1916 Hwy. 16 South

Sanderson's Restaurant, 1324 Hwy. 16 South (barbecue)

Greenville

Chamber of Commerce
2713 Stonewall Street
903-455-1510
http://www.Greenville-Chamber.org

The county seat of Hunt County, Greenville is located in the blacklands of Texas on I-30 about 45 miles from Dallas. It is home to the huge Raytheon plant and a variety of other industries.

Birding

Lake Tawakoni

This is one of the largest man-made reservoirs in the state of Texas, covering 36,700 acres. The best birding areas are located on the southern half of the lake on property controlled by the Sabine River Authority. In the spillway below the dam, a number of water birds can usually be seen, including American White Pelican, Great-blue Heron, White and White-faced Ibis, and Double Crested Cormorants. From the top of the dam, which is accessible through the Sabine River Authority compound on the north end of the dam, a wide variety of waterfowl can be seen. Permission to enter must be obtained from the office. Especially good in winter, Pacific Loon has been seen, along with Common Loon, Horned Grebes, Red-breasted Merganser, and Common Goldeneye. Across from the Sabine River Authority compound on CR 1475 is one of the best places in Texas to see Smith's Longspur in winter. In the same area is a small bird sanctuary owned by the Dallas Audubon Society that can be very profitable for small birds such as Ruby-crowned Kinglets and Tufted Titmouse. Bald Eagles have also been seen and Ospreys are here. When you enter the area on Highway 47 you will pass through a community known as the Flats, and just before you reach the dam, there is an area of Sabine River Authority land that can be birded. Prothonotary Warbler, Eastern Phoebe, Indigo Bunting, and Field and Grasshopper Sparrows are a few of the species that can be seen. On the telephone wires, Dickcissels are busy singing.

Attractions

American Cotton Museum

Located on I-30, this museum contains memorabilia of the area's historic cotton industry, and demonstrations depict the process from planting, growing, ginning, baling, spinning, and weaving cotton. Other exhibits include a tribute to local baseball great Monty Stratton, who pitched for the Chicago White Sox and even pitched in pro ball after he lost a leg in a hunting accident. There is also a display honoring *Voyager* co-pilot Jeana Yeager. Mementos of the most decorated hero of World War II, Audie Murphy, includes medals, uniforms, and photos.

Mathews Prairie Preserve

Contains 100 acres of virgin tall grass blackland prairie. An excellent spot to bird, or just enjoy the wildflowers or a look into the past of how the north central Texas area looked to early settlers. Located on FM 903, west of Greenville off of U.S. 380 West.

Festivals

October: Cotton Jubilee, phone 903-455-1510

January: Eagle Fest, Emory, Texas (about 30 miles southeast of Greenville). Take a barge tour on Lake Fork or Lake Tawakoni to view the wintering Bald Eagles or prowl the surrounding woods for owls. Enjoy the fine arts and crafts show, birds of prey demonstrations, and other entertainment. Contact the

Rains County Chamber of Commerce, P.O. Box 695, Emory, Texas 75440 or phone 800-561-1182.

April: Bluebird Festival, Wills Point, Texas (about 30 miles from Greenville). Annual Bluebird Festival offers Bluebird trails where visitors can view nesting boxes, attend nature exhibits and programs, enjoy live entertainment, an arts and crafts show, story hours, and the Bluebird Dinner Theatre. Contact: Wills Point Bluebird Festival Association, 142 N. 4th St, Wills Point, Texas 75169 or phone 903-873-4449.

Motels

Best Western Inn, 1216 I-30, phone 800-528-1234

Days Inn, 5118 I-30, phone 903-454-9200. Continental breakfast, kids stay free

Gold Key Inn, 1215 I-30, phone 903-454-7000

Comfort Inn, 1209 I-30, phone 800-228-5150

Super 8 Motel, 5010 Hwy. 69S, phone 800-800-8000. Continental breakfast

Ramada Inn, 1215 East I-30, phone 904-454-7001

Dining

Greenville has an abundance of fast food restaurants, including Taco Bell, Whataburger, McDonald's, Arby's, Wendy's, Jack-in-the-Box, Church's, Popeye's, Grandy's, KFC Chicken, CiCi's Pizza, Domino's, and Papa John's Pizza. Others include IHOP, Denney's, and several Chinese restaurants.

Catfish King, 5105 I-30, an excellent place to feed a family on a budget

Fitzgerald's The Spare Rib, 7818 Wesley, famous across the state

Royal Drive In, 6308 Wesley (great hamburgers)

Ryan's Steak House, 3210 I-30 West, buffet

Molina's Mexican Restaurant, two locations, 3811 Wesley and 8119 Wesley

Mary of Puddin' Hill Bakery, I-30 and Division St. World famous for their fruitcakes, they also serve a great deli lunch and have a wide variety of candies for sale.

Hillsboro

Chamber of Commerce
115 North Covington St.
254-582-2481
http://www.hillsboro.net

Hillsboro is well known for its many antique shops and its recently restored courthouse. It is the home of Hill County College, which houses the Confederate Research Center. Birding opportunities can be found at nearby Lake Whitney and Meridian State Parks.

Birding

Meridian State Park

This park is located in Bosque County and is about forty miles west of Hillsboro. There is limited lodging and dining facilities in Meridian, which is only three miles from the entrance. Although not a large park (503 acres), the area is another of those spots where you may see the Golden-cheeked Warbler. This is one of the oldest parks in Texas and has 5 miles of walking trails.

The best place to see the warbler is on Shinnery Ridge trail, which is on the west side of the 70-acre lake. The presence of the bird is monitored by park officials, and up-to-date information can be obtained at the headquarters. On the east side of the lake, there are two other hiking trails, the Little Forest Junior Trail and the Little Springs Nature Trail. Birding possibilities in the summer include Ladder-backed Woodpecker, Western Kingbird, Tufted Titmouse, Painted Bunting, and both Chipping and Lark Sparrows. On the water both Green and Great Blue Herons will be present, along with the beautiful Wood Duck and Belted Kingfisher. Bee Creek below the dam provides a different habitat where you may see Yellow-billed Cuckoo, Ruby-throated Hummingbird, and both Red-bellied and Downy Woodpeckers, along with White-eyed Vireo and Summer Tanager. Cedar Waxwings may be present in winter, along with a variety of sparrows such as Field, Vesper, Lark, Savannah, Fox, Song and Lincoln's. Overhead several hawks can be seen, including Northern Harrier, Sharp-shinned, and Cooper's. Wintering waterfowl include Pied-billed Grebe, both Green-winged and

Blue-winged Teal, Northern Pintail, and Northern Shoveler, just to mention a few.

Lake Whitney State Park

Lake Whitney is a massive (23,550-acre) body of water managed by the U.S. Army Corps of Engineers and has numerous developments and recreational facilities. Lodging and dining facilities are available in Whitney, but they are limited. The Lake Whitney State Park is the best place to bird. It contains almost 1,000 acres and is situated on the east shore of the lake. Most birds can be seen on the .9-mile nature trail loop just across from the landing strip and airplane tie-down area that is located in the park. It has both woodlands and wetlands and in summer can be very productive for birding with such species as: Red-bellied, Hairy, and Downy Woodpeckers; Great Crested Flycatcher; Blue-gray Gnatcatcher; Summer Tanager; and Tufted Titmouse. Less likely to be seen but sometimes present are Eastern Screech-Owl, Barred Owl, and Chuck-will's-widow. In the wetlands look for both Great and Little Blue Herons, Wood Duck, and Belted Kingfisher. In the winter Bald Eagles are present, along with a wide variety of ducks.

Attractions

Hill County Cell Block Museum

This museum served as a jail from 1893 to 1983 and has a large collection of Indian artifacts. There is also a Willie Nelson Memorabilia Room. Located in the 200 block of N. Waco.

Texas Heritage Museum

Located on the campus of Hill County Junior College, this museum displays artifacts of the Civil War era and particularly those of Hood's Texas Brigade. It also has a tremendous library of books, maps, and photographs of the war. Recent changes have expanded the display areas and features displays from World War I and II, as well as an extensive collection of Audie Murphy, the most decorated soldier of WWII, memorabilia. This can be a very educational tour for the kids.

Motels

Best Western-Hillsboro Inn, 307 I-35 W. service road, phone
254-582-8465

Comfort Inn, 1515 Old Brandon Rd., phone 254-582-3333

Holiday Inn Express, 1505 Hillsboro Drive, phone 254-582-0220

Ramada Inn, I-35 & Hwy. 32, phone 254-582-3493

Thunderbird Motel, 203 I-35, phone 254-582-8452

Dining

Thunderbird Restaurant, I-35 Service Road (very good breakfast)

Lone Star Cafe, 100 Dynasty Drive

Golden Corral, 1501 Corsicana Hwy.

El Conquistador Restaurant, (good Mexican food)

Monte's Mexican Buffet, located in The Outlet Mall on Hwy. 35

Black-Eyed Pea, Hwy. 35 service road

Fast food includes: KFC, McDonald's, Pizza Hut, Schlotzsky's,
Sonic, Wendy's, Whataburger, Burger King, Arby's, and
Braum's.

Lewisville

Chamber of Commerce
551 N. Valley Pkwy.
800-657-9571

This city, located just north of the Dallas metroplex, was first settled
in 1844 and has grown into a major center of commerce and industry due to its proximity to the Dallas/Fort Worth Airport. The Tour
18 Golf Course, a re-creation of the most famous golf holes in America, is located here, along with 150 dining locations and 1,200
motel/hotel rooms.

Birding

Lewisville Lake Park and Fish Hatchery Road

Accessible from I-35, the lake is used for recreation and can be very
busy on weekends as the park contains numerous baseball, soccer,

and football fields and a golf course. However, the scattered groves of oaks, riparian habitat, and fields along Sandy Beach Road and Trout Road can harbor a variety of migrants in spring and fall, including Yellow-billed Cuckoo, Great Crested and Scissor-tailed Flycatchers, Western and Eastern Kingbirds, Dickcissel, and Baltimore Oriole. Year-round residents are Northern Bobwhite, Mourning Dove, Downy Woodpecker, Eastern Phoebe, Loggerhead Shrike, Cardinals, Blue Jays, and Mockingbirds. A number of waterfowl species can be seen along the lakeshore such as Great Blue Heron, Great and Snowy Egrets, Yellow-crowned Night-Herons, and Mallard Ducks. Mud flats in the shallow bay south of Sailboat Point will reveal a number of shore birds. With the help of a scope, you can also see a number of lake ducks in winter. The Fish Hatchery Road, which runs below the dam, is a different environment, and a wide assortment of birds can be seen. In the summer you may see Green Heron, Ruby-throated Hummingbird, Red-bellied Woodpecker, Northern Rough-winged Swallows, Blue-Gray Gnatcatcher, Brown Thrasher, and White-eyed Vireo, just to name a few.

Attractions

Miss Lewisville Paddlewheel Boat

Take a ride on a Mississippi style paddle boat on Lake Lewisville. The boat docks at Sneaky Pete's Marina. Reservations are probably a good idea and are a necessity on weekends.

Old Town

Unique storefronts dating back to the turn of the century are a feature of this shopping mall that contains many antique shops, boutiques, and craft stores. Exit 452 from I-35 and go east on Main Street. A spot Mom would enjoy visiting.

Festivals

March: Lewisville Celtic Fest Scottish Highland Games, phone 972-353-5971

June: Festival of Sails, phone 972-318-1011

Motels

Hampton Inn of Lewisville, next door to Cracker Barrel Restaurant

Holiday Inn Express, 200 N. Stemmons Frwy., phone
972-434-1000

Homewood Suites Hotel, 700 Hebron Pkwy., phone 972-315-6123

La Quinta I-35, 1657 S. Stemmons Frwy., phone 972-221-7525

Dining

Easy Street Family Café, 190 W. Main, homecooked American

Golden Corral, 251 Stemmons Freeway, buffet

Good Eats Grill, 2225 S. Stemmons Freeway, always good family
dining

Mama's Daughter's Diner, 1288 W. Main Street, great corn bread
and pies

Mill Street Café, 727 S. Mill Street, best chicken-fried steak in
Lewisville

The Pantry Café, 1288 W. Main St.

McKinney

Chamber of Commerce
1801 West Louisiana Street
972-542-0163
E-mail: mckcoc@waymark.net

McKinney is located on Highway 75 between Dallas and Sherman. It
was first settled in 1845 and is the county seat of Collin County. The
area has experienced tremendous growth in recent years as an
expansion north of the Dallas Metroplex has reached up Highway
75. The historic downtown area has been restored and contains an
old-fashioned hardware store, along with a number of antique, arts
and crafts, and gift shops.

Birding

Heard Natural Science Museum and Wildlife Sanctuary

Located just south of McKinney, this combination museum and wildlife sanctuary plays an important role in the rehabilitation of injured

raptors in northeast Texas. The 206-acre wildlife sanctuary has bottomlands, woodlands, and prairie with over five miles of trails that make it ideal for an easy family birding expedition. Guided tours are also available. Water is contained in man-made ponds. Feeders outside the museum attract a number of birds and can be a restful spot to let the birds come to you. A bird checklist is available, and 272 species have been recorded here, including Henslow's Sparrow. The raptor center, which is separate from the refuge, is not open to the public. Inside the museum, in addition to local history exhibits, there are displays of natural history, seashell, rock and mineral, and art exhibits. The museum also conducts an extensive educational program for all ages, including a special summer Biology Camp.

Attractions

Heard Natural Science Museum

(See above description included with Heard Wildlife Sanctuary.)

Collin County Youth and Farm Museum

Featuring a collection of antique farm equipment and artifacts from North Texas farms during the 1930s. Located 4 miles northwest of the city on County Road 166.

Storybook Ranch

Features hayrides and a western museum town called "Drybones." An opry house, bank, saloon, hotel, barber shop, marshal's office, and jail are available to the public on Thursday nights from 6 P.M. to 9 P.M. for dinner in the lodge and hayrides. Phone 972-562-8308 for more information.

Festivals

May: MayFair Art Festival, phone 972-562-6880

September: Harvest Fest & Great McKinney Bed Races, phone
972-562-6880

Motels

Amerihost Inn, 951 N. Central Expressway, phone 972-547-4500

Days Inn, 2104 N. Central Expressway, phone 972-548-8888

Holiday Inn, 1300 N. Central Expressway, phone 972-542-9471

Super 8 Motel, 910 N. Central Expressway, phone 972-548-8880

Dining

CiCi's Pizza, 320 N. Central Expressway, inexpensive way to feed a family

El Chico of McKinney, 1222 N. Central Expressway, good Mexican food

Mama Emilia's Italian Restaurant, 119 W. Virginia Street

Rhineland Haus, 1330 N. McDonald, great German food

Steak Kountry Restaurant, 143 S. Central Expressway & 153 Westgate Shopping Center

Pantry Restaurant, 214 E. Louisiana St., open for lunch only

Mineral Wells

Chamber of Commerce
P.O. Box 1408
511 E. Hubbard
940-325-2557
http://www.mineralwellstx.com

The waters were known during the late 19th and early 20th centuries for their supposed healing powers and attracted, and still do, many health seekers.

Birding

Lake Mineral Wells State Park

This 2,809-acre park has an abundance of hiking trails, sixteen miles to be exact, but only six are reserved for hiking only, while ten are used for horseback riding and bicycling. With children, the six-mile trail will probably be more than enough while visits to the camping areas and the spillway area below the dam will produce a number of birds. Residents include Red-shouldered Hawk, Northern Bobwhite, and three species of woodpeckers: Red-bellied, Ladder-backed, and Downy. Both Carolina and Bewick's Wrens are present, along with Field and Lark Sparrows. In summer you may see Mississippi Kite overhead, and Black-chinned Hummingbird, Scissor-tailed Flycatcher, and White-eyed Vireo are also visitors. There are a number of birds to be seen (or heard) at dusk, including Common Nighthawk. Colorful birds include the Indigo and Painted Buntings, and Red-tailed Hawk should be overhead. The wetlands along Rock Creek are the best place to bird, and much of it can be done from the trail north of the Cross Timbers Camping Area.

Green Herons, Great Egret, and Yellow-crowned Night-Heron, along with Great Blue and Little Blue Herons can be seen in the summer, and in winter look for Pied-billed Grebe, Gadwall, American Wigeon, Ring-necked Duck, Lesser Scaup, and Bufflehead, along with others, on the water. During migration, the area below the spillway, which is a low-water crossing, will attract shore birds.

Attractions

Crazy Water Well

At the intersection of U.S. 281 and 180 is the site of the first mineral water well in the county, and several historical markers give the history of the area.

Famous Water Company

This bottling company was founded in 1913 by Edward P. Dismuke and is still in operation. Some of the products bottled here have included Dismuke's Pronto-lax, Dismuke's Famous Mineral Crystals, Dismuke's Eye Bath, and Dismuke's Residuum.

B.A.T.S. Tour

The Beneficial Animal Teaching Society has tours to Bat World, a museum about bats and field trips. This can be very educational for the children. For information phone 817-325-3404.

Palo Pinto Museum

An old jail and log cabin, which contains area artifacts and history, is open weekend afternoons in the summer. Located one block south of the courthouse in Palo Pinto, which is 12 miles west of Mineral Wells on U.S. 180.

Motels

Budget Host Inn/Skyline Motel, 3601 East Hubbard, phone 800-BUD-HOST

Days Inn, 3701 E. Hubbard, 940-325-6961

Executive Inn, 2809 Hwy. 180 West, phone 940-328-1111

Ramada Limited, 4103 Hwy. 180 East, phone 800-2RAMADA

Dining

A number of fast foods are available, including Braum's, Dairy Mart, Dairy Queen, Domino's, Mr. Jim's Pizza, Pizza Hut, Subway, Taco Bell, and Whataburger.

Baris Italian Restaurant, 2805 Hwy. 180 W.

Little China, 200 N.E. 27th Street

Mineral Wells Steakhouse, 100-D S.E. 1st Street

Pulido's Mexican Restaurant, 100 N.E. 22nd Street

Rodriquez & Son Restaurant, 1507 S.E. 1st Street

Shotgun's Bar B-Que, 215 N.E. 27th Street

Plano

Convention & Visitors Bureau
2000 E. Spring Creek Pkwy.
800-81-PLANO
http://www.tourtexas.com/plano/p4lano.html

Once a sleepy little community of less than 4,000, this city has become a metropolitan area with an explosion of growth due to its proximity to Dallas on Highway 75, leading north. It is known as the Balloon Capital of Texas with the hot-air balloon festival each September. Historic downtown has been restored with a plaza and many specialty shops. Dining and lodging facilities are almost unlimited.

Birding

Plano Outdoor Learning Center

This small birding area is unique in that it is located in the northeast section of the Dallas Metroplex. It contains almost undisturbed areas of bottomland hardwood forest along Rowlett Creek. The Learning Center is operated by the Plano Independent School District, and the trails are heavily used by schoolchildren after 9 A.M., so any birding should be done before that time. A loop that runs from the learning center, through mowed meadows, and across the prairie into the woods along Rowlett Creek is the best place to bird. In the meadow you may see, in spring and summer, breeding birds including Mourning Dove, Common Nighthawk, Barn Swallow, Blue Jay, American Crow, Eastern Bluebird, American Robin, Northern Mockingbird, Brown Thrasher, Northern Cardinal, and Eastern Meadowlark, along with a number of other species. During spring migration, a number of warblers and vireos can be seen in the forest along the creek. In the winter you may find Yellow-bellied Sapsucker, Northern Flicker, Red-breasted and White-breasted Nuthatches, Brown Creeper, Cedar Waxwing, and Purple Finch. To find the center, take exit 30 off U.S. 75 in Plano. Follow Parker Road east to Jupiter Road south to Royal Oaks, then east to Shiloh Road and north one block.

Attractions

Interurban Railway Station Museum

This station, which once served an electric railway system that from 1908 to 1948 ran from Denison to Waco, has been restored and contains memorabilia of railway history. Located in Haggard Park, 901 E. 15th Street.

Mountasia Fantasy Golf

A 54-hole miniature golf course that offers challenges such as caves, waterfalls, and other obstacles. Lots of family fun and the clubhouse has a video game room in case the kids need a break from birding. Located at 2400 Premier Drive, off U.S. 75.

Southfork Ranch

The children won't remember, but mom and dad might enjoy visiting the site of the shooting of the TV series *Dallas*. See the gun that shot J. R. or Lucy's wedding dress or the Lincoln Continental Jock Ewing drove. You got to be a fan, but if you are, the ranch is located off Hwy. 75 North. Take exit 30 and drive east on FM 2514/Parker Rd. about six miles and then turn right on FM 2551 (Hoggs Road) to the ranch.

Festivals

September: Annual Southwestern Bell Plano Balloon Festival, phone 972-422-0296

Motels

The once sleepy little town of Plano has become a metropolitan city on its own, and the lodging facilities are numerous on North Central Expressway (Highway 75). This has recently been widened but can still be a congested thoroughfare during morning or evening rush hours.

Dining

As with the housing, many dining establishments, from fast food to deluxe, are available along North Central Expressway.

Pancho's Mexican Buffet, 3200 Alma Drive

Cheddar's, 2400 N. Central Expressway

Dickey's Barbeque Pit, 1211 14th St. and 1441A Coit Rd.

Good Eats Café, 1101 N. Central Expressway

Mr. Jim's Pizzeria, 2357 Jupiter Rd.

CiCi's Pizza, 1414 Jupiter Rd., 2011 W. Spring Creek, and 2220 Coit Rd.

Sherman

Chamber of Commerce
P.O. Box 1029
903-893-1184
http://www.shermantexas.com
E-mail: shermanchamber@texoma.com

Located north of the Dallas area on Highway 75, Sherman is 15 miles from the Hagerman National Wildlife Refuge on the expansive Lake Texoma, which spans the Texas-Oklahoma state line.

Established as the county seat of Grayson County in 1846, this city was the winter headquarters for the Missouri bushwhacker Quantrill and his gang in 1863. It was named in honor of Texas Republic officer Gen. Sidney Sherman, who coined the phrase "Remember the Alamo." It is the home of Austin College.

Birding

Hagerman National Wildlife Refuge

This 11,320-acre refuge was built to provide food and protected nesting habitat for waterfowl during the winter and migration seasons. Known for the great flocks of migrating geese that stop here due to the abundance of food supplied to them, the refuge is also home to a great many other migrants in April and early May, among them Bobolink and Yellow-headed Blackbird. Nesting neotropical migrants include Yellow-billed Cuckoo, Ruby-throated Hummingbird, Eastern Wood-Pewee, Great-crested and Scissor-tailed Flycatchers, Western and Eastern Kingbirds, and many others. A Kiskadee Flycatcher was a rare visitor recently, and Chuck-will's-widow is a rare sighting. The Goode picnic area north of the refuge headquarters is a great place for a family lunch in the summer, and if you look overhead, you may see a Swainson's Hawk. Water birds are plentiful in winter, including Common Loon, American White Pelican, and of course, the geese, from Greater White-fronted and Snow to the less common Ross'. Gulls are abundant in January and February, along with Forster's Tern. At the dam site near Denison, Bald Eagles are a regular visitor. Eastern and Spotted Towhees, along with Vesper, Fox, LeConte's, Song, Lincoln, and Swamp

Sparrows can be seen in the fields. The marshes and mud flats will provide a good look at many shore birds and waders. Be sure and stop at the refuge for a map and bird list, for this is a very large refuge and is worthy of spending a little extra time to see the wide variety of birds.

Attractions

Red River Historical Museum

Located in Carnegie Library, this museum preserves the history of Grayson County with pictures and artifacts.

C. B. Roberts House

Built in 1886, this beautiful Victorian home of a prominent Sherman family has been restored and preserved by the Sherman Preservation League and is a part of an area of Victorian homes along S. Crockett Street. Driving maps are available from the Chamber of Commerce.

Motels

Comfort Suites, 2900 Hwy. 75 N., phone 903-893-0499

Hampton Inn, 2904 Michelle, phone 903-893-9333

Days Inn, 1831 Texoma Parkway, phone 903-892-0433

Holiday Inn, 3605 Hwy. 75 S., phone 903-868-0555

LaQuinta Inn & Suites, 2912 Hwy. 75 N., phone 903-870-1122

Dining

Der Sandwich Shop, 110 E. Houston. Great sandwiches, just off the square. Don't miss it.

El Chico Restaurant, 2815 N. Hwy. 75. Good Mexican food

Kathleen's Kitchen, 1915 N. Travis

La Mesa Mexican Restaurant, 2124 Texoma Parkway

City Limits, 4521 Texoma Pkwy.

Others include Juicy Pig Café, Dragon Seed II, Meg's Restaurant, and Conrad's Pies & More.

Sulphur Springs

Tourism & Visitors Bureau
P.O. Box 347
888-300-6623
http://www.tourtexas.com/sulphursprings

Once known as Bright Star, the name was changed in 1871 and refers to the many mineral springs in the area. Hopkins County is the leading producer of dairy products in Texas and the U.S. with 490 dairies. The 1894 courthouse of red granite and limestone is worth the visit.

Birding

Cooper Lake State Park

Cooper Lake is located 14 miles north of Sulphur Springs. Commerce is closer to the west end of the dam and could be used as a base for birding, but the actual birding sites are on the north side (Doctor's Creek Unit) and the south side (South Sulphur Park Unit). This is another of those lakes built for water conservation and recreation and is quite large (19,280 acres) and relatively new (1991). The best time to bird this area is during migration as very few if any water birds will be present in the summer, although you may see American White Pelicans, Ring-billed Gull, and several terns such as Caspian, Forster's, Least, and Black. In the fall, however, Common Loons visit, as do both Horned and Eared Grebes, and Bald Eagles have been seen. The best place to look for waterfowl is the dam, but parking is only available below the dam. In the summer at both the Doctor's Creek area and the South Sulphur Park, a great variety of birds may be seen, including Wood-Pewee, Acadian and Great Crested Flycatchers, Eastern Kingbird, and both American and Fish Crows. Pileated Woodpeckers may also be present, along with Northern Parula and several warblers such as Yellow-throated, Pine, Black-and-white, and Kentucky.

Attractions

Hopkins County Museum and Heritage Park

This collection is located in the historic Wilson House and contains a collection of Civil War memorabilia, hundreds of dolls, folk art animations, miniatures of important buildings, and Caddo Indian relics. The park covers eleven acres and includes a working blacksmith shop, country store, and post office, along with syrup and grist mills and a number of log buildings. Located at 416 North Jackson St., phone 903-885-2387 for more details and dates of special events.

Music Box Gallery

One of the largest collections of music boxes in the world, the collection ranges from antique and unique to the commonplace. Some were owned by movie stars and famous people. Housed in the City Library. For more information, phone 903-885-4926.

Southwest Dairy Center

Exhibits depict milk production and processing, from the early farm kitchen to the modern transport and production of dairy products. At the end of the tour, you will enjoy ice cream treats or relax at lunch in The Creamery, the museum's old-fashioned soda fountain. Another one of those unusual places to visit that will be educational for the kids.

Mossman Guitars

A unique place to stop by if you are interested in guitars. Visitors can watch the century-old methods and equipment for building quality guitars and might even get a concert. 1813½ Main Street.

Motels

Best Western, I-30 East, phone 903-885-7515

Holiday Inn, 1495 Industrial Drive E., phone 903-885-0582

Comfort Suites, 1521 Industrial Drive E., phone 903-438-0918

Budget Inn Motel, 1529 Industrial Drive E., phone 903-885-2105

Dining

Fast foods are plentiful, such as: Burger King, Braum's, Chicken Express, Dairy Queen, Jack-in-the-Box, KFC, McDonald's, Pizza Inn, Sonic, Subway, and Taco Bell.

Bodacious Bar-B-Q, 1220 Mockingbird Lane

Burton's Family Restaurant, 1515 Shannon Rd. E.

College Street Burgers and Fries, 208 College St.

Furr's Family Dining, 1300 Mockingbird Ln.

K-Bob's Steak House, I-30 and Shannon Rd.

Ta Molly's Mexican Restaurant, 1216 Mockingbird Ln. (excellent and inexpensive)

Waco

Convention & Visitors Bureau
100 Washington Avenue
phone 800-WACO-Fun
http://www.wacocvb.com

Waco is the home of Baylor University, McLennan Community College, and Texas State Technical College. The city was named after the Waco Indians, who found the cool waters of the Brazos River a popular place. A Texas Ranger fort was established in 1837, and today the area depends largely on the rich agricultural industry.

Birding

Cameron Park

This park is the best-known birding area in Waco and can be reached by taking Hwy. 84 from I-30. It borders on the west bank of the Brazos River and offers habitat favorable for migrants such as flycatchers, vireos, warblers, tanagers, and orioles, as well as a number of resident birds, such as Mourning Dove, Yellow-billed Cuckoo, and both Red-bellied and Downy Woodpeckers. In the open areas, you may see Mississippi Kite, and both Swainson's and Red-tailed Hawk, along with Common Nighthawks in the early morning or at dusk. This is a particularly "comfortable" place to bird with children.

Waco Lake

Just west of Cameron Park lies Waco Lake, a small lake inside the city that has several excellent birding spots. Research Wetlands, Flat Rock Park, Airport Park, and Speegeville Parks I & II are located on the northwest side of the lake. The HOT (Heart of Texas) Soccer Complex can be a great place to find birds during migration, and Bosque Park will have a number of gulls and terns in the winter. Airport Park will harbor wintering Common Loons, grebes, and terns, including the Black Tern. At Flat Rock Park you may see American White Pelican, and in summer both Double-crested and Neotropic Cormorants will be present.

Waco Water Treatment Plant

The water treatment plant in most cities is a good place to find birds, and Waco is no exception. Located on the southeast side of town on FM 434, this is a good place to relax and drive the levees to see a great many water birds in the ponds and drying beds.

Tradinghouse Creek Reservoir

This power plant lake is rather new, but the cattails and riparian woodlands, along with the adjacent fields, are beginning to attract a number of birds and birders. In winter the Hooded Merganser has been seen on the lake, and in the fields along FM 3222 and FM 2957, Horned Lark, American Pipit, and McGown's, Lapland, and Chestnut-collared Longspurs can be seen. Sprague's Pipit and Smith's Longspur are also possibilities.

Mother Neff State Park

Named for Mrs. Isabelle Eleanor Neff, mother of Governor Pat M. Neff (1921-1925), this is the oldest park in the state, with 259 acres that include 2.75 miles of hiking trails through prairie, limestone hills, and creek bottoms. It is also the site of the champion Texas oak tree and a cave used by Tonkawa Indians. Birding along the Leon River is best at migration times as many flycatchers, vireos, warblers, tanagers, and orioles may be seen. In the winter Northern Flicker, Brown Creeper, both House and Winter Wrens, Yellow-rumped Warbler, Purple Finch, and Pine Siskin may be present, along with Chipping, Field, Fox, Song, Lincoln's, White-throated, White-crowned, and Harris's Sparrows. This park is actually located about 20 miles southwest of Waco near Moody, and Gatesville is only 22 miles away. Moody has places to eat and gas is available, but no lodging. Gatesville has all three if you prefer to stay in a smaller town.

Attractions

Cameron Park Zoo

The 51-acre natural habitat zoo is home to a collection that includes gibbon apes, Sumatran tigers, white rhinos, giraffes, zebras, antelopes, and many other species. It is also the site of a herpetarium. Two restaurants are on site, Gibbon Island and African Treetops Village.

Dr Pepper Museum

Perhaps the favorite soft drink of southwesterners, it was first mixed in The Old Corner Drug Store in the 1880s and was called "Waco." The museum is housed in the 1906 bottling plant and features an operating soda fountain and Dr Pepper memorabilia and interactive audio visual displays.

Texas Ranger Hall of Fame & Museum at Fort Fisher

This is a must visit if you are in the Waco area. The museum stands near the site of the original fort built by the Texas Rangers in 1837 and has displays relating to ranger history and a collection of guns and weapons from the Old West, Indian artifacts, and western art. The 35-acre park includes camping and picnic areas. Located on Lake Brazos.

Texas Sports Hall of Fame

Some of the Texas sports personalities honored here include Byron Nelson, Lee Trevino, Don January, Babe Didrikson Zaharias, George Foreman, and Nolan Ryan. Video presentations in the Tom Landry Theater features historic sporting events. Within the same area are the Texas Baseball Hall of Fame, Tennis Hall of Fame, and Texas High School Hall of Fame for football, basketball, and baseball. Located at Fort Fisher Park near the Texas Ranger Hall of Fame.

Motels

Best Western Old Main Lodge, I-35 @ 4th Street, phone
  800-299-9226
Comfort Inn, 1430 I-35 South, phone 800-228-5150
Holiday Inn, 1001 MLK Jr. Blvd., phone 800-HOLIDAY
Lexington Inn, 115 I-35, phone 800-537-8483
Super 8, 1320 I-35 S., phone 800-800-8000
Victorian Inn, 720 S. MLK Jr. Blvd., phone 800-935-1029

Dining

Burger Barn, 1700 Colcord Ave.

Trujillo's Comeor Y Cantina, 2612 La Salle Ave.

Mr. Gatti's Pizza, 1300 N. Valley Mills Dr. and 1845 Brook Circle

Buzzard Billy's, 208 S. University Parks Dr. (Cajun food)

Ryan's Family Steakhouse, 301 S. Valley Mills Drive

Fast food restaurants are abundant with four Whataburger locations.

Wichita Falls

Convention & Visitors Bureau
100 Fifth St.
phone 940-716-5500
http://www.wichitafalls.org

Located just south of the Red River and the Oklahoma state line, this city was named for the Wichita Indians who lived near the waterfall on the Wichita River. The home of Sheppard Air Force Base and Midwestern University.

Birding

Lake Arrowhead State Park

This 524-acre recreational park was created in 1965 with the damming of the Little Wichita River to form Lake Arrowhead, a 13,500-acre reservoir for the city of Wichita Falls. The park is located on the northwest side of the lake and has several trails to hike. It is the best place to bird, since much of the land around the lake is private and recreational activities can be numerous on weekends and holidays. In spring and summer birds can be seen in the grasslands along the trails, just to the right of the entrance. Golden-fronted Woodpecker, Ladder-backed Woodpecker, Western Kingbird, Carolina Chickadee, Eastern Bluebird, Eastern Meadowlark, and Brown-headed Cowbird may be seen. At the spillway, you can see water birds, and in summer both Double-crested and Neotropic Cormorants will be here, along with herons and egrets. On the lake during winter migration, a great many water birds can be seen such as Pied-billed Grebe and Horned Grebe, along with American White Pelican, Canada Goose, Green-winged Teal, Mallard, Northern Shoveler, Gadwall, and others. In the summer the fields will hold such species as Horned Lark, Loggerhead Shrike, Field Sparrow, and Eastern Meadowlark. Overhead, look for Swainson's Hawk. In the winter good numbers of Greater White-fronted, Snow, and Canada Geese may be present, along with Sandhill Cranes. At Birdwell Tank, along West Arrowhead Drive south of the park, Great Horned Owls have nest sites, and there is a pond that will attract migrants.

Attractions

Museum and Art Center

This facility contains a planetarium and scientific, art, and historical displays. Laser shows in the planetarium are offered on Thursdays and Fridays. Phone 940-692-0923 for times.

Railroad Museum

A collection of vintage railroad cars includes a MK&T diesel switch engine, Texas & Pacific Pullman car, two World War II troop sleepers, Fort Worth & Denver baggage car, and post office car. Also includes a Burlington coach "Silver Falls" and a number of cabooses.

The Plex Entertainment Center

If you want to give the kids a treat after a hard day of birding in the hot North Texas sun, take them here where they will find miniature golf courses, go-karts, bumper boats, and a video arcade. Located at 4131 Southwest Parkway.

Wichita Falls Fire and Police Museum

Old fire-fighting equipment from the turn of the century and old police motorcycles with photos and other artifacts from both fire and police departments are displayed.

Motels

Best Western-Towne Crest Inn, 1601 Eighth St., phone
940-322-1182

Fairfield Inn, 4414 Westgate Drive, phone 940-691-1066

Holiday Inn Hotel & Suites, 401 Broad Street, phone
940-766-6000

La Quinta Inn, 1128 Central Freeway North, phone 800-531-5900

New Tradewinds Motor Hotel, 1212 Broad Street, phone
800-678-8885

Super 8 Motel, 1307 Kenley Avenue, phone 800-800-8000

Dining

Davenport's Buffet, 4407 Kemp Blvd.

Brownie's Bar-B-Q and Burger, 528 Beverly Drive

Pioneer Restaurant, 1100 Sheppard Access Rd., 1400 Tenth St.,
and 812 Holiday St.

Casa Manana, 609 Eighth St.

El Gordo's, 513 Scott Ave.

CiCi's Pizza, 2710 Southwest Pkwy.

China Star Restaurant, 1024 Central Freeway

Lots of fast foods, including three Braum's locations and five Whataburgers

Pineywoods Region

pileated
woodpecker

Huntsville

Chamber of Commerce
800-289-0389
http://chamber.huntsville.tx.us/tourism.html

Huntsville, along with its birding possibilities, has the honor of being the final resting place of the first president of the Republic of Texas, Sam Houston, who is buried in historic Oakwood Cemetery. Sam Houston University was named in his honor, and the tallest statue of an American hero (77 foot) faces out on Highway 45. A museum in his honor is a must visit. The city is also known for its prison system, and there is a Texas Prison Museum.

Birding

Sam Houston National Forest

The Sam Houston National Forest is a vast expanse (158,411 acres) and is spanned by 150 hiking trails, including the 140-mile-long Lone Star trail. Birding opportunities are numerous, particularly during the spring migration, but the forest is also home to some very special birds, such as the endangered Red-cockaded Woodpeckers, which can be seen in a number of breeding spots near the junction of FM 1375 and FR 233. Other woodpeckers to be seen are the Red-headed Woodpecker and the large Pileated. The pond at Cagle Campground will produce a variety of waterfowl, including the beautiful Wood Duck. There are also nesting Bald Eagles in the forest in the winter and spring. The hard-to-see American Woodcock is also here, along with Brown-headed Nuthatch. This is such a vast area, it is best to contact the headquarters for birding, hiking, and camping information.

Huntsville State Park

This 2,083-acre state park features 21-acre Lake Raven and has hiking and biking trails around the lake, which makes it accessible for birding. It is basically the same habitat as Sam Houston National Forest and might make an easier birding trip for families. However, it is very busy on weekends. For more information, contact:

Huntsville State Park, P.O. Box 508, Huntsville, TX 77342-0508. Phone 409-429-5644.

Attractions

Sam Houston Memorial Museum and Park

This historical complex contains eight buildings. Two are period furnished homes of Houston, including "Steamboat House," his law office, kitchen, blacksmith's shop, and gazebo, replicas of General Houston's personal effects, including items belonging to Santa Anna when he was captured at San Jacinto, 19th-century pioneer items, and an exhibit hall/gift shop.

The Texas Prison Museum

See exhibits of ball and chains, rifles, and "Old Sparky," the state's electric chair that was used between 1924 and 1964. Visitors will also see crafts and products produced by inmates. Located on the south side of the square, the exhibits change periodically.

Motels

Comfort Inn and Suites, 160 I-45 S., phone 800-228-5150

Econo Lodge, 112 I-45 N., phone 800-55-ECONO

Holiday Inn Express, 201 West Hill Park Circle, phone
    800-HOLIDAY

La Quinta, 124 I-45 N., phone 800-531-5900

Gateway Inn & Suites, 606 I-45 S., phone 800-228-2000

Best Western Inn, 3 I-45 S., phone 800-491-0447

Dining

Fast food restaurants include: Papa John's Pizza, Pizza Hut,
    Quizno's Subs, Domino's Pizza, McDonald's, Popeye's, Mazzio's
    Pizza, Mr. Gatti's Pizza, and Subway.

The Catfish Place, 3400 Hwy. 19. Country Atlantic salmon is under
    $14. Close out with Chef John Eschenfelder's chocolate paté
    dessert creation. Make reservations at 409-291-7366.

El Chico Mexican Restaurant, 170 I-45 S.

Golden Corral, 2050 11th Street

Jose's Restaurant, 3011 11th Street

The Homestead on 19th Street, 1215 19th Street (This is another of those places where you might want to abandon the budget, although the prices are not extremely high. Crab-and-corn fritters with apple-mango chutney, wild rice casserole, and fresh vegetables is about $15.)

Jasper

Jasper Information Center
246 E. Milam
409-384-2762
http://www.inu.net/jasper
http://www.jaspercoc.org
E-mail: jaspercc@inu.net

A unique East Texas town featuring a historic downtown area that includes an old county jail and Sandy Creek Park with children's playground equipment, fishing ponds, and pavilion.

Birding

Martin Dies Jr. State Park and B. A. Steinhagen Lake

A short drive from Jasper on Highway 190 will take you to the Cherokee Unit of the state park after crossing B. A. Steinhagen Lake. The 705-acre state park is managed by the U.S. Army Corps of Engineers and can be very busy with visitors on the weekends. This can be a migrant trap for songbirds and provides a good place to view Little Blue and Tricolored Herons, Snowy and Cattle Egrets, and Yellow-crowned Night-Herons. You may also see the so-called snake bird, Anhinga, and White Ibis. A lot of waterfowl can be seen in winter, including the beautiful Wood Duck. Back on the Jasper side of the lake, the Walnut Ridge and Hen House Ridge units of the park are dominated by pines and forest habitat. In the summer, the 1-mile loop trail in the Walnut Ridge Unit is great for birding.

Attractions

Hidden Falls Ranch

Take a break from birding and go for a horseback or pony ride. Or just enjoy the campgrounds, hiking trails, hayrides, and cookouts. North of Jasper about 9 miles on FM 255. For information, phone 409-698-9976.

Beaty-Orton House

Constructed of native pine, this Victorian home of John T. Beaty was built near the close of the 19th century and houses the Main Street offices. Located at the corner of Main and Water Streets.

Motels

Best Western Inn of Jasper, 205 W. Gibson, phone 409-384-7767

Holiday Inn Express, 2100 N. Wheeler St., phone 409-384-8600

Ramada Inn, 249 E. Gibson St., phone 409-384-9021

Super 8 Motel of Toledo Bend, phone 409-625-3747

Dining

Fast food includes: Burger King, Church's Fried Chicken, Domino's Pizza, Kentucky Fried Chicken, McDonald's, Pizza Hut, Popeye's, Sonic Drive-in, Subway, Taco Bell, and Whataburger.

Casa Olé Mexican Restaurant, 2120 N. Wheeler

Catfish Cabin, Hwy. 96 N.

Cedar Tree, Hwy. 96 S.

Elijah's Café, 201 W. Gibson

Golden Corral Family Steak House, 235 E. Gibson

Patrick's Steakhouse, Hwy. 96 N.

Texas Charlie's Restaurant, 500 S. Wheeler

The Stump Restaurant, Hwy. 255

Livingston

Polk County Chamber of Commerce
505 North Drew Street
936-327-4929
http://www.livingston.net/chamber

Although small in size, Livingston is important to birding in East Texas for several reasons: It is on the edge of the eastern side of the Sam Houston National Forest, in the proximity of a portion of the "Big Thicket," home of the Alabama-Coushatta Indian Reservation and Lake Livingston State Park, all of which adds up to some fine birding prospects and learning opportunities.

Birding

Lake Livingston State Park

Located west of Livingston, this 635-acre state park can produce a great variety of birds during spring migration, including many waterfowl. At the causeway on the north end of the lake, White Pelicans can be seen, along with Herring, Ring-billed, and Bonaparte's Gulls. Several species of terns may also be present. When the water is low during migration, a great number of shore birds can be seen in the mud flats. On FM 3126, just off of U.S. 190, there is a restored prairie which can produce Eastern Meadowlarks, Loggerhead Shrikes, Scissor-tailed Flycatchers, Eastern Bluebirds, and several species of sparrows, including Savannah, Song, LeConte's, and White-throated. At the south end of the lake, the spillway below the dam may be a good place to see Bald Eagles in winter.

Sam Houston National Forest

(See Huntsville)

Big Thicket National Preserve

This area covers twelve separate units and ranges from just north of Beaumont to Jasper and has a section about thirty miles from Livingston, which is the home of the Alabama-Coushatta Indian Reservation. Adjacent to the reservation some 14,300 acres of the Big Thicket National Preserve can produce many birds, even in summer, including the possibility of the endangered Red-cockaded Wood-pecker. Red-headed Woodpeckers, Blue Grosbeak, and Indigo Bunting are also possible. The Big Thicket is so expansive and there are so many birding opportunities, it is recommended that you purchase a copy of *Birding Texas* by Roland Wauer & Mark Elwonger for a more comprehensive guide to the area.

Attractions

Alabama-Coushatta Indian Reservation

Created in the 1850s under the leadership of Sam Houston, this reservation can be visited by taking a 45-minute bus tour of the heavily wooded section of the Big Thicket. You can learn the history and culture of this colorful Indian tribe on the bus tour, and there is an Indian village walking tour that demonstrates the early life of the tribe with crafts, food, and weapons. Indians perform colorful dances in full Indian dress. A popular attraction is the 25-minute ride on the Indian Chief Train. There is a gift shop and Inn of the Twelve Clans restaurant. For more information, call 800-444-3507 or visit their web site at www.livingston.net/chamber/actribe.

Polk County Museum

Early American glassware, Indian artifacts, tools, and relics of early settlers and display of a logging and sawmill industry photo exhibit are featured, along with a Civil War weapons collection. Located at 514 Mill St.

Motels

Econo Lodge, 117 Hwy. 59 S., phone 800-55-ECONO

Holiday Inn Express, Hwy. 59 S. South Point Center, phone 936-327-9600

Livingston Inn, Hwy. 59 S., phone 936-327-2394

Park Inn, 2500 Hwy. 59 S., phone 936-327-2525

Dining

Livingston has several fast food restaurants, including Subway, Pizza Inn, and McDonald's.

Bodacious Bar-B-Q, 200 South Point Loop

Café in the Park (Park Inn), 2500 Hwy. 69 S.

Catfish King, 100 Hwy. 59 N. Loop

Golden Corral, 1017 Church

Florida's Kitchen, Hwy. 190 W. FM 350 S.

Shrimp Boat Manny's, 1324 W. Church

Texas Pepper, 930 Hwy. 59 N. Loop

Longview
Convention and Visitors Bureau
410 N. Center St.
903-753-3281
http://www.longviewtx.com
E-mail: lcvb@longviewtx.com

The county seat of Gregg County was settled in the 1800s, and the discovery of oil in the 1930s turned the little town of 6,000 into a metropolis. Today the population is almost 80,000, and it is the home of LeTourneau University.

Birding

Lake O' The Pines

This Corps of Engineer flood control lake covers 18,700 acres and is located 34 miles west of Longview and 26 miles north of Marshall. It is busy on weekends. At Shady Grove or Cedar Springs Parks, a great number of birds may be seen. Permanent residents include the beautiful Wood Duck and Hairy and Pileated Woodpeckers. The dam overlook and the lakeside park are the best places to see waterfowl, and in winter Bald Eagles are present. The best birding area is below the Ferrells Bridge Dam at Lakeside and Shady Grove Parks. Like most of the lakes in East Texas, this is a heavily used recreational area. In the open fields you may see American Kestral, Wild Turkey, Eastern Kingbird, Horned Lark, Eastern Bluebird, Loggerhead Shrike, Blue Grosbeak, and Indigo Bunting. Overhead, Common Nighthawks can be seen in the evening or early morning hours, and Chimney Swifts, Purple Martins, and Tree, Northern Rough-winged, Cliff, and Barn Swallows may also be present.

Attractions

Longview Museum of Fine Arts

Located in downtown Longview at 215 East Tyler, this museum was founded in 1970 and contains a comprehensive collection of paintings, drawings, prints, photography, and sculpture, focusing on artists primarily of the Southwest, especially Texas.

R. G. LeTourneau Museum

Located on the campus of LeTourneau University, this museum honors the creator of the heavy earthmoving industry and the inventor of offshore drilling platforms. Pictures, memorabilia, diagrams, scale models, and full-size examples of his machinery are on display. For more information, phone 903-233-3672.

Gregg County Historical Museum

The museum's exhibits illustrate the development of Gregg County with artifacts, labels, and numerous historic photographs used in theme settings. Displays of timber, cotton, corn, farming, oil, railroads, printing, and early business and commerce. Rooms include a dentist's office and an early 1900s parlor and bedroom. Located at 214 North Fredonia Street.

Festivals

The Great Texas Balloon Race. Held since 1978, once in a lifetime moments can be captured at the hot air balloon race. Special interest shows are featured each year, along with a display of static military aircraft. For more information, phone 903-237-4000 or go to www.longviewtx.org.

June: Alleyfest, phone 903-753-3281

Motels

Best Western Inn, 3119 Estes Parkway at I-20, phone 800-528-1234

Comfort Inn, 203 North Spur at Hwy. 80, phone 800-228-5150

Econo Lodge, 3120 Estes Parkway at I-20, phone 800-55-ECONO

La Quinta Inn, 502 South Access Rd. at I-20, phone 800-531-5900

Super 8 Motel, 1409 East Marshall Ave., phone 800-800-8000

Travelodge, 2304 South Eastman Rd. at I-20, phone 800-222-6263

Dining

Over fifty fast food restaurants are available, from Dairy Queen to Kentucky Fried Chicken, and from Jack-in-the-Box to Taco Bell. Others include Church's Chicken, Grandy's, McDonald's, Popeye's Chicken, and Wendy's.

Bodacious Bar-B-Q (five locations)

Casa Ole, 280 N. Spur 63

Ryan's Steak House, 301 E. Loop 281

El Chico, 3301 W. Loop 281

Brenda's Good Eats, 1809 W. Loop 281

Catfish King (two locations), 1700 Judson Rd. and 2338 S. Mobberly

Cotton Patch, 1228 McCann Rd.

Lufkin
Visitor & Convention Bureau
1615 S. Chestnut Street
800-409-5659
http://www.lufkintexas.org
E-mail: lufkintx@lcc.net

Located in the heart of the East Texas Piney Woods, this city of more than 30,000 population sits between the Davy Crockett National Forest and the Angelina National Forest with the huge Sam Rayburn Lake.

Nacogdoches
Convention and Visitors Bureau
200 E. Main Street
888-564-7351
http://www.visitnacogdoches.org
E-mail: info@visitnacogdoches.org

These cities are listed together because they can be your base for birding expeditions into the Sabine National Forest and Toledo Bend

Reservoir. Although there are several small towns closer to the area, none have the dining, housing, or exploration possibilities that can be found in Lufkin or Nacogdoches. There is also lodging in Center, San Augustine, and Hemphill and camping in several areas. For more information, consult the *Texas State Travel Guide*, published by the Texas Department of Transportation.

Birding

Sabine National Forest and Toledo Bend Reservoir

Sabine National Forest includes 157,951 acres on the western side of Toledo Bend Reservoir. From Nacogdoches, a good place to start a birding trip is at the north end of the lake in the Ragstown area where you may find the endangered Red-cockaded Woodpecker. Banded trees can be found along FM 3814, designating nesting sites. Along here you may also see Eastern Towhee, along with Bald Eagles and Wood Ducks. The Toledo Bend Reservoir can be seen from several farm-to-market roads and will produce a wide variety of waterfowl year round, including Pied-billed Grebe, Great Blue and Little Blue Herons, and Yellow-crowned Night-Herons. Watch also for both Belted and Green Kingfisher. Green Herons can be seen in winter. More good birding areas can be reached easily from Lufkin by driving east on Highway 103 across the north end of the Angelina National Forest. The Foxhunter Hill area near the southern end of the forest can be productive for birders and also contains clusters of Red-cockaded Woodpeckers, which can be best seen in the morning or evenings. Other resident birds include Kestrel Hawks, Downy and Pileated Woodpeckers, Carolina Chickadee, Tufted Titmouse, Wood Thrush, and White-eyed Vireos.

Angelina National Forest and Sam Rayburn Reservoir

The northern end of this area is located just east of Lufkin. Saint's Rest Road, which can be accessed easily from either Lufkin or Nacogdoches, is an old railroad bed, and although birding can be excellent year round, the spring migration makes the birding great. In summer a wide variety of birds can be seen, including Eastern Wood-Pewee, Acadian and Great Crested Flycatchers, Brown-headed Nuthatch, Blue-gray Gnatcatcher, and Northern Parula, as well as Yellow-throated, Pine, Black and White, Swainson's, and Hooded Warblers. Townsend Park, which can be reached from Hwy. 103 by turning right on FM 2923, can also provide a pleasant area to watch birds, including waterfowl, and at the southern end of the lake, Boykin Springs, which includes a campground, has great birding possibilities.

Attractions

Lufkin

Lufkin is located in the heart of the East Texas Piney Woods and is home to a vast lumber and wood-products industry.

Ellen Trout Zoo and Park

Known for breeding the West African Crowned Crane and the Louisiana Pine Snake, this fully accredited park has a wide variety of animals and birds.

Medford Collection of Western Art

Over fifty paintings by contemporary artists Joe Becker, James Boren, Raymond Ryan, and Ross Stefan are on exhibit at city hall.

Museum of East Texas

Located in the historic Episcopal church at Second and Paul Streets, exhibits of science and history are constantly changing, along with a permanent display of works by East Texas artists.

Texas Forestry Museum

From a sawmill town exhibit to early logging machinery and wild land fire-fighting equipment, an old railroad depot with antique railroad and sawmill steam engines, this museum tells the story of the logging industry in East Texas.

Nacogdoches

The oldest city in Texas is a historian's delight. If you are interested in Texas history and roots, Nacogdoches will be a joy to visit when the birding is done.

Ghost of Nacogdoches Historical Trail

This ten-mile city trail is sponsored by the East Texas Area Council of the Boy Scouts of America. It focuses on the importance of Nacogdoches as a hub of western expansion and frontier development. Trail booklets are available at the Nacogdoches Convention and Visitors Bureau.

Milliard's Crossing

Once an Indian footpath, this trails wanders through thickets of paw-paw, dogwood, and scarlet blooming buckeye. Not only a nice stroll, but you might even see some birds.

Nacogdoches Fire Museum

Once called the "Central Fire Station," this museum is home to Nacogdoches' first commercial fire engine, old sirens, nozzles and tools, along with many photos. Located at 214 E. Pilar. Tours are made by appointment.

SFA Mast Arboretum

This arboretum on the campus of Stephen F. Austin University has nineteen acres of a wide diversity of plant life, including rare trees, shrubs, vines, and perennials.

Sterne-Hoya House

Built by a prominent leader of the Texas Revolution in 1830. Located at 211 S. Lanana.

Stone Fort Museum

While in Nacogdoches, this Spanish colonial residence is a must see. This replica of Antonio Gil Y'Barbo's stone house is on the Stephen F. Austin campus.

Festivals

Nacogdoches: Blueberry Festival, second weekend in June. A weekend full of activities and food. Phone 888-564-7351 for information.

December: Nacogdoches: Nine Flags Festival, phone 888-564-7351

Motels: Lufkin

Comfort Inn, 4402 S. First, phone 936-632-4949

Holiday Inn, 4306 South First, phone 936-639-3333

La Quinta Inn, 2119 South First Street (Hwy. 59 and Loop 287), phone 800-531-5900

Days Inn, 2130 South First Street, phone 936-639-3301

Best Western Expo Inn, N. Loop 287 at U.S. 59 North, phone 936-639-7300

Motel 6, 1110 South Timberland, phone 936-637-7850

Motels: Nacogdoches

Best Western Inn of Nacogdoches, 3428 South Street, phone 800-528-1234

Econo Lodge, 2020 N.W. Loop 224, phone 800-553-2666

The Fredonia Hotel, 200 N. Fredonia, phone 800-594-5323

Holiday Inn, 3400 South Street, phone 800-HOLIDAY

La Quinta, 3215 South Street, phone 800-531-5900

Victorian Inns & Suites, 3612 North Street, phone 800-935-0676

Dining: Lufkin

Fast food options include McDonald's, Popeye's Chicken, Sonic, Burger King, Arby's, Schlotzky's Deli, and Chick-Fil-A.

Barnhills Mesquite Grill and Buffet, 3102 S. John Redditt (also in Nacogdoches)

El Chico, 2104 S. First Street

IHOP, 4400 S. Medford

Ray's Drive In, N. Timberland and South (best hamburger in Angelina County)

Casa Olé, 2109 S. First Street

Luby's Cafeteria, 3107 S. First Street

Dining: Nacogdoches

There are the usual fast food restaurants: CiCi's Pizza, Dairy Queen, Mazzio's Pizza, Papa John's Pizza, Pizza Hut, Sonic

Drive-in, Chicken Express, Kentucky Fried Chicken, Long John Silver's, Popeye's Fried Chicken, Arby's, and Schlotzky's
Aubrey's Café, 1523 E. Main St. (home cooking)
Cotton Patch, 3117 North St. (home cooking)
Luby's Cafeteria, 3613 North St.
The Barbecue House, 4915 North St.
Casa Olé, 1116 University Drive
Golden Corral, 1315 North St.

Marshall

Chamber of Commerce
P.O. Box 520
903-935-7868
http://www.marshalltxchamber.com
E-mail: cvd@internetwork.net

Marshall, the county seat of Harrison County, is steeped in history. When Texas seceded from the union, Marshall became a huge producer of products for the Confederacy, from saddles, harnesses, and clothing to powder and ammunition. It also became the Confederate capital of the government of Missouri in exile and headquarters for the Trans-Mississippi Postal Department. Its proximity to Lake O' The Pines and Caddo Lake makes it a prime birding area in East Texas.

Birding

Caddo Lake State Park and Wildlife Management Area

This 32,000-acre lake and 478-acre state park is a wetland paradise, with cypress-filled swamplands and a hardwood forest and even open fields. The wide variety of habitat provides a wide variety of species. Waterfowl can include Red-breasted Mergansers, Greater White-fronted and Canadian Geese, Common Snipe, Virginia Rail, and Bald Eagles in winter. The swamps can be reached in summer by renting canoes at the state park. Even outside the park, the grassy fields can produce Winter and Sedge Wrens and a number of sparrows, including Vesper and LeConte's in winter. In the summer you might find American Redstart, Yellow-breasted Chat, and

Louisiana Waterthrush. Overhead, Mississippi Kites and Red-tailed Hawks can be seen, along with Purple Martins and Barn Swallows.

Lake O' The Pines

See the information under Longview. Either Marshall or Longview can be used as a base for visiting Lake O' The Pines.

Daingerfield State Park

Located just north of Lake O' The Pines, this is a much smaller park and lake but can be very profitable in the spring and summer when Dickcissel, Lark Sparrow, Loggerhead Shrike, and American Kestrel can be seen. In winter the geese, Canadian, Greater White-fronted, and Snow, can be seen in the fields outside the park and Bewick, House, and Sedge Wrens are also present, along with a variety of sparrows, including Fox, Song, Swamp, and White-crowned. An excellent place for a picnic lunch.

Attractions

Harrison County Historical Museum

Old Harrison County Courthouse exhibits the history of Marshall and Harrison County as well as Caddo Indian artifacts, a Civil War display, George Foreman and Bill Moyers exhibits, Lady Bird Johnson display, and Y. A.Tittle exhibit.

Marshall Pottery and Museum

Demonstrations of pottery making and firing are featured in this, the largest manufacturer of glazed pottery in the U.S. Founded in 1896, the museum has exhibits of the history of the plant and a video presentation that shows pottery as an art form. Other exhibits include an antique pottery wheel and photographic displays of pottery's origin.

Starr Family State Historical Site

Maplecroft was the name of the house built in 1870 by James S. Starr, son of Dr. James Harper Starr, early financier, surgeon general of the Republic of Texas in 1837, secretary treasurer for the republic, and postmaster general for the Confederate States. Located at 407 W. Travis Street.

Festivals:

Stage Coach Days Festival. Held in early May, this celebration includes a parade, stagecoach rides, entertainment, arts and crafts, and lots of food.

Fire Ant Festival. Believe it or not, a festival celebrating fire ants! Events include a parade, arts and crafts, fire ant calling (?), ugly face contest, fire ant roundup, and entertainment. And of course, food. Held in early October.

Wonderland of Lights. Starting in late November and continuing through December 30th, this celebration includes over 9 million lights throughout the city. Activities include home tours, carriage rides, outdoor ice skating, lighted Christmas parade, and Cowboy Christmas celebration, with entertainment on the courthouse square.

Motels

Best Western Inn of Marshall, 5555 East End Blvd., phone 903-935-1941

Hampton Inn, 5100 S. East End Blvd., phone 903-927-0079

Motel 6, 300 I-20 East, phone 903-935-2380

Super 8 Motel, 6002 East End Blvd., phone 800-800-8000

Budget Inn, 502 East End Blvd., phone 903-938-7984

Comfort Inn, U.S. 59 and I-20, phone 800-228-5150

Dining

Fast food options include: Burger King, McDonald's, Schlotzsky's, Sonic, and Subway

El Chico, 205 East End Blvd. North

Lupe's Mexican Restaurant, 1205 South Hwy. 59

Bodacious Bar-B-Q, 2018 Victory Drive

Porky's Smokehouse & Grill, 504 East Carolanne at Hwy. 59 South

Golden Corral, 5012 East End Blvd. South

Barnstormer's, 1000 East End Blvd. South

Tyler

Tyler Convention & Visitors Bureau
315 N. Broadway
800-235-5712
http://www.tylertexas.com
E-mail: dpamell@tylertexas.com

Tyler is best known as the rose capital of the world and for the "Apache Belles" dance/drill team of Tyler Junior College. But the city that roses built has blossomed into a thriving metropolitan city. The Tyler State Park sits amid one of the finest forested sections of Texas and is a busy recreation area with facilities that include camping, a nature trail, fishing, swimming, boating, and of course, birding. Tyler is also located just a few miles south of Lake O' The Pines.

Birding

Tyler State Park

Located just east of the city of Tyler, this 994-acre park features a spring-fed lake that is a popular recreational site. There is a hiking trail that is good for birding all year for such species as Belted Kingfisher, Northern Flicker, Carolina Wren, Tufted Titmouse, Gray Catbird, and Indigo Bunting. Wood Ducks, Lesser Scaup, and Pied-billed and Horned Grebes can be seen in winter.

Lake Palestine

Located southwest of Tyler, this 25,500-acre impoundment is primarily for recreation and is a favorite fishing, boating, and water sport haven. There is a marina with bait and tackle shops and a swimming beach. If you are looking for an area to combine a family fishing trip with birding activities, this would be a great selection, but not for birding only.

Attractions

Brookshire's World of Wildlife and Country Store

Visit Brookshire's to show the kids what life was like before computers and television. The Wildlife Museum displays over 250 species of animals. World of Wildlife Museum includes the Country Store, which depicts what grocery stores were like in 1928 with products and fixtures common to that period, along with a 1926 Model T Ford delivery truck and old-time gasoline pump. Outside is an antique fire truck. A great place for reptiles and fish.

Caldwell Zoo

This 35-acre zoo has elephant and giraffe houses, monkey island, birds, bears, alligators, and an aquarium. The Texas exhibit has a cow for milking. This zoo was started as a backyard project in 1938 and is designed to bring enjoyment to children. It includes a petting zoo. Located at 1600 W. SW Loop 323 and Old Jacksonville Hwy.

Carnegie History Center

Located in the old library building, this center exhibits artifacts from Tyler's historic, social, and economic culture. Displays are of Indian, Republic of Texas, and Civil War eras. Located at 125 S. College Street.

Discovery Science Place

Children will enjoy the hands-on learning center with exhibits of science concepts. Fun for the entire family. Located at 308 N. Broadway Street. Call 903-533-8011 for information.

Harrold's Model Train Museum

Over 1,500 pieces of model railroad, with scenery and villages. A must stop for the railroad enthusiast. Located on Loop 323 on Lavender Road.

Hudnall Planetarium

Located on the campus of Tyler Junior College, this planetarium is one of Texas's largest and contains exhibits of space vehicles.

Municipal Rose Garden and Museum

Approximately 38,000 rose bushes are displayed, representing about 500 varieties. Tyler is the rose capital of the world, and the 22-acre garden is at its peak from May to November. The Rose Museum features educational exhibits of the industry.

Festivals

Azalea and Spring Flower Trail. Features tours of historic Tyler, arts and crafts shows, a quilt show, Art 'n Bloom, and more. Walking trails and shuttle tours. Held in late March, early April.

Texas Rose Festival. Held in mid-October, this festival includes the coronation of the rose queen, rose show, a parade, and tours of the rose nurseries.

Motels

Best Western-Tyler Inn and Suites, 2828 W. Northwest Loop 323, phone 903-592-5672

Econo Lodge, 2739 Northwest Loop 323, phone 903-531-9513

Fairfield Inn, 1945 W. Southwest Loop 323, phone 903-561-2635

Motel 6, 3236 Brady Gentry Pkwy., phone 800-4-motel6

Days Inn, 3300 Hwy. 69 N., phone 903-595-2451

Super 8, 2616 N. Northwest Loop 323, phone 903-593-8361

Dining

J. W. Finn's Market Café, 2324 S. Southeast Loop 323

Armadillo Willy's, 215 W. Southwest Loop 323

Jason's Deli, 4740 S. Broadway

Pauline's Country Buffet, 3040 W. Gentry Pkwy.

Papacita's Mexican Restaurant, 6704 Broadway

Bruno's Pizza, 1400 S. Vine Ave.

Central Plains Region

bald eagle

Austin

(See Edwards Plateau)

Eagle Lake

Chamber of Commerce
121 N. McCarty Ave.
979-234-2780

This town was named in honor of the Karankawa Indian brave who brought an eagle for his Indian maiden. It is a big hunting ground for duck and goose hunters where thousands of the birds are killed at hunting clubs and is best avoided during hunting season.

Birding

Attwater Prairie Chicken Refuge

A 3,400-acre sanctuary for the once endangered Greater Prairie Chickens. Tours can be arranged for viewing the birds by calling the Chamber of Commerce or the refuge at 979-234-3021. The refuge is located on FM 3013 between Eagle Lake and Sealy. (Also see Bay City/Matagorda County, Upper Coast and Eagle Lake.)

Attractions

Prairie Museum

Dedicated to the preservation of artifacts relating to the natural history and cultural traditions of Colorado County. Located at 408 East Main St. Open on weekends only.

Motels

The Eagle Lake Lodge, P.O. Box 195, phone 888-TX LODGE

Eagle Hill Inn & Retreat, 307 East State St., phone 800-324-3551

Hunter's Lodge, 104 E. Waverly, phone 979-234-7252

Dining

Austin's Bar B Q, 507 Main Street

Dairy Delite, 810 East Main

Sportsman's Restaurant, 201 Boothe Drive
2K's Taqueria, 514 East Main
Dairy Queen, 100 Boothe Drive

Edna
Chamber of Commerce
317 W. Main Street
361-782-7146

This city was built on the Robert Guthrie league granted by the Mexican government through Stephen F. Austin in 1824. It was first called Macaroni Station and today is a center for rice, cotton, corn, and milo production. It is located on the Great Texas Coastal Birding Trail.

Birding

Lake Texana State Park

This 11,000-acre lake extends about 18 miles from the Navidad River Valley above Palmetto Dam, which was completed in 1980. There are about 125 miles of shoreline, and it is a favorite spot for fishermen and boaters on the weekends and holidays. The Texana State Park contains 575 acres and has a nature trail on the northwestern edge of the campground. In the winter, a drive around the loop that circles the entire lake is the best way to bird and will provide you with a look at many water birds, such as Mottled Duck, Northern Pintail, Blue-winged Teal, Canvasback, Common Goldeneye, Bufflehead, and Hooded Merganser. Three species of grebe may be seen, Pied-billed, Eared, and Western. Bald Eagles are sometimes seen in the pastures and fields along FM 3131 and FM 1593, and they can also contain great flocks of geese, including Greater White-fronted, Snow, and even a few Ross's, along with hundreds of Sandhill Cranes. Hawks are frequently seen overhead, from Northern Harrier to Sharp-shinned to Cooper's and Red-tailed. In the spring, migrants can be plentiful in the state park where you might see a different variety of water birds such as Yellow-crowned Night-Heron, White Ibis, Black-bellied Whistling-Duck, and

Black-necked Stilt. The huge Pileated Woodpecker is a resident in the woods below the dam.

Attractions

Otto Lawrence Children's Museum

A great place for the children to learn from hands-on exhibits with replicas of an old country schoolhouse, country store, and post office and a display of vintage clothing and homemade games. Located in the historic Jackson County Jail at the corner of Cypress and Ed Linn Streets.

Texana Museum and Old Jail House

Includes exhibits of artifacts, art items, and documents pertaining to early life in the area. The exterior of the museum has murals of the early history. Located at 403 N. Wells on Texas 111 North.

Motels

Inns of Edna, 600 E. Houston Hwy., phone 361-782-5276

Jackson Inn, 191 Loop 521, phone 361-782-0808

Dining

Dos Hermanos Mexican Restaurant, 106 East Houston Hwy. Service Road

Frontier Bar-B-Que, 608 N. East

Lariat, 1022 S. Wells

Palmetto Restaurant, 906 West Main

Prasek's Hillje Smokehouse, Rt. 3, Box 18, Hwy. 59 South, El Campo

Fast food options include Whataburger, Sonic, Pizza Hut, Gary's Corner Store/Deli, and Church's Chicken.

Gonzales

Chamber of Commerce
414 St. Lawrence Street
Located in an 1887 Jail House
830-672-6532
http://www.gonzalestexas.com

The first battle of the Texas Revolution was fought here. The town was settled in 1825 by Green C. DeWitt and named for Rafael Gonzales, the Mexican governor of the state of Cohhuila-Texas. The streets are named for saints. It is the seat of Gonzales County and the center of pecan, cattle, and poultry production.

Birding

Palmetto State Park

This relatively small park (263 acres) lies on the San Marcos River and was named for the dwarf palmetto that grows in the park's Ottine Swamp. The habitat here is varied, ranging from blackland prairie to post oak savannah to coastal plains. There are several hiking trails that will lead the birder into each of these areas, and a number of birds can be seen. Prothonotary, Swainson's, and Kentucky Warblers nest on the Palmetto Trail (.33 mile), and in summer the Pileated Woodpecker, Black-chinned Hummingbird, Yellow-breasted Chat, Northern Parula, Summer Tanager, Blue Grosbeak, and both Indigo and Painted Buntings will be present. Also in summer, a walk on the River Walk (.66 mile) will produce such species as Wood Duck, Purple Gallinule, and Green Kingfisher. At the campgrounds you can find Eastern Screech-Owl, Barred Owl, and Chuck-will's-widow, and you are more likely to hear them than see them. Oxbow Lake on the northwestern side of the park is another good place for owls at dusk. The Hiking Trail is a good place to see Red-shouldered Hawk, Ash-throated Flycatcher, Bewick's Wren, and Blue-gray Gnatcatcher. Birding along Park Road 11 can give you a look at a different assortment of birds, from Dickcissel to Loggerhead Shrike and Field, Lark, and Grasshopper Sparrows. In the winter, geese and Sandhill Cranes sometimes are present, along with a variety of sparrows, including LeConte's, Fox, Swamp, and Harris'.

Attractions

Gonzales Memorial Museum

Located on E. St. Lawrence Street, this museum commemorates the first battle of the Texas Revolution against Mexico, with a monument dedicated to those who fought there and the 32 who later fought at the Alamo. A replica of the famous gun that was used and the flag with the "Come and Take It" motto are part of the display.

Historic Sites

An old jail built in 1887 has been restored with cells, dungeon, gallows, and jailer's quarters. The museum has an extensive gun collection and is the home of the Chamber of Commerce and the historical society. This entire area is steeped in the history of Texas and is another of those great opportunities for the children to learn. Eggleston House, built in 1848, is near the Memorial Museum and has been restored and furnished with antiques. Confederate Square and Texas Heroes Square are downtown.

Festivals

"Come and Take It" Celebration: In early October, a four-day event honoring those who fought in the Texas Revolution.

Motels

Inn of Gonzales, 1804 Sarah Dewitt Drive, phone 830-672-9611

Lexington Motel, Hwy. 90 Alternate, phone 830-672-2807

Regency Inn & Suites, 1811 Sarah Dewitt Drive, phone
    830-672-5555

Dining

Café on the Square, 705 St. Joseph Street

Cassie's Steak & Grill Restaurant, 401 St. George

Matamoros Taco Hut, 201 St. Joseph Street

Opie's Cow Palace Restaurant, 1801 W. U.S. Hwy. 90A

Toni's Foods, 209 St. Lawrence Street

Fast Foods: Whataburger, Subway, Sonic, Pizza Hut, and Dairy
Queen

La Grange
Chamber of Commerce
171 S. Main St.
800-LA GRANGE or 409-968-5756

Developed in 1831, La Grange is the county seat of Fayette County.
The Historic Oak on the north side of the town has been the muster-
ing point for men in six conflicts. The city is a pivotal point on the
Texas Pioneer Trail.

Birding

Fayette Lake

This 2,400-acre lake is actually a cooling basin for the coal-fired
Fayette Power Plant, but Oak Thicket and Park Prairie Parks are
managed separately from the Lower Colorado River Authority and
can be an excellent, though not large, place to bird. Oak Thicket
Park is located on the northeast side of the lake just off of Hwy. 150
and can be reached easily from either Fayetteville (8 miles) or La
Grange (10 miles). La Grange has lodging, Fayetteville does not. In
the park you have a selection of habitats and a good look at the lake
where a scope would be a handy thing to have along. There is a
viewing platform at the campground, and in winter there will be a
lot of water birds such as Pied-billed Grebe, Double-crested Cormorant, Great Blue Heron, and Green-winged Teal. Ducks will include
Mallard, Northern Pintail, Ruddy, American Wigeon, Lesser Scaup,
and Bufflehead to name a few. Belted Kingfisher may be seen on the
edge of the water, and in the reeds look for Red-winged Blackbird.
Onshore resident birds are both Mourning and Inca Doves, Red-
bellied Woodpecker, Carolina Chickadee, Tufted Titmouse, and
Northern Cardinal, among others. There is a 2.5-mile Rice-Osborne
Bird and Nature Trail, which starts just inside the park entrance.
This area was only opened in 1996 and has not been birded by great
numbers. In the Park Prairie Park there are a few ponds and open
fields that will produce in summer Eastern Bluebird, both Western

and Eastern Kingbirds, Purple Martin, and Cliff and Barn Swallows. In the fields you may see Dickcissel and Field and Lark Sparrows. Several raptors can be seen such as Northern Harrier, Sharp-shinned, Cooper's, Red-tailed, and Ferruginous Hawks, along with Crested Caracara and American Kestrel.

Attractions

Fayetteville Area Museum (in Fayetteville)

This museum features displays from the German-Czech heritage, including Baca Band memorabilia and early kitchen and drugstore items. Located in an old building on the courthouse square, it is only open on Sunday afternoons in the spring and fall, and at other times by appointment. Phone 979-378-2210.

Monument Hill State Historic Site (La Grange)

A monument honors the men who drew a black bean and died after the Mier Expedition against Mexico and 41 of Captain Nicholas Dawson's soldiers who were killed by Mexicans at Salado Creek. There is a visitors center and self-guided tour, a nature trail, and pic-nic facilities. Phone 979-968-5658 for details.

The Jersey Barnyard

This is another fun place where the kids can also learn about the dairy business with cow milking demonstrations that you can try and a petting and feeding zoo with goats, donkey, bunnies, ducks, calves, and more. Belle the singing cow from Blue Bell Creameries is here, and after a hayride, the children can enjoy Blue Bell ice cream in the Jersey General Store. Located at 3117 Hwy. 159.

Festivals

September: Main Street Arts and Crafts Show, phone 979-968-8701

Motels

Carter Motel, 243 Ellinger Road, phone 979-968-8331
Cottonwood Inn, 1494 W. Hwy. 71, phone 979-968-3175
Oak Motel, 227 S. Jefferson, phone 979-968-3133
River Valley Motor Inn, P.O. Box 840, phone 979-968-8314

Executive Inn, 1708 Hwy. W. Hwy. 71, phone 979-968-2600

Antlers Inn, I-10 and 609, Flatonia, phone 361-865-2906

Dining

Fast food options include Golden Fried Chicken, McDonald's, Sonic, Whataburger, Gold'n Crisp, and Pizza Hut.

Das Kraut Haus, 2409 Hwy. 71 (Be sure the kids like German food.)

China Buffet, 1545 S. Jefferson

Guadalajara Mexican Restaurant, 403 N. Jefferson

Schulze's Southern Grill, 6585 Jefferson

Tim's on the Square, 155 N. Main

Taylor

Chamber of Commerce

512-352-6364

The original town was laid out in 1876, and the town was incorporated in 1882. Today it is a center for agriculture and manufacturing. It was originally called Taylorville and was named in honor of Edward M. Taylor of the Houston Belt and Terminal Railroad.

Birding

Alcoa Lake

This is a private lake or cooling pond owned by the Aluminum Company of America and is open to birders who check in when they arrive at the security office. Birding must be done only from the roadways, and taking pictures is forbidden. In spite of the regulations, it is the best spot to bird in the area. A five-mile drive on FM 1766 through oak woodlands and fields can be very productive during either fall or spring migration when some birds remain to nest and become residents. Birds you might see here are Ruby-throated Hummingbird, Eastern Wood-Pewee, Acadian and Great Crested Flycatcher, and White-eyed Vireo. Along the roadsides Wild Turkey, Northern Bobwhite, and Greater Roadrunner may be present, and overhead, look for American Crow. There is a pond about 4 miles from the entrance on the right with a view of one corner of the lake to the left, and both are excellent birding places year round. In summer Pied-billed Grebe, Little Blue Heron, Green Heron, and Great, Snowy, and Cattle Egrets will be here, along with Wood Duck and Black-bellied Whistling-Duck. The tiny Least Bittern can be seen in summer, also, and the American Bittern, Virginia Rail, Sora, and Marsh Wren are sometimes seen in winter. The Rusty Blackbird may also be here in the cattails, but look out for the alligator!

Granger Lake

Granger Lake covers 4,400 acres and is managed by the U.S. Army Corps of Engineers. The bird list is similar to that of Alcoa Lake in the spring and summer, but wintering water birds can vary. Fourteen species of sparrows have been identified here, and in October thousands of Franklin Gulls gather. The best places to bird are Wilson H. Fox Park, Friendship Park, or north of the dam. Both McCown's and Chestnut-collared Longspurs can be seen in the fields along the county roads in winter.

Attractions

Moody Museum

The birthplace of Texas governor Dan Moody, who took on the Ku Klux Klan in Williamson County, the home was built in 1887 and contains the original furnishings of the Moody family. Located at 114 W. Ninth Street and open only on Sunday afternoons.

Motels

Regency Inn, 2007 N. Main St., phone 512-352-2666
Taylor Village Motor Inn, 1907 N. Main St., phone 512-352-8565
Western Inn, 15255 Hwy. 79 W., phone 512-352-5292

Dining

Sirloin Stockade, 200 W. Lake Drive
Lakeview Inn Restaurant, 4701 CR 424
Rudy Mikeska's BBQ, 300 W. 2nd Street
Fast Foods: Dairy Queen, Golden Chick, McDonald's, Pizza Hut, Sonic, Subway, and Taco Bell

Upper Coast
Region

sabine gull

Brazoria County

Southern Brazoria County
Visitors & Convention Bureau
159 North Brazosport Blvd.
Clute, TX 77531
800-WET-GULF

or

Brazosport Convention & Visitors Council
420 W. Hwy. 332
Brazosport, TX 77531
888-477-2505
http://www.tourtexas.com/brazosport

Perhaps one of the best-kept secrets of birding in Texas is Brazoria County, an area that includes the cities of Angleton, Alvin, Brazoria, Clute, Danbury, Freeport, Jones Creek, Lake Jackson, Oyster Creek, Pearland, Quintana, Richwood, Surfside Beach, Sweeny, and West Columbia. The Migration Celebration, held in the spring each year, is one of the most productive birding experiences you can have. During spring migration, a fall-out at the Quintana Sanctuary, in spite of its small size, can produce a huge variety of warblers and other migrants. There is also a joint venture between Dow Chemical Company and the birding community that should be a standard for other large companies. Dow has actually reserved a portion of one of its parking lots to accommodate a colony of nesting Black Skimmers, and they designated one of their engineers, an avid birder, to supervise.

Birding

Brazoria National Wildlife Refuge

Two hundred and forty-seven species of birds have been identified in this 42,000-acre refuge located on the Gulf Intracoastal Waterway. There is a six-mile self-guided auto tour and hiking trail. It is a nesting area for Mottled Ducks and wintering ground of Snow Geese. Open first full weekend of every month. Contact refuge headquarters in Angleton before visiting 979-849-6062.

Brazosport Nature Center and Planetarium Nature Trail

The entrance to this trail is located at the east side of the Brazosport Arts and Science Center, home of the Nature Center and Planetarium, and runs through the river bottom land. A copy of the *Trail Guide to a River Bottom Woodland* may be obtained at the nature center or: Brazosport Center for the Arts and Sciences, 400 College Drive, Lake Jackson, TX 77566. tgn.net/-snark/ncap/ucap2.html. Phone 409-265-3376.

San Bernard National Wildlife Refuge

A 24,000-acre refuge is located between Cedar Lake and San Bernard River on the Intracoastal waterway. Many herons, egrets, shore birds, and Mottled Ducks will be found on the mud flats or ponds. A three-mile Moccasin Pond auto loop and Scissor-tail Trail are good for a short look, or walk the Bobcat Woods Trail, an elevated boardwalk with a view of Cockleburr Slough. This refuge contains coastal prairie, woodlands, salt and freshwater marshes, and lakes. For information on access, contact headquarters at Brazoria National Wildlife Refuge (above).

Quintana Neotropical Bird Sanctuary

A small but very productive sanctuary is located south of Surfside. This is an excellent birding area for small children, as not a lot of walking is required to see many birds. Benches in the sanctuary face water sources that will draw the birds to you. During spring migration, this is one of the hot spots on the Texas coast. Recent rarities include the Black-whiskered Vireo. Other include Summer and Western Tanagers, Rose-breasted Grosbeaks, Gray Catbird, Oven Bird, and an extensive list of warblers that can appear in the spring during a "fall-out." Many ducks, egrets, and shore birds can be seen on the way to the sanctuary.

Attractions

Sea Center Texas

The Sea Center, a cooperative endeavor of Dow Chemical Company, the Coastal Conservation Association, and the Texas Parks and Wildlife, is located at 300 Medical Drive in Lake Jackson and is free. It is open six days a week, closed on Monday. Call 409-292-0100 for more information. It contains a 50,000-gallon Gulf of Mexico aquarium. Gordon, a grouper that weighs 250 pounds, swims to the delight of onlookers, along with red drum, tarpon, and other open water fish. A 12-foot-wide touch pool allows visitors to touch marine animals such as blue crabs, hermit crabs, starfish, urchins, clams, snails, and anemones. A walkway includes exhibits of salt marsh habitat, along with an artificial reef tank and culture ponds.

Brazosport Center for the Arts and Sciences

Located at 400 College Drive, this center is the home of the Brazosport Art League, the Brazosport Museum of Natural Science, the Brazosport Center Stages Theater, and the Brazosport Nature Center and Planetarium. The Museum of Natural Science features halls on malacology, archaeology, mineralogy, and fossils and wildlife. Over 14,000 shells are displayed in the Hall of Malacology. The museum is open Tuesday through Saturday from 10 A.M. to 5 P.M. and on Sunday from 2 P.M. to 5 P.M. There is no fee.

Brazoria County Historical Museum

Housed in the 1897 Brazoria County courthouse in Angleton, this museum contains the Austin Colony Exhibit. The first of Stephen F. Austin's authorized 300 Anglo settlers in what was then Tejas y Coahuila, Mexico, arrived at the mouth of the Brazos River in 1821. Many of the events leading to the Texas Revolution developed here. There is an exhibit of weapons and tools from prehistoric times to 1836 and artifacts of daily life such as rare books and paintings. Other exhibits are housed in the building, along with the Adriance Research Center, which preserves thousands of pictures and family histories.

Varner-Hogg Plantation

Martin Varner was one of Texas's original 300 colonists when he started his plantation on the Brazos River in 1824. The property changed hands several times until 1901, when it was purchased by Texas governor James S. Hogg. The two-story brick home was donated to the state in 1958 by his daughter, Ima Hogg, and today is a state historical park. Guided tours are conducted on Wednesday through Sunday. Call 409-345-4656 for more information.

Surfside Beach

Twenty-one miles of unspoiled shoreline will give you a break from birding as you enjoy a wide variety of water sports, charter fishing, a crabbing pier, or just soaking up the South Texas sun while the kids build sand castles. Whether fishing at Jetty Park or walking the beach, you can still enjoy watching the shore birds, gulls, and terns.

Train Museum

Displayed at a child's eye level, this 12 ft. by 32 ft. scaled model layout of Brazoria County in the year 1955 is the focal point of the museum, which is located at 418 Plantation Drive in Lake Jackson. Operated by the Brazos Valley Railroad Society, the museum is open from 10 A.M. to 3 P.M. on Saturdays and 1 P.M. to 4 P.M. on Sunday. Anyone interested in the history of railroading will not want to miss this, and it is very educational for children.

Festivals

April: Migration Celebration is a spring birding festival on the upper Texas coast, focusing on the incredible return of neotropic migrants from Latin America. Guided trips take guests to see amazing concentrations of warblers, tanagers, grosbeaks, and buntings. Informative speakers, entertaining shows, and a trade exposition complete the event. Contact: Southern Brazoria County Visitor & Convention Bureau, 1239 W. Highway 332, Clute, Texas 77531 or phone 800-938-4853. www.tourist-info.org

July: (Clute) Annual Great Texas Mosquito Festival, phone 800-371-2971

Motels

Comfort Suites, 296 Ausner Jackson Pkwy., 979-297-5545

Days Inn, 1809 Velasco, Angleton 800-325-2525 (Continental breakfast, under 16 free)

Days Inn, 805 Hwy. 332, Clute, 800-329-7466 (Continental breakfast)

Ramada Inn, Hwy. 332, Lake Jackson, 979-297-1161 (Birder friendly)

Holiday Inn Express, Hwy. 332, Clute, 800-Holiday (Continental breakfast)

Contact the visitors bureau for a complete list of motels and bed and breakfasts.

Dining

Fast foods in the area include, Chick-Fil-A, Blimpie Subs, Papa John's Pizza, Subway, Domino's Pizza, and McDonald's.

Café Laredo, 403 This Way, at Hwy. 332, Lake Jackson, Mexican food

Cactus Grill, 107 West Way Brazos Emporium, Lake Jackson, family steak house

Dido's, County Rd. 519, Brazoria, seafood and steaks

Ryan's Family Steakhouse, 119 Hwy. 332 W., Lake Jackson

El Chico, 100 Hwy. 332 W. in Brazos Mall, Lake Jackson

Salt-N-Peppers Co., 1415 Hwy. 332, Clute

Bay City and Matagorda County

Chamber of Commerce
P.O. Box 768
201 7th St.
979-245-8333

Matagorda County is another of those birding spots that does not get a great deal of attention. But it is an important stop on the Great Texas Birding Trail, partially due to its proximity to the Attwater's Prairie-Chicken National Wildlife Refuge and also because it is within twenty-five miles of the coast and a multitude of birding opportunities such as the Family Mad Island Marsh Preserve, which is managed by the Nature Conservancy of Texas.

Birding

Matagorda County Jetty Park

This is an area that can attract a great number of birds during spring migration. Within the city of Matagorda, many exotic trees have been planted that attract the birds, and a drive along the Colorado River along FM 2031, with frequent stops in the many pull-out areas, will produce a great many wading birds such as White and White-faced Ibis and Roseate Spoonbills. In the winter a walk out to the end of the pier that reaches out into the Gulf could give you a look at Northern Gannet and perhaps some jaegers in the summer. This is also a good place to see the Magnificent Frigatebird overhead.

South Texas Project Prairie Wetlands

Located just north of Matagorda, this 110 acres has three seasonally flooded wetlands. From the observation tower at the entrance, you will see a great assortment of ducks and geese in winter. Migrant shore birds will be abundant in the spring, along with many other water birds.

Attwater's Prairie-Chicken National Wildlife Refuge

Established to protect the endangered Greater Prairie Chicken, this grassland can also be the home of many species that also prefer the habitat, such as Sprague's Pipit, Sedge Wren, and both Grasshopper and LeConte's Sparrows. Contact the Eagle Lake Chamber of Commerce at 409-849-6443. Contact the Attwater's Prairie-Chicken National Wildlife Refuge at 409-234-3021 for information on when the area can be birded. Guidelines are in place to protect the birds. (Also see Eagle Lake, Central Plains.)

Attractions

South Texas Project Visitors Center

The children can learn all about nuclear power generation through displays and programs. There is also a telescope for viewing the plant. Tours by reservation. Phone 361-972-5023 for more information.

Matagorda County Museum and Children's Museum

The kids will love the Children's Museum, which features exhibits and activities especially designed for them in the basement of the museum. Upstairs there are displays of clothing, books, Texas maps, furniture, paintings, and a carpentry tool collection from the late seventeenth century.

Motels

Econo Lodge, 3712 7th Street, Bay City, phone 409-245-2173

Holiday Inn Express, Hwy. 60, Bay City, phone 979-323-9500

Best Western Matagorda Hotel, Hwy. 35 West, Bay City, phone
    800-245-5404

Dining

Fast foods in Bay City include Blimpies, Church's, Dairy Queen,
    Hardee's, Jack-in-the-Box, KFC, Sonic, Subway, Taco Bell, and
    Whataburger.

Golden Corral, 3521 7th Street

Mr. Gatti's Pizza, 4011 7th Street

Pizza Hut, 2701 7th Street

Gem's Pancake House, 3729 7th Street

Glenn's Country Style Barbecue, 2901 6th Street

Beaumont/Orange/Port Arthur

Convention and Visitors Bureau
P.O. Box 3827
801 Main Street
Beaumont, TX 77704
800-392-4401
http://www.beaumontcvb.com

Known as the Golden Triangle, each of these cities sits on the leg of a triangle that forms not only a bountiful birding paradise, but harbors one of the most important areas in Texas history. Birding or just visiting, you can make any of the three your base of operations for a day, weekend, or extended visit. Children can learn not only about birds, but some of the rich heritage of Texas.

Birding

Cattail Marsh

Located on Babe Zaharias Drive, this 900 acres of wetland is a birder's paradise.

Texas Point National Wildlife Refuge and Sabine Pass Battleground

This 8,952 acres of coastal marshlands is located about seventeen miles south of Port Arthur, near Sabine Pass. Much is not accessible, but by driving west on Quinn and north on South 8th, you can watch the marshes for rails, wrens, and sparrows. Take FM 3322 west to Sabine Pass and go west on TX 87 to the nature trail that is located on the south side of FM 87, 2.4 miles west of Sabine Pass. The woods here are stunted and may contain Orchard Orioles and buntings. The Sabine Pass Battleground is an excellent place for a picnic lunch as well as a history lesson (see below).

Texas Ornithological Society's Sabine Woods

Located on the north side of TX 87 a little over four miles from Sabine Pass, this area of live oaks is a great place during the spring migration as many land birds take refuge here. In the early fall thousands of Ruby-throated Hummingbirds fill the lantana bushes.

Sabine Pass

Take Highway 87 to Sabine Pass. As you drive along the shores of Sabine Lake, you will probably see cormorants, gulls, and terns. Just before entering Sabine Pass, you will drive over the Sabine Pass marshes, where you may see White and White-faced Ibis, Least Bitterns, Roseate Spoonbills, Clapper Rails, and Yellowthroat, along with Seaside Sparrows.

Sea Rim State Park

Stop at the boathouse at the entrance off Highway 87, and look for Cave, Barn, and Cliff Swallows. Go west on Highway 87 to the entrance. The boardwalk east of the headquarters is an excellent place for children to bird in comfort and safety. Many marsh birds will be found here, including most of the rail family.

McFaddin National Wildlife Refuge

Located about twelve miles from Sabine Pass on Highway 87, this is a haven for waterfowl, but access is limited. There is an observation blind behind the headquarters on Pond 11.

Attractions

Babe Didrikson Zaharias Museum and Visitors Center

Located at 1750 I-10 and MLK Parkway, Exit 854, this museum honors America's greatest female athlete, Mildred "Babe" Didrikson Zaharias, who was three-time basketball All-American, won three Olympic gold medals, and was a pioneer for women in the sport of golf. Open daily 9 A.M. to 5 P.M. Phone 800-392-4401.

Fire Museum of Texas

Home of the 24-foot spotted fire hydrant, which was donated by Walt Disney's Studios to celebrate the movie *101 Dalmatians.* Founded in 1927, this former fire station displays antique fire bells, leather buckets, nozzles, badges, photographs, and vintage fire engines. A class on fire prevention and safety is conducted in the Fire Safety Activity Center, which includes toy collections and a puppet theater. Open Mon.-Fri. 8 A.M. to 4:30 P.M. Located at 400 Walnut.

Spindletop/Gladys City Boomtown

On January 10, 1901, the modern petroleum industry was born when the gusher drilled by Anthony F. Lucas blew in at 10 A.M. This oil town has been re-created complete with clapboard buildings, which include an information center, post office, photo studio, livery stable, blacksmith shop, surveyor's office, and wooden oil derricks. Open Tues.-Sun. 1 P.M. to 5 P.M. Located on University Drive at U.S. 69. Admission charge.

Sabine Pass Battleground State Historical Park

An excellent opportunity to combine a picnic lunch, birding, and a lesson in Texas history. Located south of Port Arthur, this 56-acre state historical park is maintained to commemorate the Battle of Sabine Pass during the Civil War in which Richard Dowling, with a few Confederate soldiers, repelled an attempted invasion of Texas by Union naval gunboats. A picnic area is available, along with restrooms and soft drink machines. During migration in the spring, such birds as Indigo and Painted Buntings may be present, along with orioles, grosbeaks, and a variety of warblers and vireos. Permanent residents include Seaside Sparrow, Clapper Rail, Marsh Wren, and White-faced Ibis, along with a great number of shore birds.

Motels

Best Western-Beaumont Inn, 2155 N. 11th Street, phone
    409-898-8150
La Quinta Inn-Beaumont, 220 I-10 North, phone 800-531-5900
Best Western Inn-Orange, 2630 I-10, phone 409-883-6616
Motel 6 Orange, 4407 27th Street, phone 800-4-Motel6
Budget Inn, 2311 MacArthur, Orange, phone 409-883-0204
Holiday Inn-Park Central, Port Arthur, 2929 Johnson Blvd., phone
    409-724-5000

Dining

Pancho's Mexican Buffet, 850 S. Eleventh St.
Luther's Bar-B-Que, 5860 Eastex Freeway
Casa Olé Mexican Restaurant, 335 I-10 N. and 5898 Eastex Frwy.
CiCi's Pizza, 5882 Eastex Freeway
Jason's Deli, 112 Gateway St. & 414 Dowlen Rd.

Galveston

Convention and Visitors Bureau
2428 Seawall Blvd.
888-425-4753
http://www.tourtexas.com/galveston

The pirate Jean Laffite established a settlement here in 1817, and during the War Between the States, it was the home of the Confederate Navy. The city was incorporated in 1838 and suffered the worst disaster of the United States when a hurricane killed between 5,000 and 7,000 people. The island city has 32 miles of beach and is a popular vacation spot for many, including a tremendous spring break crowd of college students.

or

Bolivar Peninsula

Chamber of Commerce
P.O. Box 1170
1760 Hwy. 87
409-684-5940 or 800-386-7863
http://www.crystalbeach.com/chamber.html

Birding

Anahuac National Wildlife Refuge

This 24,293-acre refuge has more than 40 nesting species. Maintained as a haven for wintering and migrating waterfowl, the refuge has a large variety of resident birds and is home to the American alligator. This is one of the best waterfowl refuges on the Texas coast. Enter the refuge at the main entrance located on FM 1985 and take the tour loop. At Shoveler Pond you may find Least Bitterns in the summer, and Marsh Wrens are common in the cattail marshes. Common Moorhens and Purple Gallinules are abundant and breed here. In addition to the alligators, you may see nutrias. The rails can be found here, including Clapper, King, Virginia, and Sora. Yellow Rails are also present but harder to find.

High Island Boy Scout Woods

One of the ultimate goals of every birder, this sanctuary is owned and operated by the Houston Audubon Society. It is an ideal place to bird with small children, for there are boardwalks and a place to sit down and watch for birds. The variety of species is greater in the spring during migration, but fall (late August to November) can also produce some rare finds. Summer birding will not be as productive but still well worth the stop.

Eubanks Woods Bird Sanctuary

This area is best during spring migration. A boardwalk will let you get to the woods even in wet weather, where the young oaks can harbor a variety of migrants.

Bolivar Flats Shore Bird Sanctuary

This is a must stop. Expansive tidal flats are covered with thousands of shore birds, terns, and gulls. It can also provide a little break in birding if you are interested in walking along the beach and picking up seashells. Birds to be seen here include most of the shore birds of North America. Among them: American Avocets, Black-necked Stilts, Red Knots, Marbled Godwits, American Oystercatchers, and both White and Brown Pelicans. Most terns and gulls are present, along with Dowitchers, Lesser Yellowlegs, and a variety of sandpipers. It will take some time to observe all the birds and identify them, and the day can be topped off with a ferryboat ride to Galveston.

The Railroad

On the west side of Galveston Island are several areas worth stopping at. A six-mile road runs alongside the Galveston Municipal Golf Course, and many shore birds can be found there, including Long-billed Curlew, Black-bellied Plover, and Buff-breasted, Upland, and Baird's Sandpipers. An eight-mile road runs into a street named Sportsman's Road, but local birdies call it the "Railroad," because of the abundance of rails that can be seen there, including Soras in season. You can also see Common Snipe, Ruddy Turnstone, and Willets.

Galveston Island State Park

This park contains coastal wetlands as well as salt meadows and coastal prairie, along with 1.5 miles of beach. There are bird blinds. The Clapper Rail Trail is always productive, and Marsh and Sedge Wrens can be seen. The bird list is extensive. In summer you may even see a Magnificent Frigatebird. This is a good place to have a picnic lunch. Camping facilities are also available.

Attractions

Lone Star Flight Museum

Here is a collection of more than two dozen vintage aircraft that have been restored, including a B-17 Flying Fortress, P-47 Thunderbolt, P-38 Lightning, a Spitfire, and many others. The Conoco Hall of Power displays historic engines, photos, air combat memorabilia, and wartime vehicles. Open daily from 10 A.M. to 5 P.M. except for major holidays. Located at 2002 Terminal Drive.

Moody Gardens

You may want to set aside a full day to visit at least a part of this 156-acre exhibit that includes the Aquarium Pyramid, which has two million gallons of water to showcase ocean waters of the North Pacific, where visitors view the ocean habitats from two levels. The Rainforest Pyramid rises ten stories high and displays the rain forest, including butterflies and exotic wading birds, along with the flowers and fauna, waterfalls, caves, and tropical fish of the rain forest. The Discovery Pyramid includes an IMAX theater with a simulated space ride developed in conjunction with NASA that takes visitors on a moving, shaking ride in space. The Palm Beach section of the gardens includes white sand beaches, swimming lagoons, and paddle boats. The Yellow Submarine and Octopus Slide features a 30-ft. submarine with fully operational periscope, water gun, and dive horn. For more information, call 800-582-4673.

Texas Seaport Museum

Located at Pier 21 at the north end of Kempner (22nd) Street, this museum is home of the square-rigged, 400-ton barkentine *Elissa*, which was built in Scotland in 1877 and was a visitor to Galveston during her sailing days. Two wide-screen presentations on the legends and lore of the sea and the restoration of the *Elissa* are shown.

Center for Transportation and Commerce (Railroad Museum)

Located on Rosenberg Street at the foot of the Strand, this railroad museum displays vintage railroad cars and engines on once active tracks, historic Santa Fe Depot restored in 1932 art deco style, HO-gauge working model of the Port of Galveston with tracks, ships, and port activities. Six theaters present the history of Galveston shipping, railroading, and commerce. Open daily from 10 A.M. to 5 P.M. There is an admission charge.

Moody Mansion

This elegant historic home was built in 1892. It will probably be of more interest to the adults than children. Built of red brick, Texas limestone, and terra-cotta tile, the interior features stained glass, beautifully carved wood trimmings, and fancy plaster work. Also contains a collection of antiques, silver, photographs, and works of art. Open Mon.-Sat. 10 A.M. to 4:30 P.M. Admission charged.

The Strand

Along the Strand you will find beautiful Victorian, Gothic, and Greek Revival homes and buildings. Take a carriage ride to shopping and restaurants, or ride the trolley to the Seawall. For more information, call 800-725-6174.

Motels

As in all resort areas, prices can range from inexpensive to very expensive, depending on the location and the season. It is best to always check prices when planning your trip. Staying at a motel outside of the resort area will almost always be less expensive. Avoid spring break.

Best Western Beachfront Inn, 5914 Seawall Blvd., phone
   409-740-1261

Gaido's Seaside Inn, 3800 Seawall Blvd., phone 800-525-0064

Motel 6, 7404 Avenue J. Broadway, phone 800-4-motel6

Ramada Inn, 5201 Gulf Freeway, La Marque, phone
   800-2-RAMADA

Comfort Inn, 2300 Seawall Blvd., phone 409-762-1166

Days Inn, 6107 Broadway St., phone 409-740-2491

Dining

Mario's Seawall Italian Restaurant, 628 Seawall Blvd.
   (lunch buffet)

Yaga's Tropical Café, 23114 Strand

Cadillac Authentic Mexican Food Restaurant, 1502 Wedwall Blvd.

Hill's Pier 19, 20th St. and Wharf St. (sit down dining or po-boys to go)

El Nopalito, 614 42nd Street (Tex-Mex)

Houston

Greater Southwest Houston Chamber of Commerce
713-666-1521
http://www.gswhcc.org

or

Greater Houston Convention and Visitors Bureau
800-365-7575
E-mail: ghcvbtou@compassnet.com
http://www.houston-guide.com

or

Katy Chamber of Commerce
281-391-2411
E-mail: katycofc@fbtc.net

As one of the largest metropolitan cities in the state, Houston has the unique situation of being two birding areas in one. The first is the inner city, where a very strong Audubon Society has promoted the development of parks and sanctuaries where visitors, even on business trips, can find the time and place to bird. The second birding opportunity is the expansive areas surrounding the city that allows the vacationer the ability to bird without dealing with the big city traffic (which can be very hectic) by staying in suburban motels. For detailed directions to these areas, it is recommended that you obtain a copy of "The Great Texas Coastal Birding Trail" map of the upper coast, published by the Texas Parks and Wildlife and the Texas Department of Transportation.

Birding Areas

Sam Houston Park

Located within walking distance of downtown Houston, this 19-acre park, with its gardens filled with native plants, freshwater wetlands, and mature oaks and pecan trees, is a haven for migrants that sometimes become confused by the towering buildings of downtown. Although particularly good for birding during the spring migration, the park is home to a number of resident birds.

Buffalo Bayou Park

Located west of the downtown area, this area features a hiking trail and woodlands that attract migrants.

White Oak Park

Located near downtown at White Oak Lake, this restored bayou habitat is home to Yellow-crowned Night-Herons and Green Herons, along with a number of woodland birds.

Hermann Park

This is the home of the Houston Zoo and features a birdhouse built like an Asian jungle that contains more than 200 species of tropical birds. The park is also home to the Museum of Natural History, the Burke Baker Planetarium, the Wortham IMAX Theatre, and the Cockrell Butterfly Center. This is a very educational complex and could merit a day of exploring. Picnic facilities are available. Wild birds may also be seen, including Red-headed Woodpecker, and during the winter a number of ducks can be seen on the lakes.

Russ Pittman Park and Nature Discovery Center

Located in the southwest sector of Houston, this spot is particularly good for wintering hummingbirds, which are attracted to the feeders that are placed by the nature center staff. Not only has the common Ruby-throat been recorded here, but also Black-chinned, Broad-tailed, and Rufous. Like the other sanctuaries within the city, migrants are attracted to this rest stop during the spring. For more information on the center, call 713-667-6550. Or write: Nature Discovery Center, 7112 Newcastle, Bellaire, Texas 77402-0777.

Attractions

Museum of Texas History

Located across from Texaco Heritage Plaza, this Heritage Society's collection of memorabilia covers Texas history from 1519. The exhibits change frequently and range from Spanish treasure to space exploration. In an adjacent building is the Long Row, a reconstruction of a shopping strip built in 1837 that contains gift shops and a tearoom.

Funplex

This complex contains a roller rink, bowling, miniature golf, arcade, rides, and three movie screens, all indoors and air conditioned. Located at 13700 Beechnut. Phone 281-530-7777.

Gulf Coast Railroad Museum

Displays and memorabilia of the history of railroading in the Houston area, along with Texas and the U.S., are presented inside the museum's visitor center, a former Santa Fe heavyweight end-door baggage express car. Located at 7390 Mesa Rd. Phone 713-631-6612.

Children's Museum of Houston

Hands-on exhibits cover science, history, culture, and the arts for children from five months old to fourteen years. Includes an outdoor discovery garden and greenhouse. Located at 1500 Binz. Admission charged.

Houston Museum of Natural Science

This area features exhibits of space, geology, archaeology, and natural history. Located at 1 Hermann Circle Dr. Includes: Burke Baker Planetarium, Cockrell Butterfly Center, Lillie and Roy Cullen Gallery of Earth Science, Wortham IMAX Theatre, and the Hall of Health.

San Jacinto Battleground State Historical Park

This is the site of the battle that won Texas its freedom from Mexico on April 21, 1836, when Sam Houston's army defeated Gen. Santa Anna's army, capturing the general. The tour includes a 35-minute lesson on the history of Texas and would be profitable for children. This is also the resting place of the battleship *Texas*, which is moored at the battleground. This ship served as the flagship for the 1944 D-day invasion of Europe.

For other tourists sites in the Houston area, consult the *Texas State Travel Guide*, published by the Texas Department of Transportation, or *Exploring Houston with Children* by Elaine L. Galit and Vikk Simmons.

Lodging and dining facilities are abundant in the city. Staying in a motel on the outer limits of the metropolitan area is advisable to avoid the heavy traffic and constant road work. In a city this large you will always find a variety of dining opportunities in the area of the motels.

Palacios
Chamber of Commerce
312 Main Street
361-972-2615

Founded in 1903, it was so named because shipwrecked Spaniards supposedly saw a vision of *tres palacios*, which means three palaces in Spanish. A bayfront park is a popular fishing and picnic area, and it is the home of the oldest Baptist youth camp in the state, Texas Baptist Encampment.

Birding

Cash's Creek

In the Cash's Creek area, located north of Palacios on FM 2853, there is an abundance of pastures and crop lands, and in the winter they can be filled with geese, including Greater White-fronted, Canada, and even Ross'. Most, however, will be Snow Geese. These fields can also contain a great variety of shore birds during the spring migration, and in winter White-tailed Kite, Northern Harrier, White-tailed Hawk, Red-tailed Hawk, Crested Caracara, and American Kestral may be present. Peregrine Falcons have also been seen here.

Palacios Waterfront and Trull Marsh

A leisurely drive along the waterfront on East Bayshore Drive can be spectacular because of the mix of habitat, from open bay to grassy yards, to saltwater wetlands and brush. Drive through the Texas

Baptist Encampment, oldest in the state, and watch for a great many shore birds, and in winter many species of ducks can be seen on the bay. But year-round birds are Pied-billed Grebe, Neotropic Cormorant, a variety of herons and egrets, both White and White-faced Ibis, Roseate Spoonbill, and Mottled Duck. In the summer Fulvous Whistling-Duck, Black-necked Stilt, and Painted Buntings are usually present. At Trull Marsh the boardwalk and observation platform are good places for easy birding where the kids can see a variety of duck species, as well as a wealth of shore birds including Greater Yellowlegs and Long-billed Dowitcher.

Palacios Marine Education Center and Nature Trail

The Marine Education Center on Camp Hulen Road, west of Marerum Boulevard, has a nature trail through vegetation to the bay and an observation deck. This area is especially good during spring migration.

Attractions

Marine Fisheries Research Station

This research center studies the adaptability of saltwater species to fresh water. Tours are mainly of interest to those with a special interest in marine biology.

Luther Hotel

This turn-of-the-century hotel is a recorded Texas Historic Landmark and is open to the public. In its prime it was the base for early land developers and featured a rambling front porch where a formally attired orchestra played during the mealtimes.

Motels

Luther Hotel, 408 S. Bay Blvd., phone 361-972-2312
The Deluxe Inn, 1505 First, phone 361-972-2547

Dining

Luther Hotel Dining Room, 408 S. Bay Blvd.
Palacios Mexican Restaurant, 511 Main St.
Shimek's Restaurant, 1001 Henderson St.
Yang Chow, 1009 Henderson St.

Port Lavaca/Calhoun County

Chamber of Commerce
2300 Hwy. 35 Bypass
P.O. Box 528
361-552-2959

Calhoun County is a wonderland of beautiful beaches and combined with the birding possibilities, is an ideal location for a family vacation. Within the triangle formed by Port Lavaca, Port O'Connor, and Seadrift, there are a number of great birding areas as well as a multitude of attractions along the Gulf Coast.

Birding

Port Lavaca Bird Sanctuary

Located on Highway 35 east of Port Lavaca, the Port Lavaca Lighthouse Beach and Bird Sanctuary features the Formosa Wetlands Walkway that leads to the Alcoa Birding Tower. In the marshes along the boardwalk can be found Clapper Rails, along with Seaside and Nelson's Sharp-tailed Sparrows (in winter). This is a good place to take a scope if you have one, for from the tower you should see Brown Pelican and a number of gulls and terns. In the bay you may also find Common Loons and American Oystercatchers. Watch the sky for Ospreys.

Magnolia Beach

Located west of Port Lavaca on TX 316, the prairies in this area can be profitable in the winter for Sandhill Cranes and Snow Geese. White-tailed Hawk has also been seen here, along with a number of other hawk species. The rice paddies (in the spring) contain a number of migrating shore birds such as Wilson's Phalarope, Hudsonian Godwit, and Buff-breasted Sandpiper. Rails can be seen in the marshes, and even the elusive Black Rail has been spotted here.

Port O'Conner/Matagorda Island State Park

This beautiful island paradise has recorded 320 species of birds, including Whooping Cranes, White-tailed Hawk, and Peregrine Falcon. It is reached by ferry service at 16th Street and Maple in Port

O'Conner. Be sure to go early in the morning, and call ahead to make reservations on the ferry. Matagorda Island State Park, P.O. Box 117, Port O'Conner, TX 77982. 361-983-2215 or 361-983-4358. Even the ferry ride, which the children will enjoy, can be a birding opportunity as you will see a wide variety of gulls, terns, waders, and shore birds in the flats along what is known as the Army Cut at the beginning of the trip. This island is one of the most preserved natural habitats on the coast, and it is limited to pedestrian and bicycle traffic. Check with the Texas Department of Wildlife about special tours. The area is rather expansive (56,668 acres of undeveloped barrier reef that is 38 miles long), so don't plan on seeing it all in one day. Hot spots to bird include the Lighthouse area and the North Cedars. Thirty-seven species of shore birds have been recorded here. April and May are the best times to bird for spring migrants, August and September for fall migrants, and from November to March for winter birds. The list for each season is extensive, and this is one of the best birding areas on the Texas Coast. It is included in the Great Texas Coastal Birding Trail, Central Texas Coast map (see Appendix C).

Guadalupe Delta Wildlife Management Area

Located on Highway 35, this is another area that lends itself to family birding with an observation platform near the entrance. The rest of the area is closed to the public except for special events. However, a short stop here, especially with a scope, can produce sightings of herons and egrets, along with a great number of shore birds. Wood Storks are present in late summer, and though seldom seen, the Marsh Wren can be heard.

There are several other birding hot spots in Calhoun County. Consult the Great Texas Coastal Birding Trail map for the Central Texas Coast, published by the Texas Department of Transportation and Texas Department of Parks and Wildlife.

Attractions

Halfmoon Reef Lighthouse

Built in 1858 on Matagorda Bay, this lighthouse was kept dark during the War Between the States to protect blockade runners and was reactivated in 1868. It was damaged by a hurricane in 1942, but the light was kept burning. In 1943 the condemned building was moved to Point Comfort and moved again in 1979 to the site on Highway 35, next to the Chamber of Commerce.

Indianola County Historic Park

Located on the site of old Indianola, this town survived shelling and capture during the War Between the States but was destroyed by a hurricane in 1875. Today, only stones projecting from the tide waters mark the spot, along with a granite statue of Rene Robert Cavelier, Sieur de la Salle, the French explorer who first arrived here more than 300 years ago.

Calhoun County Museum

Located in the Calhoun County courthouse annex, 201 Austin Street, this is a display of the relics, artifacts, and mementos of the early days of the area. Open Mon. through Fri., 1:30 to 4:30 P.M.

Motels

Chapparrel Motel, 2086 N. Hwy. 35, phone 361-552-7581
Days Inn, 2100 N. Hwy. 35, phone 361-552-4511
Holiday Motel, 2805 S. Hwy. 35, phone 361-552-5868
Royal Inn, 150 N. Hwy. 35, phone 361-553-6640

Dining

Port Lavaca has several fast food restaurants, including Dairy Queen, Church's Fried Chicken, Domino's Pizza, McDonald's, Pizza Hut, Sonic, Taco Bell, KFC, and Whataburger
The Lunch Box, 111 N. Hwy. 35
El Patio, 548 W. Main
Gordons, 2615 N. Hwy. 35
Gazebo, 2100 N. Hwy. 35 (Days Inn)
The Marina, 116 N. Commerce
Skillet, 2090 N. Hwy. 35

Coastal Bend

brown
pelican

Aransas Pass

Chamber of Commerce
130 West Goodnight
361-758-2750 or 800-633-3028
http://www.aransaspass.org

Aransas Pass is perhaps best known for its shrimping, along with commercial and sport fishing. Located on the mainland but connected to Mustang Island by causeway and ferry, it maintains a strong link in the tourist industry of South Texas. The vast amounts of water, particularly the flats along the causeway, also make it a prime area for birders.

Birding

Farm Road 1069

From Aransas Pass, take Farm Road 1069 toward Ingleside and cross Highway 35. On the left will be County Road 134, which is a dead end street but has ponds that can produce Least Bittern and Purple Gallinules, along with many species of ducks in winter. Go back to the main road and drive to Kenny Lane and make a left turn. Marshes here are likely to have White-faced Ibis, Mottled Duck, American Avocet, Black-necked Stilt, and both Black-bellied and Fulvous Whistling Ducks.

Dale Miller Causeway

Driving out of Aransas Pass toward Port Aransas, you will cross a very shallow bay with many sandbars. This is a good place to find a variety of shore birds, including Snowy Plover. You may also see American Oystercatcher and Reddish Egret. A scope can come in handy here.

Attractions

Deep Sea Fishing

If time and budget permit, a family deep-sea fishing trip can be booked. These can be strenuous and are not recommended for very small children. You can book one out of Aransas Pass by contacting one of the following fishing guides:

Elliott Guide Service, Box 122, Portland, 78374, phone 361-643-7351

Fisherman's Wharf, 900 Tarpon, Port Aransas, 78373, phone 361-749-5760 or 800-605-5448

Haire Guide Service, 1662 Mooney Ln., Ingleside, 78362, phone 361-776-1933 or 800-758-2890

Outdoor Texas, 259 South Commercial, Aransas Pass, 78336, phone 361-758-1560

Festivals

Shrimporee: September celebration with live entertainment, children's section, contests, parade, games, and a lot of shrimp eating, from fried to Cajun style and everything in between. Contact the Chamber of Commerce for dates and more information, 800-633-8320.

Motels

Days Inn, 410 E. Goodnight, phone 361-758-7375

Homeport Inn, 1515 Wheeler, phone 361-758-3213

Super 8 Motel, 500 E. Goodnight, phone 361-758-7888 or 800-800-8000. Free breakfast

Travelodge, 545 North Commercial, phone 361-758-5305

Seven RV parks are listed in the brochure available from the Chamber of Commerce.

Dining

Dairy Queen, McDonald's, Sonic, and Whataburger offer family meals at reasonable prices.

Crab-N, Highway 35 Business (fresh local seafood, steaks)

Groovies Sandwiches and Salads. In Dolphin Alley

Mac's Barbecue, 1933 Wheeler (barbecue beef, pork, chicken, sausage)

Old Towne Grille, 410 S. Commercial (steaks, burgers, sandwiches, seafood)

Nopalitos, 306 E. Goodnight (Mexican food)

Corpus Christi

Convention & Visitors Bureau
1201 N. Shoreline Blvd.
800-678-6232
http://www.corpuschristi-tx-cvb.org

Visitor Centers
6667 Texas 77 at I-37
361-241-1464

1823 Chaparral
800-766-BEACH

14252 South Padre Island Drive
361-949-8743

Perhaps more than any other major city in Texas, Corpus Christi has birding areas that are "family friendly." In only a matter of minutes, you can drive from Hans Suter Park to the Packery Channel, to the Corpus Christi Botanical Gardens or to Indian Point, and from Hazel Bazemore Park drop by Tule Lake and then still make it to Blucher Park near downtown. And all within range of a variety of other entertainment locales, many motels, and inexpensive dining.

Birding

Blucher Park

Located immediately behind downtown Corpus Christi just off Carrizo Street, this small park is a stop-off for many migrating passerines and hummingbirds. The local Audubon Outdoor Club of Corpus Christi conducts bird walks every Saturday and Sunday during April from 7:30 to 9:30 A.M. An excellent place to see many migrants, and a fall-out can produce a variety of birds.

Hans Suter Wildlife Park

Located on the edge of Cayo del Oso (Oso Bay), this park can be reached by going south on South Padre Island Drive (SPID), turn right on McArdle Road, and at Ennis Joslin Road turn left. An excellent place to see a wide and ever-changing variety of waterfowl, with easy assess to the water on a boardwalk. Here you will see many shore birds and waders. Roseate Spoonbills, Reddish Egrets,

Black-necked Stilts, and White Pelicans are usually present. Watch the waterway that runs parallel with the boardwalk and you may see Blue-winged Teal, Pied-billed Grebes, Northern Shovelers, and other species of ducks.

Hazel Bazemore Park

Located in the Calallen area on Highway 624, this drive-through park can produce a wide variety of birds such as Groove-billed Ani, Carolina Wren, two species of thrashers, and both Olive and Lark Sparrows. On the small lake, Mergansers can sometimes be found, along with a number of other water birds. There is a bird blind overlooking the lake. Picnic tables and playground equipment are available, and this is an excellent place to have lunch. During hawk migration thousands of Broad-tails can be seen taking off and forming their huge "kettles."

Tule Lake

Located on Up River Road behind the oil refineries, this brackish lake is the temporary stopover for a multitude of waterfowl. Plovers are here in the winter, and Wood Storks can sometimes be seen in the summer. The lake is on private property; observation of the birds must be done while parked on the shoulder of the road, and care must be taken to provide safety. A viewing scope will help you see the birds here.

Laguna Madre

Located in the Flour Bluff area of Corpus Christi, go south on South Padre Island Drive (SPID) and turn left on Waldon Road, go to Graham Road, turn left again to Laguna Shores Road. This is the west edge of the Laguna Madre. You should see many waders and shore birds. Proceed south on Laguna Shores Road and watch for birds in the mud flats and tidal pools including American Oystercatchers and Black-necked Stilts. Populations of shore birds increase during migration and winter months. You may see Reddish Egrets, Marbled Godwits, Ruddy Turnstones, and a number of plovers in winter or during migration.

Skimmer Nesting Grounds

Located at the west end of the Kennedy Causeway, you will see an area on the south section of the highway that is closed to traffic. This is the nesting area of the Black Skimmer. These beautiful birds will be there with chicks in June and July.

Indian Point

Go over the big bridge toward Portland from Corpus Christi (TX 35/U.S. 181) and exit at Old Portland Road. The entrance to Indian Point is surrounded by tidal flats that can harbor a wide assortment of shore birds and many of the herons and egrets, including the Reddish. Several species of rails are found here, and the sand flats to the right of the parking lot are generally filled with shore birds, from Dowitchers to Ruddy Turnstones. Two new boardwalks have been built out into the bay, primarily for fishermen, and there is a small fee for their use. Most of the gulls and terns can be seen with binoculars without going out on the walks. However, a scope can be put to good use here. When leaving Indian Point, you can turn left on the old Portland Road to Sunset Lake where loons, grebes, and a number of diving ducks can be seen. However, the road is in poor condition and requires careful driving.

Packery Channel

Drive over the John F. Kennedy Causeway on Highway 358 (South Padre Island Drive, or SPID) to the lower end of Mustang Island. Located on Laguna Madre, this is good place to park the car and walk. The low brush is home to a wide variety of resident birds and during the spring migration, can be a rest stop for many warblers. Burrowing Owl has been seen here.

Corpus Christi Botanical Gardens

Located off South Padre Island Drive at Staples Street on Oso Creek, this highly maintained park features South Texas habitat, along with wildflower and butterfly displays.

Some Texas "brush" birds, such as Groove-billed Ani, at least two species of thrashers, and the cardinal-like bird the Pyrrhuloxia can be seen here. There is a lake where grebes abound and Couch's Kingbird may be seen. Contact Corpus Christi Botanical Gardens,

8545 S. Staples, Corpus Christi, Texas 78413. Phone 361-852-2100 for open times.

Attractions

Aquarium, Texas State

The aquarium features close-up views of the wonders of the Gulf of Mexico in a wide variety of habitats, including an artificial reef community created by the massive leg of an offshore oil rig. Over 250 species of marine life are included in the 350,000 gallons of seawater.

Open Mon.-Sat. 9 A.M. to 5 P.M.; Sunday 10 A.M. to 6 P.M. Located at 2710 N. Shoreline Blvd. (Surfside Exit from U.S. 181) Admission fee. 800-477-GULF.

Asian Cultures Museum and Educational Center

Displays include a five-foot bronze Amida Buddha, fine Japanese Hakata figures, lacquerware, and porcelains, along with native costumes from the Far East, utensils, games, and toys. Open Tues.-Sat. 10 A.M. to 5 P.M. Located at 1809 Chaparral. Admission. 361-882-2641.

Corpus Christi Zoo

About 300 animals are on display. There is a kid's petting zoo, a 240-pound 15-foot Royal Burmese python, and a Siberian tiger. Open daily, but call for hours. 361-814-8000.

USS Lexington Museum on the Bay

A floating museum of naval history is aboard the USS *Lexington*, World War II aircraft carrier that saw action from Tarawa to Tokyo. Tours include the hangar deck, fos'cle, commanding/admiral quarters, sick bay, galley, flight deck, and bridge. Open daily 9 A.M. to 5 P.M. Admission. 800-LADY-LEX.

Corpus Christi Museum of Science and History

A great education for children on the natural history of the Gulf Coast, including shells and artifacts. Hands-on exhibits. Open Mon.-Sat. 10 A.M. to 5 P.M. 1900 Chaparrel. Admission. 361-883-2862.

Festivals

Buccaneer Days, phone 361-882-3242

Motels

Best Western, Corpus Christi Inn, 2838 S. Padre Island Drive, phone 361-854-0005

Days Inn, 6301 S. Padre Island Drive, phone 361-992-3100

Holiday Inn, Emerald Beach, 1102 Shoreline Blvd., phone 361-883-5731 (children eat free)

Super 8 Bayfront, 411 N. Shoreline Blvd., phone 361-884-4815

Comfort Suites, 3925 S. Padre Island Drive, phone 361-225-2500

For an expanded list of accommodations, contact the Chamber of Commerce or obtain a copy of the Texas Department of Transportation publication "Texas Accommodations Guide" www.txlodging.com or call 800-452-9292 for a free copy.

Dining

Snoopy's Pier, 13313 South Padre Island Drive under the John F. Kennedy overpass. Eat inside or out on the patio. A different setting and good seafood.

The Lighthouse Bar and Grill, Lawrence Street T-Head downtown, 444 N. Shoreline. Somewhat expensive for family dining, but food is very good.

Crystals Restaurant-Confectionery Bar, 4119 Staples. Variety menu at a reasonable price

Joe Cotton's Bar-B-Que, Hwy. 77 in Robstown. Inexpensive. The best barbecue in South Texas

Miller's Bar-B-Q, 2233 Airline Rd. Good family dining at a very reasonable price

CiCi's Pizza, 4102 Staples

Blackbeard's on the Beach, 3117 Surfside. Good seafood at good price

County Line Barbeque, 6102 Ocean Drive. Dinner with a view

Kingsville

Chamber of Commerce
635 King St.
361-592-6438
http://www.kingsville.org

Tourist Information
361-592-4121

There are a number of excellent birding spots in the Kingsville area, but the King Ranch tours are probably the most profitable. Keep in mind that you will be in Texas brush country and it can be very hot and dry in the summer. These tours can be extensive, and making Kingsville your home base is a good idea as there are a number of good motels and dining facilities. The city is also a history buff's dream come true, for the King Ranch represents a great part of the heritage and history of the South Texas brush country.

Birding

Drum Point

Drive south on U.S. 77 to FM 628, then east to County Road 2250 and turn north about one mile. Continue to County Road 1132, turn north and drive along the bluff. Drum Point is located after the pavement ends and the road turns to caliche. A good spot to have a scope to see most of the herons and egrets, and in winter waterfowl are abundant, including Lesser Scaup and Bufflehead.

Kaufer-Hubert Park

Located one mile south of where FM 628 turns southeast, it is where Vattman Creek empties into Baffin Bay. Lots of shore birds. Trailer hookups are available for campers.

Dick Kleberg Park

A great place to be during spring migration. Located on the south side of the city between U.S. 77 and U.S. 77 Business. Permanent residents include Great Kiskadee Flycatcher, Golden-fronted Woodpecker, and Green Jays. In winter you may see Vermilion Flycatcher.

Sarita Rest Stop

This is a good place to stop if you are going from Kingsville to Harlingen. For one thing, it is the last rest stop for many miles, and many rare migrants have been sighted here such as Clay-colored Robin and Tropical Parula.

King Ranch Tours

Founded in 1853 by Captain Richard King, the King Ranch is a vast expanse (825,000 acres) of South Texas brush country. Famous for developing the Santa Gertrudis breed of cattle, the ranch has been opened only in recent years for guided bird tours. There is a wide variety of tropical and migratory birds, along with white-tailed deer, javelinas, and coyotes. For information on the tours, contact the King Ranch at the visitor center on Highway 141 West, phone, 361-592-8055, or visit their web site at www.king-ranch.com. Special tours are conducted to look for the Ferruginous Pygmy Owl and the Tropical Parula. Other birds you might see are White-tailed Hawk, Burrowing Owl, Sprague's Pipit, and LeConte's Sparrow. Fees for a day's tour could get expensive for a family, but half-day tours are also available.

Louise Trant Bird Sanctuary

Located south of Kingsville on Hwy. 77 just as you enter the little town of Riviera, this small wetlands is operated by Corpus Christi Audubon Society and is especially good in winter for waterfowl such as Sora, Common Moorhen, and an assortment of herons and egrets. Red-billed Pigeon and Masked Duck have also been recorded here. Can be viewed from the highway, but better to go to the back side for safety reasons.

Attractions

King Ranch Museum

Located in Kingsville at 405 N. 6th Street, the museum contains Toni Frissell's award winning photographic essay of life on the King Ranch in the 1940s and a collection of saddles from around the world, the King Ranch commemorative issue of Colt Python .357 Magnum pistol, antique carriages, and vintage cars, including a custom-designed Buick Eight hunting car built in 1949. Hours are 10-4 Mon. through Sat., 1-5 Sun. Admission fee. Phone 361-595-1881.

King Ranch Saddle Shop

Following the Civil War, Captain King began operating his own saddle shop, building the very best saddles, harnesses, and other equipment for use on the ranch. The saddle shop is located in downtown Kingsville in the historic John B. Ragland Mercantile Building. Phone 800-282-King for fees and schedules.

Kleberg Hall of Natural History

A great place to take small children, the display features animals and plants of South Texas and has a discovery area where children can examine "hands on." Open Mon. through Sat., 9 A.M. to 4:30 P.M. Located on the campus of Texas A&M-Kingsville University. Phone 361-595-2810.

Motels

B Bar B Ranch Inn, 8 miles south of Kingville on Hwy. 77, phone 361-296-3331. A bed and breakfast with 16 bedrooms and near birding hot spots.

Best Western-Kingsville Inn, 2402 E. King Ave., phone 361-595-5656

Budget Inn, 716 S. 14th, phone 361-592-4322

Comfort Inn, 505 N. Hwy. 77, phone 361-516-1120

Days Inn, 715 S. U.S. 77, Bishop, phone 361-584-4444

Econo Lodge/Quality Inn, 221 S. U.S. 77 Bypass, phone 361-592-5251

Economy Inn, 1415 S. 14th, phone 361-592-5214

Dining

Barth's Restaurant, on Hwy. 77 at the Holiday Inn. Good family dining

El Jardin Restaurant, 330 E. Henrietta. Good Tex-Mex

Gem's Pancake House, 129 S. Brahma Blvd.

Kings Inn, located on Baffin Bay. Go south from Kingsville on Hwy. 77 to FM 628, turn left and go to Riviera Beach. Forget the budget, this is dining at its finest. Seafood served family style with salad, french fries, onion rings, tomatoes, and the best tartar sauce you have ever eaten.

Sirloin Stockade, 1500 S. Brahma Blvd. Very good buffet

Fast food options include Pizza Parlor, Sonic, Burger King, McDonald's, and Taco Bell.

Downtown at Harrel's Kingsville Pharmacy is an old-fashioned drugstore soda fountain.

Port Aransas

Tourist and Convention Bureau
421 W. Cotter
361-749-5919 or 800-45-COAST

This tourist attraction is located on Mustang Island, connected to the mainland by a causeway and a twenty-four-hour-a-day ferry service. Beautiful beaches cause the population to swell in the summertime as thousands of travelers seek the warm waters for relaxation or for the abundance of fishing services available.

Birding

Mustang Island

From Aransas Pass, take Highway 361 to the free ferry to Port Aransas. The ferryboat ride itself is a treat for children, and along the way you are almost certain to see Brown Pelicans and several other shore birds. Follow Cotter Avenue to the jetty where you will see a variety of gulls, terns, and shore birds. Sandwich Terns and Sooty Terns have been spotted here. A walk out on the jetty will give children a chance to see starfish, sea anemones, and snails. On the jetty, you may see Magnificent Frigatebird, and in winter Eared Grebes may be present.

St. Joseph's (San Jose) Island

Reached only by boat, this island is part of the great barrier beach system. The island is covered with sand dunes and little vegetation.

This is a good place to take a lunch and look at the many shore birds on the mud flats such as Red Knots, Sanderlings, Whimbrels, and several plovers. Often dolphins can be seen offshore. For more information on the boat, for which a fee is charged, call Woody's Boat Basin at 361-749-5252. The boat runs hourly 6:30 A.M. to 6:00 P.M.

Mustang Island State Park

Located 14 miles south of Port Aransas, this state park contains 3,704 acres. A good place to take a break and enjoy swimming, camping, and just walking the beach looking for shells. Restrooms and picnic tables are available. Shore birds are abundant, along with a multitude of Laughing Gulls which children will enjoy feeding. A bird list is available at the headquarters. The park address is: Box 326, Port Aransas, TX 78373.

Port Aransas Wetland Park

Located on Highway 361, this park was established by the city of Port Aransas, TXDOT, and Texas Parks and Wildlife. There is an observation platform overlooking the freshwater basin that will contain many species of waterfowl and shore birds. During migration, a number of land birds may be seen.

Attractions

Birding Center

The Birding Center is located on Ross Street behind the wastewater treatment plant and features boardwalks and raised observation towers for viewing the shallow water. Weekly guided tours, called Birding on the Boardwalk, are held each Wednesday at 9 A.M. at the Birding Center. Alligators and nutria, a rodent-like animal, also call the center home.

University of Texas Marine Science Institute

The Visitors Center is open to the public Monday through Thursday at 11 A.M. and 3 P.M. and features seven aquariums with typical Texas coastal habitats and the organisms that live there. Displays show current and past research projects and preserved specimens or photographs of local flora and fauna. Admission is free. For more information call the center at 361-749-6729.

Trolley Rides

Visitors are invited to take advantage of the free trolley rides that run hourly courtesy of the Port Aransas and Corpus Christi Regional Transit Authority. From 10 A.M. to 5:55 P.M., you may flag down the trolley along the route that begins at Pioneer RV Park on SH 361 and is marked by colorful route signs. Brochures of the route are available at the Chamber of Commerce.

Festivals

Annual Whooping Crane Festival. Held in late February, this yearly festival has exhibits, birding bus and boat tours, and world-renowned speakers, along with nature arts and crafts, demonstrations, art classes, and more. Contact: Port Aransas Chamber of Commerce/Tourist Bureau, 421 W. Cotter, Port Aransas, TX 78373 or phone 800-452-6278. www.portaransas.org

Motels

Captain's Quarters Inn, 235 W. Cotter, phone 361-749-6005, or 888-Aransas

Tropic Island Resort, 315 Cut-off Road, phone 361-749-6128 or 888-221-7179

Driftwood Motel, 300 W. Avenue G., phone 361-749-6427 or 800-753-6409

Pioneer RV Resort, 120 Gulfwind Drive, phone 888-480-3246 (cottages are available)

Dining

Tortugas, 500 Cut-off Road. Featuring slow cooked BBQ and fresh seafood

Castaways Seafood & Grill, 312 N. Allster at Beach St. Lunch, kids under 5 menu

Pizzeria, 222 Beach St. Family atmosphere, salad bar, spaghetti

Beach-N-Burger-N-More, 314 Avenue G. Daily lunch specials, Blue Bell ice cream

Rockport-Fulton Area

Chamber of Commerce
800-826-6441 or 361-729-6445
404 Broadway
http://www.rockport-fulton.org

These separate but historically and environmentally connected cities could well be called the birding capital of Texas. Located on the peninsula between Copano Bay and Aransas Bay and sheltered from the Gulf of Mexico by St. Joseph's Island, the area is a haven for migratory birds as well as home to a wide variety of waterfowl.

Birding

Aransas National Wildlife Refuge

Best known as the winter home of the endangered Whooping Cranes, this refuge can be reached by driving north from Rockport on SH 35 to FM 774. Turn right and follow the signs to the entrance. The visitor center has interesting exhibits, and an alligator can usually be seen just across from it. Only a small portion of the 54,829-acre refuge is open to the public, but an observation tower can give an overview of the tidal marsh. A spotting scope can be of benefit here, for most of the birds are going to be seen at long distance. Nesting birds of the refuge include Common Pauraque, White-tailed Hawk, Crested Caracara, Purple Gallinule, Groove-billed Ani, and several species of sparrows. Over 325 species of birds have been seen here. P.O. Box 100, Austwell, TX 77950, phone 361-286-3559.

Live Oak Peninsula

Going into Rockport from the south, follow Highway 35 to the north edge of town and a split in the road. Just past the turnoff to Rockport Beach Park is Little Bay. There will always be a variety of shore birds and gulls here. It is also home to the Connie Hagar Wildlife Sanctuary, which has greater numbers of birds in the winter, including loons, grebes, and a number of waterfowl. Connie Hagar was a lady who made twice-daily birding excursions and kept detailed records. She had listed 413 species, and in her memory, the north section of Rockport has been named the Connie Hagar Wildlife Sanctuary.

Goose Island State Recreation Area

Located twelve miles northeast of Rockport, the park has marshes, meadows, and live oak trees. Picnic areas are also available and restrooms. Resident birds include Roseate Spoonbills, American Oystercatchers, Black-crowned Night-Herons, Clapper Rails, and at least three species of terns, along with Black Skimmers and Seaside Sparrows.

Little Bay

A drive along Fulton Beach Road, particularly from mid-April to mid-May will produce such species as Yellow-bellied Flycatcher, Gray-cheeked Thrush, and Philadelphia Vireo, along with a wide variety of herons and egrets, Long-billed Curlews, Marbled Godwits, and Snowy and Piping Plovers. Redhead and Canvasback Ducks can be seen and Red-breasted Mergansers.

Demo Bird Garden and Wetlands Pond

Located at the TXDOT highway rest area about a mile south of the intersection of Highway 35 and FM 3036. You can walk around the hummingbird garden and learn about many of the native plants. There is a boardwalk that ends at a willow grove and wet slough, which is an excellent spot to see many land birds.

Attractions

Whooping Crane Tours

Although it is sometimes possible to see the Whooping Cranes from the observation tower at Aransas Wildlife Refuge, the best way to see the endangered birds is by boat. Not only will you see the birds during the winter season, but the boat trip will also provide a look at a number of wading birds along the way.

Captain John Howell's Pisces
1015 North Allen #B
Rockport, TX 78382
361-729-7525 or 800-245-9324

My Wharf Cat
Fisherman's Wharf
P.O. Box 387
Port Aransas, TX 78373
361-729-7525 or 800-782-BIRD

Fulton Mansion

Located on Fulton Beach Road, this elegant structure was built by George and Harriet Fulton in 1874. They amazed their neighbors with its ornate trim work and furnishings but even more so because of its indoor plumbing, central heat, and gas lighting system. Guided tours are conducted Wednesday through Sunday. Wear flat, soft-soled shoes to protect the mansion's floors and rugs. Admission fee.

The Big Tree

While birding on Goose Island, a must see is the Big Tree. This giant live oak is a charter member of the Live Oak Society of America and has been the subject of Ripley's "Believe It Or Not." The tree is more than 35 feet in circumference, 44 feet high, and has a crown spread of 89 feet. It is estimated to be over 1,000 years old.

Texas Maritime Museum

Experience the rich maritime heritage of Texas from Spanish exploration to the search for offshore oil and gas. With changing exhibits, interactive displays, and educational public programming, visitors experience how Texas has relied on the sea. Located across from Rockport Harbor. Open Tues.-Sat. 10 A.M. to 4 P.M. closed major holidays. 1202 Navigation Circle at Rockport Harbor. Admission fee. 361-729-1271.

Festivals

Texas State Kite Festival, third weekend in May

Air Show and Fireworks, July Fourth

Rockport Seafair, Columbus Day weekend

Hummer/Bird Celebration: Held in mid-September each year. Celebrate the jewel of the bird world, the hummingbird. The fall migration of hundreds of Ruby-throated Hummingbirds will dazzle even die-hard hummer fans. Look closely for the Buff-bellied and Rufous Hummingbirds, too. The entire family will enjoy bird banding demonstrations, trips to see pelagic species, evening speakers, and nature workshops. Contact: Rockport/Fulton Area Chamber of Commerce, 404 Broadway, Rockport, TX 78382 or phone 800-826-6441. www.rockport-fulton.org

Motels

Best Western Inn by the Bay, 3902 Hwy. 35 N., Fulton, phone 361-729-8351 or 800-235-6076

Days Inn Rockport, 1212 E. Laurel, Rockport, phone 361-729-6379 or 800-DAYSINN

Holiday Inn Express, 901 Hwy. 35 N., Rockport, phone 361-727-0283 or 800-HOLIDAY

Over 20 RV parks and camping areas are listed in the brochure available from the Rockport/Fulton Area Chamber of Commerce. 800-826-6441.

Dining

Visit Charlotte Plummer's on Fulton Harbor and forget the budget. This is one of the best seafood restaurants on the coast. Specializing in fish and shrimp dishes, they also have a good salad bar and a children's menu, 202 N. Fulton Beach Road.

Duck Inn, 701 Broadway at Hwy. 35 N.

There are a number of fast food restaurants in Rockport and Fulton including Burger King, Dairy Queen, KFC/Taco Bell, McDonald's, Subway, and Whataburger.

Brush Country

roadrunner

numbers of White Pelicans and flocks of Black-bellied Whis-tling-Ducks, along with large flocks of geese can be seen in this area.

Pernitas Point

From the Corpus Christi State Park, turn right and go to Hwy. 359, and just after you pass through the little town of Sandia (don't blink or you will miss it), turn right on FM 534 and go about ten miles and watch for a sign for Pernitas Point and turn right again. You will come to a low water bridge. Do not park on the bridge. From the point you may see a variety of waterfowl, including Great Blue Heron, Snowy Egret, and Green Heron. Wood Storks have been seen here, and the small wooded area at the end of the bridge can hold a number of warblers during migration.

Lake Alice

Located at the end of Texas Street on the north side of the city, this 90-acre lake is a water reservoir for the city of Alice, and there is restricted public access, as only pedestrian traffic is allowed past the parking areas. The west side of the lake is the most productive, and resident birds include Great Kiskadee, Groove-billed Ani, Least Grebe, Black-bellied Whistling-Duck, Long-billed Thrasher, Green Jay, and Olive Sparrow. In the winter you may see Sandhill Cranes, Sprague's Pipit, Say's Phoebe, and an assortment of ducks and geese. During migration Couch's, Western, and Eastern Kingbirds have been recorded, along with a number of warblers and shore birds. As many as 90 species have been seen here in one day.

Attractions

South Texas Museum

This small museum features displays on the history and traditions of the South Texas area, including displays that trace the habitation from the American Indian to the 20th-century farm, ranch, railroad, and oil activities. Emphasis is on the South Texas ranch, with dis-plays of household articles and artifacts, also mounted wildlife and livestock specimens. 66 Wright Street.

Motels

Best Western-Executive Inn, 1350 S. U.S. Hwy. 281, phone
361-664-2133

Days Inn, 555 N. Johnson Street, phone 361-664-6616

King's Inn, 815 S. U.S. Hwy. 281, phone 361-664-4351

Dining

Chente's Mexican Restaurant, 107 Cecilia Street (excellent)

Nortex Bakery & Fast Food, 1801 N. Texas Blvd. (the sauce is very
hot, great bakery goods)

Panda Chinese Restaurant, 300 E. Front Street

Kettle Restaurant, 820 S. U.S. Hwy. 281

Fast food choices include: McDonald's, Popeye's, Dairy Queen,
Dairy Burger, Pizza Hut, and Pizza Inn

Goliad

Chamber of Commerce
205 S. Market
800-848-8674
http://www.goliad.org

Steeped in Texas history, this area is a great place to visit, whether
you bird or not. The value of the history lessons learned here will
help the children in school for years to come and will make them
realize their freedom came through great sacrifice by many men.

Birding

Goliad State Park

This 2,208-acre park is a delight to visit both from a birding standpoint and in view of the historical value of the area. The park is
located on the San Antonio River and has excellent camping facilities. The best place to bird is the river road, which winds from the
Mission Espiritu Santo along the river to the northeast side of the
park. This is the edge of the southern limits of the breeding grounds
for several species such as Ruby-throated Hummingbird, Red-
bellied Woodpecker, Great Crested Flycatcher, American Crow, Blue

Jay, and Carolina Chickadee and is the northern limit for Buff-bellied Hummingbird, Golden-fronted Woodpecker, Brown-crested Flycatcher, Long-billed Thrasher, and Olive Sparrow. In summer you may see Yellow-billed Cuckoo, Black-chinned and Buff-bellied Hummingbirds, Dickcissell, Bell's Vireo, Northern Parula, and Yellow-breasted Chat. At dusk in spring and early summer you may see Eastern Screech-Owl, Great Horned and Barred Owls, and both Lesser and Common Nighthawks. Pauraque and Chuck-will's-widow are not as common, and you are more likely to hear than see them. Open fields adjacent to the park will harbor Cattle Egret, Wild Turkey, Northern Bobwhite, Greater Roadrunner, and Cactus Wren. Several species of hawks can be seen, along with both Cliff and Cave Swallows.

Attractions

Presidio La Bahia

Established in 1749 near Mission Espiritu Santo, this fort was one of the most important on the Spanish frontier, and its restoration has been completed. The massive stone walls served as a prison for Fannin's men during the 1836 Texas Revolution before they were taken out and massacred. A museum houses articles discovered during the restoration. Its chapel is being used for religious services.

General Zaragoza State Historic Site

This is the reconstructed birthplace of one of Mexico's most famous military figures, Gen. Ignacio Zaragoza. He defended the central Mexico city of Puebla against a superior French army, which planned to establish a French colony in the area. The battle date, Cinco de Mayo, is a national holiday that is celebrated both in Mexico and Texas.

Grave of Col. James W. Fannin Jr. and Men

A monument marks the grave of Colonel Fannin and the 352 men who were killed after surrendering to Mexican forces during the Texas Revolution. The men were killed on the orders of General Santa Anna on Palm Sunday, March 27, 1836, and their deaths became a rallying point for the Texas army under General Sam

Houston, along with the cry, "Remember the Alamo." Another great place for the kids to get a lesson in Texas history.

Festivals

May: Honoring the famous General Zaragoza. For information, phone 361-645-3563.

June: Goliad Longhorn Stampede where breeders re-enact the history of the longhorn steer in Texas.

Motels

Antlers Inn, 813 West Pearl, phone 361-645-8215

Budget Inn, Hwy. 77 & 59, 105 S. Jefferson, phone 361-645-3251

Dining

Fast food restaurants, including Church's Fried Chicken, Dairy Queen, and Whataburger

Clara's Café, 515 S. Jefferson

Flore's Bakery and Taqueria, 1107 U.S. Hwy. 59 North

Irma's, one block west of Hwy. 59 at 183

Jorge's Pizzeria, 741 W. Pearl

La Bahia Restaurant, U.S. Hwy. 183/77A South

The Farmer's Table, Hwy. 119 and FM 884 in Weesatchie

Laredo

Convention & Visitors Bureau
501 San Austin
800-361-3360
http://www.visitlaredo.com

Laredo is the nation's largest inland port as a wide variety of products flow across the border from Mexico. The city was founded in 1755 by a Spanish land grant and became the county seat of Webb County in 1848. Rich in the culture of both nations, Laredo and Nuevo Laredo are like twin cities.

Birding

Lake Casa Blanca State Park

This relatively new state park was once the Laredo City Park. It has a 1,656-acre lake and is well known for its excellent black bass fishing. The park is still being developed, and there is no bird checklist available. It is located at the junction of U.S. 59 and PR 20, on the northeastern side of Laredo. The best place to bird is the north shore road where open water between fingers of the lake and cattail marshes can be seen. This wetlands habitat can produce such species as Pied-billed Grebe, Neotropic Cormorant, and both Great Blue and Tricolored Herons year round, along with Great, Snowy, and Cattle Egrets. Also present are Black-bellied Whistling-Duck and both Ringed and Green Kingfishers. In the summer you may see Green Heron and Least Tern. In winter such water birds as Blue-winged Teal, Mallard, Northern Pintail, Ruddy Duck, Northern Shoveler, American Wigeon, Lesser Scaup, and Spotted and Least Sandpipers may be seen. The shoreline at the end of North Shore Road is good for migrants in the spring and fall. The grasslands near the entrance are good for many more resident birds such as Golden-fronted and Ladder-backed Woodpeckers and Vermilion Flycatchers. You may even see Great Kiskadee and Pyrrhuloxia, and Couch's Kingbird has been spotted.

Attractions

Laredo Children's Museum

A hands-on experience for the kids in experimentation and exploration in the areas of history, culture, art, and science. A guided tour involves the children with the Primaries: Yippee, Rudie, and Booboo. Located at West End Washington Street on the campus of Laredo Jr. College. Phone 956-725-2299.

Fort McIntosh

This fort was established by the Army in 1848 and was in use until 1946. Built for protection from Indian attacks, it was the base for the border patrol. An old guardhouse, chapel, warehouse, and commissary remain. Located at foot of Washington Street on the banks of the Rio Grande.

Republic of the Rio Grande Building/Museum

This building, with rock walls two feet thick, once served as the capital of the unsuccessful Republic of the Rio Grande and has displays in the museum of guns, saddles, and household goods from the frontier days. Located at 1000 Zaragoza Street on San Austin Plaza. A good place for the kids to learn a history lesson no one else in their school will know about.

Festivals

February: Washington Birthday Celebration. This ten-day festival is celebrated on both sides of the border with parades, fireworks, dances, and a coronation ceremony.

Motels

Econo Lodge, 2620 Santa Ursula, phone 956-722-6321, 800-55-ECONO

Hampton Inn, 7903 San Dario, phone 800-HAMPTON

La Haciendo Motor Hotel, 4914 San Bernado, phone 956-722-2441

La Quinta Inn, 3610 Santa Ursula, phone 800-531-5900

Motel 6 (two locations), phone 800 4-Motel6

Dining

Santa Maria Party House (burgers), 1909 Santa Maria Ave.

J. & A. Restaurant, 4220 Loop 20

La Mexicana Restaurant, 1902 Santa Ursula Ave.

Quick Bite Restaurant and Seahorse Bar, 3401 San Bernardo Ave.

The Pantry Café, 1288 W. Main Street

Guapo's Sports Café, 107 Calle Del Norte

Golden Corral, 5930 San Bernardo

Sirloin Stockade, 5310 Sandario

Fast food choices include Domino's Pizza, Pizza Hut, Dairy Queen, Subway, Burger King, Fuddruckers, KFC, Jack-in-the-Box, Wendy's, Whataburger, and Taco Bell.

San Antonio

Chamber of Commerce
602 E. Commerce St.
210-229-2100
http://www.sachamber.org

San Antonio is the number one tourist attraction in Texas with its many historical sites and recreational parks such as Fiesta Texas, Sea World, and Splashtown. Founded in 1718, there was an Indian village on the site and Spain established Mission San Antonio de Valero, or the Alamo. The rich combination of Texian and Mexican history makes this metropolis a magnet for people from all over the world. The HemisFair was held here in 1968, and the Henry B. Gonzales Convention Center was a part of that fair and attracts many conventions to the city. The extension of the San Antonio River and its development as a tourist attraction is another draw, with dinner on the river and a ride in one of the river boats a must for most tourists. There are a multitude of museums and festivals that attract thousands. It also happens to have a number of special birding sites.

Birding

Mitchell Lake

If you get caught up in all the tourist attractions of San Antonio and only have time to bird one area, Mitchell Lake is the place to go. Once a sewage treatment plant for the city, the 660 acres is divided into a number of ponds called "polders" and there are also grasslands. The area can be covered mostly by driving and, although not necessary, a scope can be a great help in seeing birds here. The area is controlled by the San Antonio Audubon Society, and access can only be gained by contacting the society and making arrangements to enter. The lake is located south of the city and can be reached by taking Exit 46 from Loop 410 SE and turning south onto Mourland about .7 miles to the gate. The Audubon Society schedules a field trip every fourth Saturday and visitors are welcome. Call the society at 956-733-8306. The birding begins as soon as you enter the gate, and along the entrance road you may see Northern Bobwhite, both White-winged and Mourning Doves, Ladder-backed Woodpecker, Cave Swallow, and both Long-billed and Curve-billed Thrashers. Overhead look for Black and Turkey Vultures, Harris's and Red-tailed Hawk, and Crested Caracara. Several species of sparrows may be seen in the grasslands, along with Eastern Meadowlark and House Finch. During the migration season of both spring and fall, a great many neotropical migrants can be seen such as flycatchers, thrushes, vireos, warblers, tanagers, and sparrows. A few even stay and nest here, such as Painted Bunting and Blue Grosbeak, plus both Orchard and Bullock's Orioles. In the winter, House, Winter, and Sedge Wrens will be present, along with at least ten species of sparrows. But the stars of the show at Mitchell Lake are the water birds. By driving or walking the 5-mile loop route from the entrance, you may see year-round residents such as Pied-billed Grebe, American White Pelican, Black-crowned Night-Heron, White-faced Ibis, and ducks, including Black-bellied Whistling, Ruddy, Mallard, Northern Shoveler, and Gadwall. The shore birds can be spectacular and include Black-necked Stilt and American Avocet, along with Greater Yellowlegs. The herons and egrets are here, along with American Bittern, and in summer you might see the Least Bittern. Gulls and terns that frequent the area are Bonaparte's and Ring-billed. Again in the summer look for Yellow-crowned Night-Heron, White Ibis, Roseate Spoonbill, Wood Stork, and Purple Gallinule. The bird list is extensive, and it is advised that you consult *Birding Texas* for more information.

Braunig Lake and Calaveras Lake

Both of these lakes, located on the other side of Highway 37 from Mitchell Lake, are warm watered due to power plants managed by the San Antonio River Authority, and a fee is charged for admission. Boating and fishing are popular here, and it can be busy on weekends. But both areas can be worth the effort, and such species as Golden-fronted Woodpecker, Painted Buntings, and orioles are possible in summer. In summer you may also see Harris's, Red-shouldered, and Red-tailed Hawks, as well as Crested Caracara.

At Calaveras you may see some birds that don't appear at Mitchell or Braunig, and its three-mile shoreline can produce Least Grebe, Wood Duck, Anhinga, Green Kingfisher, and Eastern Kingbird. Depending on the time you have to spend in the area, a good rule of thumb is: If the birding is good at Mitchell, forget the others, but check the hotline; sometimes vagrants have been seen in these areas.

Brackenridge Park

Listed as a recreational site, Brackenridge Park also has potential for birding. The tropical birdhouse at the zoo has a free flying area, and the African Flight Cage can be entered and the birds viewed from inside their "cage." These are not wild birds, but some wild birds can be seen in the park. At the San Antonio Botanical Center just east of the park, Wood and Black-bellied Whistling-Ducks are found on the lake in summer. And of course, there are always a number of scavengers to be found in the picnic areas.

Attractions

The Alamo

Established in 1718 as Mission San Antonio de Valero, the Alamo became renowned during the Texas war of independence from Mexico, when 189 defenders, including Davy Crockett and William Travis, held off the army of General Santa Anna until it fell on March 6, 1836. Rich Texas history is preserved here in this well-maintained monument to their sacrifice that enabled Sam Houston time to build an army and defeat the Mexicans at San Jacinto and win independence for the Republic of Texas. The Long Barracks Museum and Library contains artifacts and mementos and offers a narration on the fall of the Alamo.

Brackenridge Park/San Antonio Zoo

The park has a winding walkway with stone bridges and includes the Japanese Tea Garden, a sunken display of foliage that on occasion offers entertainment. There is also a sky ride and miniature diesel trains that offer transportation to the foot-weary tourist. The zoo contains over 3,000 animals and is a sanctuary for such endangered species as the Whooping Crane, snow leopard, and white rhino. Natural habitats have been created in the cliffs of an old rock quarry along the San Antonio River. Special displays of Australian animals and Africa's Rift Valley, which contains elephants, zebras, and cheetahs, are available, and a boat ride is a relaxing way to see many of the animals and plants from around the world. There is also an aquarium with a wide variety of sea creatures.

Institute of Texan Cultures

Twenty-seven ethic and cultural groups are featured in this exhibit that shows their food and clothing, music and festivals. There is a multimedia show four times daily, and it is an excellent place for the children to learn of the heritage of Texas.

El Mercado

Mother will enjoy this shopping mall that is a reproduction of a typical market from Mexico with lots of shops that sell jewelry, clothing, leather goods, cascarones, pottery, music, and art. Dine on authentic Mexican enchiladas and enjoy the festivities.

Missions of San Antonio

A map is available at the Visitor Information Center that shows the location of some of the missions of the area other than the Alamo. A short drive will take you to Mission Nuestra Señora de la Parisima Conception, Mission San Francisco de la Espada, Mission San Jose y San Miguel de Aguayo, and Mission San Juan Capistrano. All are ancient reminders of the Spanish influence on the culture of the area and the importance of religion in the lives of the early settlers.

Ripley's Believe It or Not!

Explore over 500 oddities from the collection of Robert Ripley, who made a career of finding the bizarre and unusual aspects of society, from the world's smallest painting to a hand-carved 1,000-piece miniature circus and authentic dinosaur eggs.

San Antonio Children's Museum

Located within walking distance of the Alamo in downtown San Antonio, this museum offers hands-on experiences for children as they learn about historical landmarks, role play in a life-size airplane, operate a front-end loader, and milk Alamo, the cow, in the Okie Dokie Kiddie Corral. Great for smaller kids and very educational.

River Walk

Shop, dine, or just take a quiet ride down the river in comfort past the giant cypress and palm trees. Half-hour scenic riverboat cruises can be accessed from the convention center, Rivercenter Mall Lagoon, and city streets including Alamo, Lojoya, Presa, Navarro, St. Mary's, Market, Commerce, and Crockett. Dining on the River Walk is a must when you visit San Antonio, and if you eat outside, you have to contend with the pigeons (Rock Doves) for your food.

Sea World, Six Flags Fiesta Texas, and Splashtown

Each of these recreational attractions will take a day to see, but if you plan it into your trip, it can be a lot of fun for all the family. Brochures can be obtained at the visitors center or from the Chamber of Commerce.

Others: San Antonio has so many museums, historical sites, and recreational areas that you will have to choose which ones you have time to work into your birding trip, if any. Others include: Monarch Collections (doll museum); Pioneer, Trail Drivers, and Texas Rangers Memorial Museum; Plaza Theater of Wax; Texas Transportation Museum; and the Witte Museum of History and Science. For more information on these and other attractions, consult the Texas Department of Transportation's *Texas State Travel Guide* or *Exploring San Antonio with Children* by Docia Schultz Williams.

Festivals

May: Cinco de Mayo, a Mexican holiday commemorating Mexico's victory over the French army at the Battle of Puebla in 1862. For information, phone the San Antonio Hispanic Chamber of Commerce at 210-255-0462.

April: Fiesta San Antonio, a time of festivities celebrating Texas Independence from Mexico.

July/August: Held on the grounds of the Institute of Texan Culture in Hemisfair Park, this festival has a wide variety of music, from gospel to Cajun, and booths for antiques and crafts.

Motels

As with all big cities, the lodging facilities are almost unlimited. In San Antonio, you need to make reservations well in advance as a major convention can fill motel rooms in a hurry. For birding purposes, a motel on the south side of town would be preferred, but major highways can get you anyplace in the city quickly, except at morning and evening rush hours, which are to be avoided at all costs. For an extensive list of motels, consult the Texas Department of Transportation's "Texas Accommodations Guide."

Dining

As with lodging, the dining facilities are numerous, and in areas where motels are located, visitors can pick and choose where and what kind of food they desire. Dining on the River Walk is an experience you don't want the kids to miss, and in addition to the fast foods, a few special spots include:

Barbecue Station Restaurant, 1610 N.E. Loop 410

Augie's By the Park, 10447 Nacogdoches Road (hamburgers)

Jason's Deli, 9933 W. I-10

Mi Tierra Café and Bakery, 218 Produce Row

El Jarro de Arturo Restaurant, 9307 Broadway

EZ's Restaurant, three locations (good pizza)

Three Rivers
Chamber of Commerce
105 N. Harborth
361-786-4330

This small city gets its name from the Atascosa, Nueces, and Frio Rivers that converge there. It is a commercial center for farming and ranching, and its proximity to Choke Canyon Reservoir and State Park makes it an attraction for sportsmen. The lake is the main attraction.

Birding

Choke Canyon State Park

Opened in 1986, this 26,000-acre reservoir for the city of Corpus Christi is an active recreational lake, with fishing and boating very heavy, especially on the weekends. The Calliham Unit has a recreational complex with a gym, basketball courts, and baseball diamond. During the spring migration, the best place to bird is the area below the dam in the riparian habitat along the Frio River on the South Shore Unit of the park. More than 65 species of neotropical migrants have been recorded here, including 15 vireo and warblers. Nesting birds include Black-chinned Hummingbird, Green Kingfisher, Couch's Kingbird, and Prothonotary Warbler. In the picnic area, three species of swallows nest, Cliff, Cave, and Barn. Resident birds include Crested Caracara, Scaled Quail, Groove-billed Ani, Bewick's Wren, Long-billed Thrasher, Pyrrhuloxia, and Olive Sparrow. Vermilion, Ash-throated, and Scissor-tailed Flycatchers may be seen in the grasslands, and in summer look for Loggerhead Shrike, Lark Sparrow, and Painted Bunting. The James E. Daugherty Wildlife Management Area (just northeast of Tilden) has a birding trail, but the area is primarily for hunting and you will need to check the seasons before birding here.

Attractions

Tips State Recreation Park

A small (31-acre) park off Texas 72 on the Frio River that has camping, fishing, and picnic areas.

Motels

Best Western, Hwys. 281 and 72 South, phone 361-786-2000

Executive Inn, Hwy. 281 North, phone 361-786-3563

Nolan Ryan's Bass Inn, Hwy. 72, West, phone 512-786-3521 (on the lake)

Staghorn Inn, Hwy. 281 N., phone 361-786-3541 (on the lake)

Live Oak Lodging, 1400 Harborth Ave., phone 361-786-4440

Dining

Fast foods: Dairy Queen, Pizza Hut, and Golden Fried Chicken

Mi Casita Café, 501 Thornton St.

Nolan Ryan's Waterfront Restaurant, Hwy. 72 West

Staghorn Restaurant, 1105 Hardball Ave.

Sunrise Sunset Café, 72 W. Thornton & Dribble St.

Taqueria's Guadalajara, 800 Harbor St.

Zamzow's Deli & Market, 801 Thorton St.

Rio Grande Region

Kiskadee
flycatcher

Brownsville

Chamber of Commerce
1600 E. Elizabeth St.
956-542-4341

Sitting on the very tip of Texas, this city has a bicultural charm that blends the best of two countries. The tropical environment makes it a favorite visiting spot for not only birders, but for vacationers as well. Just across the border in Mexico there are enough shops to satisfy the most avid shopper. And on the U.S. side, there are a number of birding hot spots. The city is also rich in Texian history since it is the home of Fort Brown, which was established in 1846 by Zachary Taylor to confirm the Rio Grande as the national boundary after the Republic of Texas became a state. The port of Brownsville was opened in 1936 and is a deep-water seaport connected to the Gulf of Mexico.

Birding

Brownsville Landfill

It may not be a favorable place to take young children, but if you want to see the Tamaulipas Crow (formerly Mexican Crow) the dump is the best bet. At the gate you need to let the attendant know you are looking for the crow, and keep in mind the landfill is not open on Sunday. A variety of gulls may also be seen here, including Ring-billed, Herring, and Laughing. Other gulls that have been seen here are California, Thayer's, Lesser Black-backed, Slaty-backed, and Glaucous, so it behooves you to look over the gull population closely. The hard-to-see Chihuahuan Raven is also present; look closely for the white patch on the back of the neck.

Boca Chica Beach

Birding areas here (about 12 miles from Brownsville) are rather remote and primitive, but the drive can be productive. The usual shore birds and gulls are present, but the star of the show is the Botteri's Sparrow, which can be seen on the coastal flats, and the Red Knot, which is present on the beach. The birding here is good all year. Hwy. 4, on your way to the beach from Brownsville, can be birded as the habitat is home to a good many resident birds such as Crested Caracara, the noisy Plain Chachalaca, Green Jays, Verdin, and three species of wrens, Cactus, Carolina, and Bewick's. Woodpecker possibilities include the Golden-fronted and the Ladderback, and Groove-billed Anis are an irregular visitor. During migration, the birding in this area can be fantastic, with a great number of flycatchers, orioles, tanagers, and vireos.

On the south side of the road are a number of ponds (resacas) that will harbor waterfowl such as Pied-billed Grebe, Neotropic Cormorant, herons, and egrets, including both Black-crowned and Yellow-crowned Night Herons.

Black-bellied Whistling Ducks will be present, along with Ringed and Green Kingfishers. The snake bird, Anhinga, may also be seen, along with Purple Gallinule. A variety of ducks are present in summer, along with rails. On the coastal flats, in addition to the Red Knot, you may see both White and White-faced Ibis, Roseate Spoonbills, and Wood Storks. Overhead look for Osprey, White-tailed Kite, White-tailed Hawk, American Kestral, Merlin, and Peregrine Falcon. Several species of terns, along with both White and Brown Pelicans may also be present. A glimpse of a Magnificent Frigatebird is even a possibility.

Sabal Palms Audubon Sanctuary

This 527-acre sanctuary preserves the largest remaining stand of Sabal Palms that once covered the Rio Grande Valley. It is operated by the National Audubon Society and has two trails of about one-half mile each. One of the best places to see birds is at the visitors center where there are feeders, but a walk to the resaca (oxbow lake) is worthwhile. Some of the birds you may see are Buff-bellied Hummingbird, Hooded Oriole, White-tipped Dove, Green Kingfisher, Couch's Kingbird, Plain Chachalaca, Green Jay, Long-billed Thrasher, and Olive Sparrow. If you have an interest in butterflies, the sanctuary is also home to several species.

Los Ebanos Parrot Roost

On West Los Ebanos Street, near the railroad tracks, both Red-headed and Yellow-headed Parrots often roost, and Green Parakeets are seen within the city. Roland Wauer reports that these roosting spots change, but the parakeets can be seen in the vicinity of the Brown Hotel on a regular basis. It is best to call the birding hotline at 210-969-2731 for updated information.

Attractions

Gladys Porter Zoo

Let the kids enjoy contact with Nigerian dwarf goats, miniature mules, and domestic chickens in this unique display, perhaps the most unusual zoo in Texas. The animals here are displayed in natural settings surrounding by natural flowing waterways. Forty-seven endangered species are shown here among the 420 species, with a total of over 1,500 animals, ranging from Galapagos tortoises, black-necked swans, Caribbean flamingos, spider monkeys, and Cuban crocodiles. There are also orangutans, tigers, giraffes, elephants, zebras, lions, gorillas, chimpanzees, and a rare Jentink's duiker, an antelope. There is also an aquatic section featuring lizards, snakes, gila monsters, and both fresh and saltwater fish. Open daily from 9 A.M. For more information, phone 956-546-2177. There is an admission charge.

Historic Brownsville Museum

A restoration of a 1928 railroad depot, this museum is well known for its Spanish Colonial Revivalist style and has many photographs, exhibits, and artifacts from the area, including military history.

Matamoros, Mexico

Why not visit Old Mexico since it is so near? Just across the Gateway Bridge there are shops with lots of bargains in Mexican products, from hand-crafted pottery and leather goods to silver jewelry. Best bet is to park at the metered parking available in Brownsville and walk over the bridge, or park in the public parking at the corner of E. Elizabeth and Taylor Streets.

Palmito Ranch Civil War Battlefield

Col. John S. Ford did not get the word that Lee had surrendered at Attomattox a month earlier, and so the final battle of the Civil War was fought near Brownsville at Palmito Ranch. Only after they had captured Federal prisoners did the southern soldiers learn that the war was over. Located 12 miles east of Brownsville on Hwy. 4.

Palo Alta Battlefield National Historic Site

On May 8, 1846, cannon under the command of General Zachary Taylor opened fire on the forces of Mexican General Mariano Arista, and the war with Mexico was begun. This battlefield was dedicated as a national historic site on May 8, 1993, the 147th anniversary of the battle. The exhibits present the battle from the viewpoints of each side. Located north of Brownsville near the intersection of FM 1847 and FM 511.

Festivals

Dia de las Palmas. Held in mid-April, Dia de las Palmas is an open house that is free of charge and open to the public. Bird, butterfly, and plant tours are offered, as well as exhibits, displays, and guest speakers. Contact: Sabal Palm Audubon Society Center and Sanctuary, P.O. Box 5169, Brownsville, TX 78523-5169 or phone 956-541-8034. www.audubon.org/local/sanctuary/sabal

Charro Days: Held in late February, a festival of costumes, parades, carnivals, music, dancing, and food

Motels

Days Inn, 715 N. Frontage Rd., phone 956-541-2201

Super 8 Motel, 55 Sam Perl Blvd., phone 800-800-8000

Comfort Inn, 825 N. Expressway, phone 800-228-5150

Best Western, 845 N. Expressway, phone 956-546-5501

Red Roof Inn, 2377 N. Expressway, phone 956-604-2300

Ramada Inn, 1900 E. Elizabeth Street, phone 956-541-2921

Holiday Inn, 1900 E. Elizabeth Street, phone 956-546-2201

Dining

El Torito, 625 N. Expressway and 2514 Boca Chica Blvd.

Furr's Cafeteria, 7102 N. Expressway

Golden Corral, 2912 Boca Chica Blvd.

Luby's Cafeteria, 2124 Boca Chica Blvd. (also in Sunrise Mall)

Miguel's Restaurant, 2474 Boca Chica Blvd.

Wallbangers, 1900 N. Expressway

Fast food runs the gamut, from McDonald's to CiCi's Pizza, and Taco Bell to Whataburger.

Edinburg

Chamber of Commerce
602 W. University Drive
Edinburg, TX 78539
956-383-4974
http://www.edinburg.com/chamber
or call the visitors center at 800-800-7214

The seat of Hidalgo County and center for a vast citrus and vegetable culture, Edinburg is also the home of the University of Texas-Pan American.

Birding

Edinburg Lake

Located north of Edinburg just off of Hwy. 281 on FM 2812, Edinburg Lake is best for a drive-through in winter, when ducks and shore birds will be present. Northern Jacana has been seen here, along with Masked Duck and Black-crowned Night-Herons. After returning to Hwy. 281, turn north again and you will see several ponds on both sides of the road, which can be good places to see a number of shore birds. In the mesquite on the side of the road, Vermilion and Ash-throated Flycatchers may be present, as well as Curve-billed Thrasher and Pyrrhuloxia. In summer you may see Painted Buntings. This is a good evening drive birding excursion if you are making your base in McAllen, Mission, or Edinburg.

Attractions

Hidalgo County Historical Museum

The emphasis here is on Hispanic history in the area, including a pioneer ranch home, clothing, early documents, and photos. The museum is located in a restored county jail at 121 E. McIntyre Street and is open from Tuesday through Friday 9 A.M. to 5 P.M., Saturday 10 A.M. to 5 P.M. and on Sunday from 1 P.M. to 5 P.M.

Motels

Echo Hotel and Conference Center, 1903 S. Closner Blvd., phone 800-422-0336

Edinburg Executive Inn, 2008 S. Closner Blvd., phone 956-380-6201

Holiday Inn Express, 1806 S. Closner Blvd., phone 956-383-8800

Dining

Grand View, 1903 S. Closner Blvd. (Echo Motor Hotel) All you can eat buffet

Hec and Bec Restaurant, 317 E. University Drive

Kuntry Kitchen, 2207 S. Hwy. 281

Las Casa Del Taco, 321 W. University Drive

Peter Piper Pizza, 1009 S. Closner Blvd.

Harlingen

Chamber Convention & Visitors Bureau
311 E. Tyler
800-531-7346
http://www.harlingen.com

A center for the distribution of the vast crops of citrus and vegetables grown in the Rio Grande Valley, this city was incorporated in 1905 and is a subtropic paradise that attracts thousands of tourists and a great number of "winter Texans," retirees who live in mobile or motor homes and spend the winter in the valley.

Birding

Laguna Atascosa National Wildlife Refuge

This massive National Wildlife Refuge can be reached from either Harlingen (about 23 miles) or from Brownsville (about 25 miles). The 45,000-acre refuge is one of those places you must bird if you are in the area; over 400 species of birds have been reported here.

The best way to see a variety of birds is to drive the one-way 15-mile Bayside Loop, which will take you through several types of habitat, including a drive along the bay, where many shore birds will be present. A scope can be a real help here as there are places you can pull off the road and study the shore. Look overhead for Osprey in winter and both White-tailed Hawk and Aplomado Falcon may be seen here year round. You can begin your tour by taking the drive or walking the trails located at the visitors center, and during migration seasons a number of birds can be seen. Resident birds include the White-tipped Dove, Pauraque, Great Kiskadee Flycatcher, Couch's Kingbird, and Green Jay. The Yellow-green Vireo has also been seen here. The Mesquite Trail is 1.5 miles long and will take you through mesquite grasslands and, during wet years, two ponds. In the summer you may see such birds as Greater Roadrunner, both Brown-crested and Scissor-tailed Flycatcher, Verdin, Cactus and Bewick's Wren, along with Long-billed and Curve-billed Thrashers, and an assortment of sparrows, including Olive, Botteri's, Cassin's and Lark. Some of the colorful birds that can be seen are Tropical Parula, Summer Tanager, and both Varied and Painted Buntings, along with Orchard Orioles. This is also a good place to spot the Chihuahuan Raven, White-tailed Hawk, Crested Caracara, and Harris's Hawk. In winter the Mesquite Trail will have Eastern Phoebe, House and Sedge Wrens, Hermit Thrush, and Orange-crowned and Yellow-rumped Warblers and a number of sparrow species. You can drive to Osprey Overlook at the Resaca de los Curates where numbers of water birds can be seen, such as White-faced and White Ibis, the lovely Roseate Spoonbill, and the comical Black-bellied Whistling-Duck, and in summer you should see Wood Storks. The Laguna Atascosa can best be birded with a scope, and in winter the list of ducks is impressive, including Eurasian Wigeon, Oldsquaw, and both Green-winged and Blue-winged Teals. You may also see American Wigeon, Northern Pintail, Canvasback, Redhead, and Ruddy Duck. On the loop drive, scope the Laguna Madre for White Pelican and an almost limitless number of gulls and terns. Edward A. Kutac in *Birder's Guide to Texas* tells of spotting ninety-three species of birds in six hours in this refuge, and most of them without getting out of the car.

Attractions

Rio Grande Valley Museum

Includes three buildings, the historical museum of history and natural exhibits, and a constantly changing exhibits hall, video theater, and store. Also includes an 1850 Stagecoach Inn with period furnishings and the original Harlingen Hospital with medical equipment and dental and medical offices from the 1920s.

There is also the home of Lon C. Hill, the "father" of Harlingen, with original possessions of the pioneer family on display. Located just off Loop 499 at Boxwood and Raintree Streets.

Jackson Street

A restored historical section features buildings from the 1920s with restored store fronts, old-fashioned street lamps, and sidewalk benches; this is a great place to see arts and crafts and antiques.

Arroyo Queen

A great way to take a break from birding and still see a number of birds is a ride on the Arroyo Colorado on the *Arroyo Queen*, which departs four times daily from the Port of Harlingen dock. For more information, phone 956-423-3064.

Iwo Jima War Memorial

This is a working model of the famous statue on display at the Arlington National Cemetery. It was donated by Dr. Felix W. de Weldon to the Marine Military Academy. There is a visitors center that features a 30-minute film on the Battle of Iwo Jima, and there are self-guided tours as well. This is another opportunity for the kids to get a lesson in the history of America. Located next to the Harlingen International Airport at 320 Iwo Jima Blvd. For more information, phone 956-412-2207.

Festivals

Rio Grande Valley Birding Festival. Held in November to celebrate one of the most tropical ecosystems in the U.S.: the bird-rich Lower Rio Grande Valley. Local experts guide you to fabulous sights and South Texas specialties. Learn from workshops and enjoy presentations by noted experts. Contact: Harlingen Area Chamber of Commerce, P.O. Box 3162, Harlingen, TX 78551.

Motels

Best Western-Harlingen Inn, Expressway 83 at Stuart Place, phone 800-528-1234

Comfort Inn, 406 North Expressway 77, phone 956-412-7771

Holiday Inn Express, 501 South P. Street, phone 800-HOL-IDAY

Ramada Limited, 4401 South Expressway, phone 800-272-6232

Rodeway Inn, 1821 W. Tyler, phone 880-228-2000

Super 8 Motel, 115 S. Expressway 77, phone 800-800-8000

Dining

Plenty of fast foods, from Arby's to Dairy Queen to Mr. Gatti's Pizza. The Kettle at the intersection of Hwy. 83 and 77 is a great place for breakfast.

Chili's, 1725 W. Tyler

Luby's Cafeteria (2 locations), 2506 S. 77 Sunshine Strip and 822 Dixieland Road

Tilas Mexican Food, 906 Dixieland Road

Blue Shell Café, 1306 N. Ed Carey

Las Vegas Café, 1101 W. Harrison

Courtyard Steakhouse & Grill, 415 S. International Blvd.

Gabby's on the Arroyo, 35351 FM 2925

McAllen

Chamber of Commerce
10 N. Broadway
800-250-2591
http://www.mcallencvb.com

and/or

Mission
Chamber of Commerce
220 East 9th Street
800-580-2700
http://www.missionchamber.com

Mission is actually closer to the Bentsen-Rio Grande Valley State Park, but housing and dining facilities are more numerous in McAllen, and if you plan to go to Old Mexico to visit Reynosa, the McAllen, Hidalgo-Reynosa International Bridge via Texas 336 is near. The McAllen Chamber of Commerce also has information on visiting Monterrey at their office in Cintermex. Mission in particular is a popular wintering spot for thousands of senior citizens, and during that time the restaurants can get very crowded.

Birding

Bentsen-Rio Grande Valley State Park

With the possible exception of Santa Anna National Wildlife Refuge, this is the best place to bird in the valley. The picnic area is always good for scavengers and there is a resaca (Oxbow Lake) that will produce some very interesting birds, not only on the water, but in the air, as Peregrine Falcon is a regular visitor. Both Green and Ringed Kingfisher can be seen on branches extending over the water. The Rio Grande runs along the southernmost boundary of the park, and some rare birds such as Clay-colored Robin and Tropical Parula can be seen here. A walk around the trailer loop, where visitors camp out in motor homes and travel trailers, will give you a look at several species because many of the campers put out feeders. You will certainly hear the Plain Chachalaca again, and you can see Green Jay, Long-billed Thrasher, Olive Sparrow, Altamira and Audubon's Orioles, White-eyed Vireos, Pyrrhuloxia, and both Painted and Blue Buntings. The park comes alive after dark with the sounds of Barn, Great Horned, Eastern Screech-Owls, and in summer you may hear the Elf Owl. Lesser and Common Nighthawks may be seen at dusk, and the soft call of the Pauraque can be heard after dark. During migration other members of the "goat-sucker" family may be heard, including Common Poorwill, Chuck-will's-widow, and Whip-poor-will. This is also a great place to enjoy a picnic lunch.

Attractions

McAllen International Museum

Traveling art exhibits and a collection of Mexican folk art, along with colorful masks and costumes makes this a worthwhile stop. It also has Mexican paintings and sculptures and hands-on exhibits on science and natural history that the kids will enjoy. Located at 1900 Nolana.

Reynosa, Mexico

Located just 8 miles from McAllen across the International Bridge, this charming Mexican city has a population of over a half million with gift shops galore. Check with your motel as several offer van tours to and from the bridge. Driving across the bridge is not recommended unless you have had experience driving in Mexico and have adequate insurance coverage.

Mountasia

This amusement park could give the kids a lot of pleasure. Includes miniature golf, bumper cars, bumper boats, go-carts, a video arcade, and a restaurant. Located on U.S. 83.

Mission: La Lomita Chapel

The name means "Little Hill," and this small chapel was built in 1865 of adobe and was a stopover for Oblate padres who traveled by horseback between Brownsville and Roma. The chapel is still used for weddings and private services. There is an adjacent 7-acre park that has picnic facilities.

Festivals

Texas Tropics Nature Festival. Held in early April with field trips, seminars, a trade show, and outdoor adventure for the family in the heart of the migratory route for more than 465 birds and 260 butterfly species. Canoe and pontoon trips on the Rio Grande, birding at Bentsen Rio Grande State Park and Santa Anna Wildlife Refuge. Contact: McAllen Chamber of Commerce, P.O. Box 760, McAllen, TX 78505-0790 or phone 877-622-5536.

Motels

Super 8, 4401 N. Cage Blvd., phone 956-782-8880

Ramada Inn-McAllen, 1505 S. 9th St., phone 956-686-4401

Holiday Inn, 200 W. Expressway 83, phone 956-686-2471

Microtel Inn & Suites, 801 E. Expressway 83, phone 956-630-2727

Comfort Inn-Mission, 203 S. Sharyland Rd., phone 956-583-0333

Drury Inns-McAllen, 612 W. Expressway 83, phone 956-687-5100

Dining

Any number of fast foods, including Arby's, Burger King, and Chick-Fil-A (in mall)

Black-Eye Pea, 606 E. Expressway 83

Chili's Grill & Bar, 501 W. Expressway 83

Denny's Restaurant, 1110 S. 10th St. (a good place for breakfast)

Don Juan's Restaurant, 1610 N. 23rd St.

El Pato Mexican Food, (3 locations in McAllen: 1121 W. U.S. Hwy. 83, 2035 N. 23rd St., and 3019 N. 10th St.)

Weslaco

Chamber of Commerce
1701 East Pike Blvd.
P.O. Box 8398
888-968-2102
http://www.weslaco.com

This city is located in the heart of the Rio Grande Valley on Highway 83 and surrounded by huge citrus, vegetable, and cotton fields. Like most cities in the valley, it can be very crowded in the winter when as many as 6,000 wintering visitors fill the RV parks.

Birding

Santa Anna National Wildlife Refuge

If you only have time to take the family birding in one location, this is the place to go in the Rio Grande Valley. Boardwalks from the visitors center to Willow Lake make the walk an easy one, even for handicapped. (Be certain you have plenty of insect repellent.) The adventure begins even as you leave the parking lot as the vines along the entryway can harbor hummingbirds. As you cross the levee to enter the sanctuary itself, look both ways for raptors, including Hook-billed Kite, White-tailed Kite, and Harris's, Gray, and Red-shouldered Hawks. It is also a good place to see the Green Kingfisher. Listen as you walk through the curtain-like moss that hangs from the trees, and watch the ground, as the habitat is perfect for thrashers. And if you listen, you may hear the Great Kiskadee Flycatcher. At Pintail Lake there are two observation platforms, and a large variety of birds can be seen. A scope would be handy here but not necessary. The variety of water birds here changes constantly, and the Masked Duck has been seen on this pond. You should also see a number of other ducks, including both Fulvous and Black-bellied Whistling Ducks. Pied-billed Grebes are here, along with Common Moorhen. The trails throughout the 2,000-acre park are extensive and can be exhausting for children, but be sure and check out the feeding blind behind the old manager's house on your way to Pintail Lake. The red flowering shrimp plants here attract Buff-bellied Hummingbirds, and at the blind you will probably see orioles, Green Jays, and if you do not see, you will surely hear the noisy Plain Chachalacas. At Pintail Lake look for Sora, and in winter the numbers of waders, ducks, and shore birds can be extensive. In spring and summer both Purple Gallinule and Anhinga will be present, along with Least Bittern. Along the trail leading to the lake you can see a good assortment of field birds such as Groove-billed Ani, both Brown-crested and Scissor-tailed Flycatcher, Couch's Kingbird, Pyrrhuloxia, and this is a good place to see a Great Kiskadee Flycatcher. Check at the visitors center about the 7-mile tram ride around Wildlife Drive. From January to mid-April you have to take the tram, but during the rest of the year it is open for automobiles. The map available at the center will show you the most promising stops along the way.

Attractions

Valley Nature Center

A one-half-mile nature trail runs through five acres of natural habitat and vegetation with a butterfly garden, an elevated lily pond, cactus gardens, and an exhibit hall with interactive children's exhibits. An interesting and relaxing stop, and you might even see some birds. Located at 301 Roberts in Gibson Park.

Bicultural Museum

A display that depicts the lives of both Hispanic and Anglo settlers in the area. 515 S. Kansas Ave.

Motels

Best Western Palm Aire, FM 1015 and Expressway 83, phone
  956-969-2411

Flora Motel, 709 E. Business Highway 83, phone 956-968-3192

Vali-Ho Motel, 2100 E. Business Highway 83, phone 956-968-2173

Deluxe Inn, 601 North Westgate Drive, phone 956-968-0626

Holiday Inn Express, 1702 E. Expressway, phone 956-969-9920

Dining

There are plenty of places to eat, and fast food options include
  Dairy Queen, McDonald's, Popeye's, Stars Drive-In, Subway,
  Wendy's, Peter Piper Pizza, Long John Silver's, and
  Whataburger.

BBQ Warehouse, 108 N. Border

Casa Del Taco, 2708 N. Texas (Mexican and seafood)

Fiesta Tex-Mex, 615 W. Business 83 (good fajitas)

El Pato, 553 West Pike Blvd. (homemade tortillas)

Golden Corral, 300 W. Expressway 83

Luby's Cafeteria, 2001 W. Expressway 83

Zapata

Zapata County Chamber of Commerce
956-765-4871 or 800-292-LAKE

The town was named after Antonio Zapata, an early Hispanic settler and Indian fighter. Its proximity to Falcon Lake, in spite of the decline of the reservoir in recent years, makes it a prime birding area. Lodging and dining facilities are also located at Falcon Heights, which is closer to the state park, but Zapata (28 miles) has more to offer.

Birding

Falcon Lake and State Park

The decline of Falcon Lake in recent years has reduced the birding potential of the lake itself, but the surrounding area has a great deal to offer. Resident birds include Harris's Hawk, Bobwhite, Scaled Quail, and three species of doves, White-winged, Inca, and Common Ground Dove. The best place to bird is from the overlook below the spillway, and many water birds are usually found here, including Night-Herons and a variety of shore birds that are residents. Both Ringed and Green Kingfisher are present, and in winter you might see the Belted Kingfisher. Bird the river below the dam for Mexican Duck in summer, and rails are found here also. There is an old road that leads down the river to a dense habitat of brush and thorn forest. A clothesline pole marks the spot of an old hobo camp, and Ferruginous Pygmy Owl has been seen (or heard) here. Some really tropical birds can be seen on this hike, including Great Kiskadee Flycatcher and Green Jays. Plain Chachalaca can be seen (you will probably hear the noisy birds first), and even the Red-billed Pigeon has been spotted. In the park you may see Pyrrhuloxia and Chihuahuan Raven. A prime target of every birder who visits this area is the White-collared Seedeater.

Salineno

This has been a favorite birding spot for years where you can see the huge Brown Jays and, flying along the Rio Grande, the Muscovy Duck. There are several mobile homes near the river, and the lady who opened her yard for birders to see the variety of South Texas species up close passed away recently. Before entering any private property, be certain to get permission. Red-billed Pigeon has also been seen here, along with exotics such as Great Kiskadee Flycatcher, Green Jay, and orioles. Gray Hawk has also been noted here.

Santa Margarita Ranch

This ranch is located south of Salineno, and there is a small fee for birding. Most of the birds here can be seen at Salineno, and the area is quite primitive and can be very hot in summer. Probably not the best place for family birding, but if you missed the Brown Jay at Salineno, you might want to look here.

Attractions

Col. Antonio Zapata Museum

Artifacts of the past include arrowhead displays, antique furniture and clothing, and exhibits of photos from family collections. Located on South U.S. 83.

La Paz County Historical Museum

Visit a 200-year-old Mexican house, with photos from old Zapata, antique ranch furniture, doctor's equipment, and cooking utensils. Open September through May at Benavides Elementary School in San Ygnacio, about 25 miles north on U.S. 83.

Motels

Best Western Inn, S. Hwy. 83, phone 956-765-8403

Executive Inn, S. Hwy. 83, phone 956-765-6982

Redwood Lodge, S. Hwy. 83, phone 956-765-4371

Dining

Holiday Restaurant, Hwy. 83

Cuatro Milpas Restaurant, Hwy. 3 E. 3rd Ave. (steaks and Mexican)

Fast foods are McDonald's and Dairy Queen

Appendix A

Bibliography

Reference Materials

Texas Dept. of Transportation, *2001 Texas State Travel Guide*.

Texas Dept. of Transportation, *2001 Texas Accommodations Guide*.

Texas Dept. of Transportation, 2001 Texas Official Travel Map.

Texas Parks & Wildlife/Texas Dept. of Transportation, The Great Texas Coastal Birding Trail, Upper Texas Coast, Central Texas Coast, and Lower Texas Coast.

Field Guides

Griggs, Jack, *All the Birds of North America*, New York, NY: Harper's Collins Publishers, 1997.

Field Guide to the Birds of North America, Washington D.C.: National Geographic Society, 1983.

Peterson, Roger Tory, *A Field Guide to the Birds of Texas and Adjacent States*, Boston: Houghton Mifflin Co., 1963.

Rappole, John H. and Gene W. Blacklock, *Birds of Texas: A Field Guide*, College Station, TX: Texas A&M University Press, 1994.

Robbins, Chandler S., *Birds of North America: A Guide to Field Identification*, New York: Golden Press, 1983.

Stokes, Donald W. and Lillian, *Stokes Field Guide to Birds*, Boston: Little, Brown, 1996.

Birding Travel Guides

Holt, Harold R., *A Birder's Guide to the Texas Coast*. Colorado Springs, CO.: American Birding Association, 1993.

_____, *A Birder's Guide to the Rio Grande Valley of Texas*. Colorado Springs, CO.: American Birding Association, 1992.

Kutac, Edward A., *Birder's Guide to Texas*, Houston, TX: Lone Star Books, 1989.

Wauer, Roland H. and Mark A. Elwonger, *Birding Texas.* Helena, MT: Falcon Publishing, 1998.

Wauer, Roland H., *Naturalist's Big Bend,* College Station, TX: Texas A&M University Press, 1980.

Texas Travel Guide Books

Buckner, Sharry, *Exploring Texas With Children*, Plano, TX: Republic of Texas Press, 1999.

Bumagin, Michael, *Exploring Fort Worth With Children*, Plano, TX: Republic of Texas Press, 1998.

Galit, Elaine L. and Simmons, Vikk, *Exploring Houston With Children*, Plano, TX: Republic of Texas Press, 2001.

James, Gary, *The Texas Guide*, Golden, CO.: Fulcrum Publishing, 2000.

Little, Mildred J., *Camper's Guide to Texas Parks, Lakes, and Forests,* Houston: Gulf Publishing Co., 1998.

McCasland, Kay, *Exploring Dallas With Children*, Plano, TX: Republic of Texas Press, 1998.

Where The Locals Eat, Texas Edition, Nashville, TN: Magellan Press, 1999.

Williams, Docia Schultz, *Exploring San Antonio With Children*, Plano, TX: Republic of Texas Press, 1999.

General

Tveten, John L., *The Birds of Texas,* Fredericksburg, TX: Shearer Publishing, 1993.

Appendix B

Binoculars and Scopes

Listed below are a number of binoculars and scopes that are available. Prices are valid at time of printing but are subject to change. There are many other brands and models, and this list is just a representative assortment of the various types and prices. Tripods for scopes are sold separately.

Brand	Model	Size	Code	Comments	Price
Bushnell	Birder	8x40	Bus11-8400	Extended eye relief, center focus	$52
Bushnell	Natureview	8x42	Bus13-2000	Central focus	$119
Bushnell	Natureview	10x42	Bus13-2030	Compact	$104
Bushnell	Natureview	10x30	Bus13-2040	Compact, long eye relief	$107
Bausch & Lomb	Elite	8x42	B&L61-0842	Waterproof/fog proof	$1,110
Bausch & Lomb	Discoverer	10x42	B&L61-0142	Waterproof/fog proof	$506
Bausch & Lomb	Custom	7x26	B&L610726	Long eye relief, close focus	$335
Bausch & Lomb	Legacy	10x25	B&L12-0125	Compact	$66
Bausch & Lomb	Legacy	8x24	B&L12-0824	Waterproof/fog proof/compact	$190
Leica		8x20	Lei040-335	Compact	$349
Lieca		10x25	Lei040-336	Compact	$379
Leica		10x25	Lei040-340	Compact	$419
Leica		8x42	Lei040-012	Black ultra	$1,045
Leica		10x50	Lei040-067	Black ultra	$1,245
Minolta	Activa	10x30	8589-217	Zoom	$224
Minolta	Activa	7x35w	8585-117		$168
Minolta	Activa	8x40w	8585-417		$186
Minolta	Activa	10x50w	8585-517		$204
Minolta	Activa	12x50w	8585-617		$211
Swift	Sin Plover	8x40	Sin702B		$133
Swift	Sin Birder	8x40	Sin7384	Aerolite	$70

Brand	Model	Size	Code	Comments	Price
Swift	Sin Audubon	8.5x44	804ED	Extra low dispersion	$676
Swift	Sin Eaglet	7x35	825R	Waterproof	$476
Swift	Sin Kestral	10x50	826		$347
Bushnell Scope	Spacemaster	60mm	78-2317	Black zoom	$339
Lieca Scope	Apo	20-60	Lei040-912	Angled w/20-60x	$1,624
Swift Scope	Nighthawk	80mm	Sin849	Body only, eye-piece $259	$557

Appendix C

State Park Camping and Recreational Facilities

Texas is blessed with a great number of state parks that offer not only camping facilities, but recreational opportunities for the family. Those listed in this book are also great areas to go birding. Most of them will have a visitors center where you can pick up a map of the park, along with a comprehensive listing of the birds that might be seen there. The travel budget can be greatly reduced by taking advantage of these parks, either for tent camping, RV parking, or by renting one of the screened-in shelters or cabins available. Several such as Fort Davis and Balmorhea have motels available, along with dining facilities. Many of them are within a short drive of other birding areas listed in this book and can save you a great deal of money as opposed to staying in a city and eating in restaurants. All have picnic facilities. The chart below is a condensation of the information available on the state parks located in birding areas covered in this book.

	Campsites Water/Elect	Campsites Water Only	Restrooms/ Showers	RV dump station	Cabins/ Shelters	Other
Trans Pecos						
Amistad	48 total		no	Diablo E.	no	beach swimming
Balmorhea Lake	28	6	yes	yes	18-unit motel	swimming, playground
Big Bend	Primitive	no	no	no	no	swimming, nature trails
Davis Mountain	61	33	yes	yes	39-unit motel	playground, restaurant
Franklin Mountain	Primitive	no	no	no	no	rock climbing
Hueco Tanks	17	3	yes	yes	no	rock climbing, nature trail
Panhandle						
Caprock Canyon	25	10	yes	yes	no	rock climbing, playground
Copper Breaks	25	11	yes	yes	no	swimming, paddle boats
Monahan Sandhills	39	5	yes	yes	no	sand surfing, nature trail
Palo Duro Canyon	133	18	yes	yes	no	nature trail, playground
Lake Rita Blanca	31 total					
San Angelo	70	50	yes	yes	no	Camps in various locales
Edwards Plateau						
Enchanted Rock	0	46 water near	yes	no	no	rock climbing, playground
Garner	146	205	yes	yes	17 cabins 24 shelters	nature trail, river swimming
Guadalupe River	48	37	yes	yes	no	playground
Kerrville-Shreiner	45	65	yes	yes	16 shelters	swimming, playground
Longhorn & Inks	56	144	yes	yes	22 shelters	playground, swimming
Lost Maples	30	0	yes	yes	no	swimming
Pedernales Falls	69	31 primitive	yes	yes	no	nature trail, scenic views
South Llano	56	12	yes	yes	no	swimming, canoeing
Northern Plains						
Cedar Hill	400	30 primitive	yes	yes	no	playground, swimming
Cleburne	58	5	yes	yes	no	nature trail, swimming
Cooper Lake	42		yes	yes	7 shelters	nature trail, swimming
Dinosaur Valley	46	6	yes	yes	no	nature trail, swimming
Fairfield Lake	125	36	yes	yes	no	playground, swimming
Fort Parker	25	10	yes	yes	10 shelters	playground, swimming
Lake Arrowhead	48	19	yes	yes	no	playground, swimming
Lake Brownwood	75	12	yes	yes	10 shelters 17 cabins	playground
Lake Mineral Wells	0	11	yes	yes	15 shelters	swimming, lake trail
Lake Whitney	68	71	yes	yes	21 shelters	swimming
Meridan	15	8	yes	yes	11 shelters	swimming, nature trails
Mother Neff	6	15	yes	yes	no	observation tower
Possum Kingdom	82	55	yes	yes	6 cabins	playground, swimming

	Campsites Water/Elect	Campsites Water Only	Restrooms/ Showers	RV dump station	Cabins/ Shelters	Other
Pineywoods						
Caddo Lake	28	20	yes	yes	8 shelters	nature trails, swimming
Dangerfield	46	6	yes	yes	no	dinosaur exhibits
Huntsville	64	127	yes	yes	30 shelters	playground, swimming
Lake Livingston	168	16	yes	yes	10 shelters	playground, swimming
Martin Dies	177 total	44	yes	yes	46 shelters	lake swimming
Tyler	107	42	yes	yes	29 shelters	swimming, nature trail
Wright Patman	362 total		yes	yes	no	swimming
Bastrop	54	11	yes	yes	12 cabins	hiking trail, swimming pool
Beuscher	40	20	yes	yes	4 shelters	swimming, playground
Palmetto	19	22	yes	yes	no	historic, swimming
Lake Somerville	118		yes	yes	no	5-mile nature trail
Lake Texoma	15 areas		yes	yes	58 total cabins	boating, fishing
Upper Coast						
Brazos Bend	77	0	yes	yes	no	playground, nature trail
Galveston	180 total		yes	yes	10 shelters	nature trails, fishing
Matagorda	primitive		no	no	no	beach swimming area
Sea Rim	20	10	yes	yes	no	beach
Coastal Bend						
Goose Island	102	25	yes	yes	no	playground, swimming
Mustang Island	48		chemical	yes		beach
Brush Country						
Choke Canyon	40	19	yes	yes	20 shelters	swimming pool
Corpus Christi	48	60	yes	yes	25 shelters	lake swimming
Goliad	44	12	yes	yes	5 shelters	historic site
Lake Casa Blanca	8	292	yes	yes	no	playground, beach swimming
Rio Grande						
Bentzen	77	65	yes	yes	no	playground, nature trail
Falcon	62	54 water near	yes	yes	24 shelters	nature trail, lake swimming

Appendix D

Trip Planning Form

Family Bird Trip Planning Sheet

Date(s) of trip:
Beginning:_____To:_____

Destination(s):

_____

Birding Sites to visit:

_____

_____

Motel/Camping Reservations made:
Day 1:_____Day 2:_____
Day 3:_____Day 4:_____
Day 5:_____
Other:_____

Ordered material from Chamber of
Commerce(s): _____

Resources:
1. *Birding Texas* trip guide: _____   2. Field guide(s): _____
3. TXDOT travel guide: _____
a. Travel log _____   b. Maps and C of C material _____
c. Car games _____   d. Snacks _____

e. Vehicle serviced _____   f. First aid kit _____
g. Insect repellant _____   h. Bottled water _____
i. Binoculars _____   j. Scope _____
k. Flashlight _____   l. Cooler _____
m. Picnic basket _____   n. Utensils _____
o. Charcoal _____   p. Trash bags _____
q. Paper goods (napkins, towels, etc.) _____
r. Medicines _____

Clothing:
1._____
2._____
3._____
4._____
5._____

Appendix E

Bird Clubs and Organizations

Bird Clubs of Texas

Contacting a local bird club can be helpful in learning of local birding possibilities and current birding conditions for that particular area.

Bird Club	Address	City/Zip Code
Abilene Zoological Society	P.O. Box 60	Abilene 79604
Big Country Audubon Society	P.O. Box 569	Abilene 79604
Big Bend Birders	P.O. Box 1438	Alpine 79831
Texas Panhandle Audubon Society	P.O. Box 30939	Amarillo 79120
Fort Worth Audubon Society	1016 Briarcliff	Arlington 76012
Aransas & Matagorda Island	P.O. Box 74	Austwell 77950
Bay City Nature Club	Rt. 1, Box 180	Bay City 77414
Twin Lakes Audubon Society	Dept. of Biology, U. of Mary-Hardin Baylor	Belton 76513
Brazosport Soc. of Naturalists	Rt. 1, Lot 3, H&R subdivision	Brazoria 77422
Rio Brazos Audubon Society	P.O. Box 1989	College Station 77841
Fort Worth Audubon Society	2205 Glade Road	Colleyville 76034
Audubon Outdoor Club	P.O. Box 3352	Corpus Christi 78463
Coastal Bend Audubon Society	P.O. Box 4793	Corpus Christi 78469-4793
Crowley Nature Center	732 Meadow Crest Drive	Crowley 76036
Dallas County Audubon Society	3352 Camelot Drive	Dallas 75229
N. Am. Starling Fancier's Association	7225 Fair Oaks #310	Dallas 75231
Lower Rio Grande Valley Audubon	421 North 11th Street	Donna 78537
El Paso/Trans Pecos Audubon	P.O. Box 9655	El Paso 79995
Aransas Bird & Nature Club	P.O. Box 308	Fulton 78358-0308
Galveston Co. Audubon Group	P.O. Box 3113	Galveston 77552
Arroyo Colorado Audubon Society	P.O. Box 531562	Harlingen 78553-1582
Hill Country Bird Club	HC 64, Box 637	Harper 78631

Bird Club	Address	City/Zip Code
Houston Audubon Society	440 Wilchester Blvd.	Houston 77079
Houston Outdoor Nature Club-Ornithology Group	P.O. Box 270894	Houston 77084
Ornithology Group of Houston	18046 Green Hazel Drive	Houston 77084
Lower Trinity Valley Bird Club	9432 Murray J. Road	Hull 77564
Huntsville Audubon Society	Rt. 15, Box 490	Huntsville 77340
Texas Ornithological Society	401 Pinn Oak	Ingram 78025
Kingsville Bird & Wildlife Club	709 W. Ave I	Kingsville 78363
Lake Houston Area Nature Club	4431 Brood Shadow Drive	Kingwood 77345
Panhandle Bird Club	Box 545	Kress 79052
Brazosport Birders	324 Linden Lane	Lake Jackson 77566
N. E. TX. Field Ornithologist	607 Regency Drive	Longview 75604
Llano Estacado Audubon Society	P.O. Box 6066	Lubbock 79493
Prairie & Timbers Audubon Society	Heard Museum, One Nature Place	McKinney 75069
Midland Naturalists	2100 West Wadley, No. 30	Midland 79705
Pineywoods Audubon Society	Rt. 5, Box 4360	Nacogdoches 75964
Golden Triangle Audubon Society	P.O. Box 1292	Nederland 77627-1292
Travis Audubon Society	P.O. Box 1132	Round Rock 78680-1132
Bexar Audubon Society	P.O. Box 6084	San Antonio 78209
San Antonio Audubon Society	3006 Belvoir	San Antonio 78230-4410
The Main Group Bird Club	204 W. Welder, Box 573	Sinton 78387
Bastrop Co. Audubon Society	305 Turney Street	Smithville 78987
Highland Lakes Birding Society	P.O. Box 204	Spicewood 78669
Piney Woods Wildlife Society	P.O. Box 189	Spring 77383-6667
Tyler Audubon Society	4115 Chester Drive	Tyler 75701

National Organizations:

American Birding Association: P.O. Box 6599, Colorado Springs, CO 80934-6599, 800-859-2473, 719-578-1614, Fax 800-246-2329, e-mail: member@ABA.org

Audubon Society: P.O. Box 52529, Boulder, CO 80322, 800-274-4201

National Wildlife Federation: 8925 Leesburg Pike, Vienna, VA 22184, www.nwf.org

Appendix F
Rare Bird Alerts

Many bird clubs and societies maintain a system for advising birders when and where rare birds have been sighted in the state of Texas. These include phone numbers and in some cases, web sites. Keep in mind that with the ever-changing area codes, some of the information listed below is subject to change.

Statewide: RBA, 713-964-5867, Internet address: http://www.birdware.com/lists/RBA/_us/tx/txindex.htm

Abilene (Big Country Audubon Society): 915-691-8981

Austin area: RBA, 512-926-8751: Internet access: Birding in Central Texas web site: http://www.onr.com/user/andyd/Birding.html

Travis Audubon Society web site: http://www.travisaudubon.org

Beaumont area: RBA, 409-769-4029

Corpus Christi area: RBA, 361-265-0377

Lubbock area: RBA, 806-797-6690

Heart of Texas (Central Brazos Valley) area: RBA, 409-694-9850, e-mail only: bert@bafrenz.com

North-Central (Dallas/Fort Worth) area: RBA, 817-329-1270

Northeast area: RBA, 903-234-2473

Panhandle area: Internet only: jwhall@am.net

Rio Grande Valley area: RBA, 956-969-2731

San Antonio area: RBA, 210-308-6788

West Texas area: e-mail only: dsarkozi@infocom.net

Appendix G

The Great Texas Coastal Birding Trail

This trail, dedicated in September of 1995 by Roger Tory Peterson, is 500 miles long and covers the Texas coast in three sections:

A. The upper coast covers the area from the Louisiana border to Brazoria County.

B. The central coast gives birding information from the Big Boggy National Wildlife Refuge to the Corpus Christi/Kingsville area.

C. The lower coast begins at Port Mansfield and covers the area south to Boca Chica and up the Rio Grande Valley from Brownsville to Laredo.

Three beautiful maps, with the birding sites listed on the back and arranged in "loops" for convenient planning of a birding trip to the area, are available.

Over 200 birding sites are listed on the maps, and the information includes national, state, and county parks, wildlife refuges, wildlife management areas, and private property.

These guides have been developed by the Department of Transportation and the Texas Parks and Wildlife Commission, along with a number of communities along the trail.

Not only do the maps list information on birding sites, including explicit directions, but also a listing of some of the species that might be seen, suggestions on the best season to bird a particular area, and where to obtain more information on the area.

The maps may be obtained from one of the twelve Texas Travel Information Centers, at many of the convention and tourist bureaus in the area, or from the Texas Department of Transportation, Travel and Information Division, P.O. Box 5064, Austin TX 78763, phone 800-452-9292.

If your trip includes the Texas coast, these will be of great assistance to you and make your family birding expedition more profitable.

Index of Attractions

Alpine, 14
Hwy. U.S. 67 & U.S. 90, 14
Apache Trading Post, 14
Woodward Agate Ranch, 15

Balmorhea, 16
Balmorhea Lake, 16
Balmorhea State Park, 16-17

Big Bend National Park, 17

Del Rio, 19
Amistad National Recreation Area, 19
Seminole Canyon State Park, 20
Moore Park, 20
Whitehead Memorial Museum, 20
Seminole Canyon Indian Pictographs, 20

El Paso, 21
Franklin Mountains State Park, 21
Fred Hervey Water Reclamation Ponds, 22
Hueco Tanks State Park, 22
Border Patrol Museum, 22
El Paso Saddle Blanket Trading Post, 23
El Paso Zoo, 23
El Paso Science Center, 23
El Paso Museum of History, 23
El Paso/Jaurez Tours, 23
Western Park Museum, 23
Tigua Indian Reservation, 24

Fort Davis, 25
Limpia Creek and the Davis Mountain Loop, 25
Davis Mountains State Park, 25
Fort Davis National Historic Site, 26
McDonald Observatory, 26
Neil Museum, 26
Overland Trail Museum, 26

Marathon, 27
The Post, 27
Prairie Dog Colony, 28
Great Marathon Basin, 28

Presidio, 28
Fort Leaton State Historic Park, 28
Big Bend Ranch State Park, 29
Fort Leaton State Historic Site, 29

Abilene, 32
Abilene State Park, 32
Kirby Lake, 32
Seabee Park, 33
Abilene Waste Water Treatment Plant, 33
Abilene Zoo, 33
Fort Phantom Hill, 33
Grace Museum, 33
Buffalo Gap Historic Village, 34
Paramount Theater, 34

Amarillo, 35

Canyon, 35
Lake Meredith National Recreation Area, 35
Buffalo Lake National Wildlife Refuge, 36
Palo Duro Canyon State Park, 37
Amarillo Zoo, 37
Amarillo: American Quarter Horse Heritage Center and Museum, 37
Amarillo: Cadillac Ranch, 37
Amarillo: Don Harrington Discovery Center, 38
Amarillo: English Field Air and Space Museum, 38
Canyon: Pioneer Amphitheatre, 38
Canyon: Panhandle-Plains Historical Museum, 38

Big Spring, 40
Big Spring State Park, 40
Heritage Museum, 41
Potton House, 41
Vietnam Memorial, 41

Dalhart, 42
Lake Rita Blanca State Park, 42
Rita Blanca National Grassland, 42
Cactus Lake, 42
Dallam-Hartley Counties XIT Museum, 43
Empty Saddle Monument, 43

Lubbock, 44
Buffalo Springs Lake, 44
Twin Ponds and Boles Lake, 44
Mackenzie Park, 45
Lake Six, 45
American Wind Power Center, 45
Buddy Holly Center, 45

Lubbock Memorial Arboretum, 46
Omnimax and Science Spectrum, 46
Joyland Amusement Park, 46
Ellen Trout Zoo and Park, 46

Monahans, 47
Monahans Sandhills State Park, 47
Million Barrel Museum, 48
Pyote Museum and Rattlesnake Bomber
     Base, 48

Muleshoe, 49
Muleshoe National Wildlife Refuge, 49
National Mule Memorial, 50

Odessa, 51
American Airpower Heritage Museum and
     Confederate Air Force, 51
Midland County Historical Museum, 51
Museum of the Southwest Complex, 51
Odessa Meteor Crater, 52
Presidential Museum, 52

Pecos, 53
Red Bluff Lake, 53
Maxey Park and Zoo, 54
West-of-the-Pecos Museum and Park, 54

Quitaque, 55
Caprock Canyon State Park, 55
Circle Dot Caprock Adventure, 55

Quanah, 56
Cooper Breaks State Park and Pease River,
     56
Hardeman County Museum, 57
Quanah, Acme and Pacific Railway Depot,
     57
Medicine Mounds, 57

San Angelo, 58
San Angelo State Park & O. C. Fisher Lake,
     58
Hummer House Texas Gems, 59
San Angelo Children's Art Museum, 59
San Angelo Nature Center, 59
Fort Concho, 60

Austin, 62
Austin Northwest, 62
Austin Central, 63
Hornsby Bend Wastewater Treatment Plant,
     63
Austin Children's Museum, 64
Austin Zoo, 64
Republic of Texas Museum, 64
George Washington Carver Museum, 64

Lyndon B. Johnson Library and Museum, 64

Boerne, 65
Guadalupe River State Park, 65
Cascade Caverns, 66
Cave Without A Name, 66

Burnet, 67
Vanishing Texas River Cruise Bald Eagle
     Tours, 67
Canyon of the Eagles, 68
Inks Lake State Park, 68
Longhorn Caverns State Park, 68
Highland Lakes CAF Air Museum, 69
Hill Country Flyer, 69

Fredericksburg, 70
Enchanted Rock State Natural Area, 70
Admiral Nimitz Museum and Historical
     Center, 71
Fredericksburg Butterfly Ranch and Habitat,
     71
Pioneer Museum Complex, 71
Lady Bird Johnson Municipal Park, 71
Historic District, Heart of Fredericksburg, 72

Johnson City, 73
Pedernales Falls State Park, 73
Exotic Resort Zoo, 74
Lyndon B. Johnson National Historical Park,
     74

Kerrville, 75
Kerrville-Schreiner State Park, 75
Cowboy Artists of America Museum, 76
Hill Country Museum, 76
Kerrville Camera Safari, 76

Lago Vista, 77
Balcones Canyonlands National Wildlife
     Refuge, 77
Lago Vista Airpower Museum, 78

Leakey, 79
Garner State Park, 79
Lost Maples State Park, 79
Real County Historical Museum, 80

Brownwood, 84
Lake Brownwood State Park, 84
Brown County Museum of History, 85
Douglas MacArthur Academy of Freedom,
     85
Camp Bowie Memorial Park, 85

Cleburne, 86
Cleburne State Park, 86
Johnson County Courthouse, 87

Layland Museum, 87

Dallas, 88
White Rock Lake Park, 88
Southside Water Treatment Plant, 89
Cedar Hill State Park and Dallas Nature
    Center, 89
African-American Museum, 90
Age of Steam Railroad Museum (in Fair
    Park), 90
Dallas Aquarium (in Fair Park), 90
Museum of Natural History, 90
Dallas Zoo, 90
The Sixth Floor, 90

Denton, 91
Ray Roberts Lake, 92
Cross Timbers Park Project, 92
Denton County Historical Museum and
    Texas Heritage Center, 92
Denton County Courthouse-on-the-Square
    Museum, 92
Little Chapel in the Woods, 92

Fairfield, 93
Fairfield Lake State Park, 94
Freestone County Museum, 94

Fort Worth, 95
Fort Worth Nature Center and Lake Worth,
    96
Benbrook Lake, 96
Fort Worth Museum of Science and History,
    97
Fort Worth Zoo, 97
Vintage Flying Museum, 97
Pate Museum of Transportation, 98

Glen Rose, 98
Dinosaur Valley State Park, 99
Barnard Mill and Art Museum, 99
Comanche Peak Information Center, 100
Creation Evidences Museum, 100
Fossil Rim Wildlife Center, 100
The Promise, 100

Graham, 101
Possum Kingdom State Park, 101
Robert E. Richeson Memorial Museum, 102
Fort Belknap, 102

Greenville, 103
Lake Tawakoni, 103
American Cotton Museum, 104
Mathews Prairie Preserve, 104

Hillsboro, 106
Meridian State Park, 106

Lake Whitney State Park, 107
Hill County Cell Block Museum, 107
Texas Heritage Museum, 107

Lewisville, 108
Lewisville Lake Park and Fish Hatchery
    Road, 108
Miss Lewisville Paddlewheel Boat, 109
Old Town, 109

McKinney, 110
Heard Natural Science Museum and Wildlife
    Sanctuary, 110
Heard Natural Science Museum, 111
Collin County Youth and Farm Museum, 111
Storybook Ranch, 111

Mineral Wells, 112
Lake Mineral Wells State Park, 112
Crazy Water Well, 113
Famous Water Company, 113
B.A.T.S. Tour, 113
Palo Pinto Museum, 113

Plano, 114
Plano Outdoor Learning Center, 115
Interurban Railway Station Museum, 115
Mountasia Fantasy Golf, 115
Southfork Ranch, 116

Sherman, 117
Hagerman National Wildlife Refuge, 117
Red River Historical Museum, 118
C. B. Roberts House, 118

Sulphur Springs, 119
Cooper Lake State Park, 119
Hopkins County Museum and Heritage Park,
    120
Music Box Gallery, 120
Southwest Dairy Center, 120
Mossman Guitars, 120

Waco, 121
Cameron Park, 121
Waco Lake, 122
Waco Water Treatment Plant, 122
Tradinghouse Creek Reservoir, 122
Mother Neff State Park, 122
Cameron Park Zoo, 123
Dr Pepper Museum, 123
Texas Ranger Hall of Fame & Museum at
    Fort Fisher, 123
Texas Sports Hall of Fame, 123

Wichita Falls, 124
Lake Arrowhead State Park, 124
Museum and Art Center, 125

Railroad Museum, 125
The Plex Entertainment Center, 125
Wichita Falls Fire and Police Museum, 126

Huntsville, 128
Sam Houston National Forest, 128
Huntsville State Park, 128
Sam Houston Memorial Museum and Park, 129
The Texas Prison Museum, 129

Jasper, 130
Martin Dies Jr. State Park and B. A. Steinhagen Lake, 130
Hidden Falls Ranch, 131
Beaty-Orton House, 131

Livingston, 132
Lake Livingston State Park, 132
Sam Houston National Forest, 132
Big Thicket National Preserve, 132
Alabama-Coushatta Indian Reservation, 133
Polk County Museum, 133

Longview, 134
Lake O' The Pines, 134
Longview Museum of Fine Arts, 135
R. G. LeTourneau Museum, 135
Gregg County Historical Museum, 135

Lufkin, 136

Nacogdoches, 136
Sabine National Forest and Toledo Bend Reservoir, 137
Angelina National Forest and Sam Rayburn Reservoir, 137
Lufkin, 138
Ellen Trout Zoo and Park, 138
Medford Collection of Western Art, 138
Museum of East Texas, 138
Texas Forestry Museum, 138
Nacogdoches, 138
Ghost of Nacogdoches Historical Trail, 139
Milliard's Crossing, 139
Nacogdoches Fire Museum, 139
SFA Mast Arboretum, 139
Sterne-Hoya House, 139
Stone Fort Museum, 139

Marshall, 141
Caddo Lake State Park and Wildlife Management Area, 141
Lake O' The Pines, 142
Daingerfield State Park, 142
Harrison County Historical Museum, 142
Marshall Pottery and Museum, 142

Starr Family State Historical Site, 142

Tyler, 144
Tyler State Park, 144
Lake Palestine, 144
Brookshire's World of Wildlife and Country Store, 144
Caldwell Zoo, 145
Carnegie History Center, 145
Discovery Science Place, 145
Harrold's Model Train Museum, 145
Hudnall Planetarium, 145
Municipal Rose Garden and Museum, 145

Eagle Lake, 148
Attwater Prairie Chicken Refuge, 148
Prairie Museum, 148

Edna, 149
Lake Texana State Park, 149
Otto Lawrence Children's Museum, 150
Texana Museum and Old Jail House, 150

Gonzales, 151
Palmetto State Park, 151
Gonzales Memorial Museum, 152

La Grange, 153
Fayette Lake, 153
Fayetteville Area Museum (in Fayetteville), 154
Monument Hill State Historic Site (La Grange), 154
The Jersey Barnyard, 154

Taylor, 155
Alcoa Lake, 155
Granger Lake, 156
Moody Museum, 156

Brazoria County, 158
Brazoria National Wildlife Refuge, 158
Brazosport Nature Center and Planetarium Nature Trail, 159
San Bernard National Wildlife Refuge, 159
Quintana Neotropical Bird Sanctuary, 159
Sea Center Texas, 159
Brazosport Center for the Arts and Sciences, 160
Brazoria County Historical Museum, 160
Varner-Hogg Plantation, 160
Surfside Beach, 161
Train Museum, 161

Bay City and Matagorda County, 162
Matagorda County Jetty Park, 163
South Texas Project Prairie Wetlands, 163

Attwater's Prairie-Chicken National Wildlife Refuge, 163
South Texas Project Visitors Center, 163
Matagorda County Museum and Children's Museum, 164

Beaumont/Orange/Port Arthur, 164
Cattail Marsh, 165
Texas Point National Wildlife Refuge and Sabine Pass Battleground, 165
Texas Ornithological Society's Sabine Woods, 165
Sabine Pass, 165
Sea Rim State Park, 165
McFaddin National Wildlife Refuge, 166
Babe Didrikson Zaharias Museum and Visitors Center, 166
Fire Museum of Texas, 166
Spindletop/Gladys City Boomtown, 166
Sabine Pass Battleground State Historical Park, 166

Galveston, 167

Bolivar Peninsula, 168
Anahuac National Wildlife Refuge, 168
High Island Boy Scout Woods, 168
Eubanks Woods Bird Sanctuary, 169
Bolivar Flats Shore Bird Sanctuary, 169
The Railroad, 169
Galveston Island State Park, 169
Lone Star Flight Museum, 170
Moody Gardens, 170
Texas Seaport Museum, 170
Center for Transportation and Commerce (Railroad Museum), 170
Moody Mansion, 171
The Strand, 171

Houston, 172
Sam Houston Park, 172
Buffalo Bayou Park, 173
White Oak Park, 173
Hermann Park, 173
Russ Pittman Park and Nature Discovery Center, 173
Museum of Texas History, 173
Funplex, 174
Gulf Coast Railroad Museum, 174
Children's Museum of Houston, 174
Houston Museum of Natural Science, 174
San Jacinto Battleground State Historical Park, 174

Palacios, 175
Cash's Creek, 175

Palacios Waterfront and Trull Marsh, 175
Palacios Marine Education Center and Nature Trail, 176
Marine Fisheries Research Station, 176
Luther Hotel, 176

Port Lavaca/Calhoun County, 177
Port Lavaca Bird Sanctuary, 177
Magnolia Beach, 177
Port O'Conner/Matagorda Island State Park, 177
Guadalupe Delta Wildlife Management Area, 178
Halfmoon Reef Lighthouse, 178
Indianola County Historic Park, 179
Calhoun County Museum, 179

Aransas Pass, 182
Farm Road 1069, 182
Dale Miller Causeway, 182
Deep Sea Fishing, 182

Corpus Christi, 184
Blucher Park, 184
Hans Suter Wildlife Park, 184
Hazel Bazemore Park, 185
Tule Lake, 185
Laguna Madre, 185
Skimmer Nesting Grounds, 186
Indian Point, 186
Packery Channel, 186
Corpus Christi Botanical Gardens, 186
Aquarium, Texas State, 187
Asian Cultures Museum and Educational Center, 187
Corpus Christi Zoo, 187
USS *Lexington* Museum on the Bay, 187
Corpus Christi Museum of Science and History, 187

Kingsville, 189
Drum Point, 189
Kaufer-Hubert Park, 189
Dick Kleberg Park, 189
Sarita Rest Stop, 190
King Ranch Tours, 190
Louise Trant Bird Sanctuary, 190
King Ranch Museum, 190
King Ranch Saddle Shop, 191
Kleberg Hall of Natural History, 191

Port Aransas, 192
Mustang Island, 192
St. Joseph's (San Jose) Island, 192
Mustang Island State Park, 193
Port Aransas Wetland Park, 193

Birding Center, 193
University of Texas Marine Science Institute,
   193
Trolley Rides, 194

Rockport-Fulton Area, 195
Aransas National Wildlife Refuge, 195
Live Oak Peninsula, 195
Goose Island State Recreation Area, 196
Little Bay, 196
Demo Bird Garden and Wetlands Pond, 196
Whooping Crane Tours, 196
Fulton Mansion, 197
The Big Tree, 197
Texas Maritime Museum, 197

Alice, 200
Corpus Christi State Park, 200
Pernitas Point, 201
Lake Alice, 201
South Texas Museum, 201

Goliad, 202
Goliad State Park, 202
Presidio La Bahia, 203
General Zaragoza State Historic Site, 203
Grave of Col. James W. Fannin Jr. and
   Men, 203

Laredo, 204
Lake Casa Blanca State Park, 205
Laredo Children's Museum, 205
Fort McIntosh, 205
Republic of the Rio Grande Build-
   ing/Museum, 206

San Antonio, 207
Mitchell Lake, 207
Braunig Lake and Calaveras Lake, 208
Brackenridge Park, 209
The Alamo, 209
Brackenridge Park/San Antonio Zoo, 209
Institute of Texan Cultures, 210
El Mercado, 210
Missions of San Antonio, 210
Ripley's Believe It or Not!, 210
San Antonio Children's Museum, 210
River Walk, 211
Sea World, Six Flags Fiesta Texas, and
   Splashtown, 211

Three Rivers, 212
Choke Canyon State Park, 213
Tips State Recreation Park, 213

Brownsville, 216
Brownsville Landfill, 216
Boca Chica Beach, 216
Sabal Palms Audubon Sanctuary, 217
Los Ebanos Parrot Roost, 217
Glady's Porter Zoo, 218
Historic Brownsville Museum, 218
Matamoros, Mexico, 218
Palmito Ranch Civil War Battlefield, 218
Palo Alta Battlefield National Historic Site,
   219

Edinburg, 220
Edinburg Lake, 220
Hidalgo County Historical Museum, 220

Harlingen, 221
Laguna Atascosa National Wildlife Refuge,
   221
Rio Grande Valley Museum, 223
Jackson Street, 223
Arroyo Queen, 223
Iwo Jima War Memorial, 223

McAllen, 224

Mission, 225
Bentsen-Rio Grande Valley State Park, 225
McAllen International Museum, 226
Reynosa, Mexico, 226
Mountasia, 226
Mission: La Lomita Chapel, 226

Weslaco, 227
Santa Anna National Wildlife Refuge, 228
Valley Nature Center, 229
Bicultural Museum, 229

Zapata, 230
Falcon Lake and State Park, 230
Salineno, 230
Santa Margarita Ranch, 231
Col. Antonio Zapata Museum, 231
La Paz County Historical Museum, 231

Index of Birds

A

Anhinga, 63, 94, 96, 130, 200, 209, 217, 228
Ani, Groove-billed, 59, 185, 186, 195, 200, 201, 213, 217, 228
Avocet, American, 16, 40, 44, 49, 97, 169, 182, 208

B

Bittern,
    American, 156, 208
    Least, 55, 96, 156, 165, 168, 182, 200, 208, 228
Blackbird,
    Red-winged, 35, 49, 56, 70, 86, 89, 153
    Rusty, 156
    Yellow-headed, 49, 117
Bluebird, Eastern, 59, 75, 94, 115, 125, 132, 134, 153
Bobolink, 117
Bobwhite, Northern, 32, 49, 57, 62, 70, 78, 96, 99, 102, 109, 112, 155, 203, 208, 230
Bunting,
    Blue, 225
    Indigo, 22, 104, 113, 133, 134, 144, 151, 167
    Lark, 14, 28, 36
    Lazuli, 22
    Painted, 14, 40, 58, 70, 73, 77, 84, 94, 106, 113, 151, 167, 176, 208, 213, 220, 222, 225
    Varied, 18, 222
Bushtit, 14, 25, 26, 80, 102

C

Caracara, Crested, 154, 175, 195, 208, 213, 217, 222
Cardinal, Northern, 109, 115, 153
Catbird, Gray, 144, 159

Chachalaca, Plain, 217, 225, 228, 230
Chat, Yellow-breasted, 58, 75, 77, 99, 141, 151, 203
Chickadee, Carolina, 62, 96, 125, 137, 153, 203
Chuck-will's-widow, 80, 107, 117, 151, 203, 226
Coot, American, 22, 89, 96
Cormorant,
    Double-crested, 75, 88, 103, 122, 125, 153
    Neo-tropical, 122, 125, 176, 200, 205, 217
Cowbird, Brown-headed, 125
Crane,
    Sandhill, 33, 36, 40, 49, 84, 125, 149, 151, 177, 201
    Whooping, 40, 177, 196, 210
Creeper, Brown, 75, 88, 115, 122
Crow,
    American, 88, 115, 119, 155, 202
    Fish, 119
    Tamaulipas, 216
Cuckoo, Yellow-billed, 36, 44, 47, 55, 66, 68, 75, 77, 79, 88, 96, 99, 101, 106, 109, 117, 121, 203
Curlew, Long-billed, 42, 169, 196

D

Dickcissel, 36, 99, 104, 109, 142, 151, 154, 203
Dove,
    Common Ground, 200, 230
    Inca, 16, 32, 36, 44, 62, 69, 153, 230
    Mourning, 28, 47, 77, 109, 115, 121, 153, 208
    Rock, 62, 89
    White-tipped, 217, 222
    White-winged, 208, 230

Dowitcher, Long-billed, 33, 97, 169, 176, 186
Duck,
  American Widgeon, 35, 49, 53, 55, 56, 75, 84, 88, 102, 113, 153, 205, 222
  Bufflehead, 32, 55, 56, 68, 102, 113, 149, 153, 189
  Canvasback, 49, 55, 149, 196, 222
  Gadwall, 35, 49, 53, 55, 68, 75, 84, 88, 99, 102, 113, 125, 208
  Mallard, 22, 42, 49, 55, 63, 84, 88, 89, 99, 153, 205, 208
  Masked, 190, 220, 228
  Mexican, 27, 230
  Mottled, 63, 149, 158, 159, 176, 182
  Muscovy, 230
  Northern Pintail, 32, 35, 42, 49, 75, 84, 89, 102, 107, 149, 153, 205, 222
  Northern Shoveler, 35, 42, 49, 53, 55, 75, 84, 89, 107, 125, 185, 208
  Redhead, 42, 49, 84, 196, 222
  Ring-necked, 49, 84, 88, 113
  Ruddy, 22, 32, 42, 53, 56, 63, 75, 88, 153, 208, 222
  Wood, 49, 73, 79, 86, 89, 94, 96, 106, 107, 130, 134, 137, 144, 151, 156, 209
Dunlin, 97

E

Eagle,
  Bald, 43, 68, 94, 97, 102, 104, 107, 117, 119, 132, 134, 137, 141, 149
  Golden, 25, 36, 42, 48
Egret,
  Cattle, 16, 32, 89, 130, 156, 203, 205
  Great, 16, 32, 63, 88, 96, 102, 109, 113, 156, 205
  Reddish, 182, 184, 185, 186

  Snowy, 16, 32, 88, 94, 96, 102, 109, 130, 156, 200, 205

F

Falcon,
  Aplomado, 222
  Peregrine, 18, 175, 177, 217, 225
  Prairie, 14, 25, 42, 47
Finch,
  House, 25, 63, 70, 208
  Purple, 115, 122
Flicker, Northern, 35, 88, 115, 122, 144
Flycatcher,
  Acadian, 75, 80, 119, 137, 155
  Ash-throated, 18, 36, 40, 44, 80, 151, 213, 220
  Brown-crested, 19, 203, 222
  Great-crested, 75, 86, 107, 109, 117, 119, 137, 155, 202
  Great Kisdadee, 20, 117, 189, 200, 201, 205, 222, 228, 230, 231
  Scissor-tailed, 16, 28, 36, 40, 44, 55, 75, 80, 109, 113, 117, 132, 213, 222, 228
  Vermilion, 14, 16, 18, 20, 40, 58, 73, 75, 78, 189, 213, 220
  Yellow-bellied, 196
Frigatebird, Magnificent, 169, 192, 217

G

Gallinule, Purple, 96, 151, 168, 182, 195, 208, 217, 228
Gannet, Northern, 163
Geese,
  Canadian, 42, 44, 125, 141, 142, 175
  Greater White-fronted, 117, 125, 141, 142, 149, 175
  Ross's, 42, 49, 117, 149, 175
  Snow, 43, 117, 125, 142, 149, 158, 175, 177
Gnatcatcher,
  Black-tailed, 27, 29
  Blue-gray, 75, 79, 84, 86, 102, 107, 109, 137, 151

Godwit,
  Hudsonian, 177
  Marbled, 97, 169, 185, 196
Goldeneye, Common, 103, 149
Goldfinch, Lesser, 25, 63
Grackle,
  Common, 45, 89
  Great-tailed, 45, 89
Grebe,
  Clark's, 16, 53
  Eared, 16, 35, 49, 53, 56, 75, 84, 88, 119, 149, 192
  Horned, 35, 49, 53, 84, 88, 103, 119, 125, 144
  Least, 200, 201, 209
  Pied-billed, 16, 22, 32, 35, 42, 55, 56, 63, 68, 75, 84, 88, 89, 94, 96, 106, 113, 125, 137, 144, 149, 153, 156, 176, 185, 200, 205, 208, 217, 228
  Western, 16, 35, 49, 149
Grosbeak,
  Blue, 14, 18, 36, 44, 55, 58, 62, 70, 133, 134, 151, 208
  Evening, 45
  Rose-breasted, 159
Gull,
  Bonaparte's, 102, 132, 208
  California, 216
  Franklin's, 156
  Glaucous, 216
  Herring, 35, 132, 216
  Laughing, 193, 216
  Lesser Black-backed, 216
  Ring-billed, 33, 35, 55, 68, 102, 119, 132, 208
  Slaty-backed, 216
  Thayer's, 216

H

Hawk,
  American Kestral, 42, 53, 57, 134, 137, 142, 154, 175, 217
  Black, 18, 35
  Broad-tailed

  Cooper's, 32, 47, 78, 99, 106, 149, 154
  Ferruginous, 14, 28, 36, 42, 48, 154
  Gray, 18, 228, 231
  Harris's, 14, 208, 222, 228, 230
  Northern Harrier, 36, 47, 53, 99, 106, 149, 154, 175
  Red-shouldered, 78, 79, 88, 112, 151, 208, 228
  Red-tailed, 14, 29, 42, 48, 49, 53, 57, 79, 113, 121, 142, 149, 154, 175, 208
  Rough-legged, 14, 36, 53
  Sharp-shinned, 47, 99, 106, 154
  Swainson's, 28, 42, 47, 117, 121, 125
  White-tailed, 175, 177, 190, 195, 222
  Zone-tailed, 80
Heron,
  Great Blue, 16, 32, 42, 58, 68, 73, 75, 79, 84, 86, 88, 96, 99, 102, 103, 106, 107, 109, 113, 137, 153, 201, 205
  Green, 16, 44, 66, 73, 86, 96, 99, 102, 106, 113, 137, 156, 173, 200, 205
  Little Blue, 86, 96, 102, 107, 113, 130, 137, 156
  Tricolored, 96, 130, 205
Hummingbird,
  Black-chinned, 16, 21, 44, 47, 59, 66, 68, 77, 79, 80, 84, 86, 101, 113, 151, 173, 203, 213
  Buff-bellied, 203, 217, 228
  Ruby-throated, 106, 109, 117, 155, 165, 173, 202
  Rufous, 173

I

Ibis,
  White, 63, 96, 103, 130, 149, 163, 165, 176, 208, 217, 222
  White-faced, 63, 103, 163, 165, 167, 176, 182, 208, 217, 222

J

Jacana, Northern, 220
Jay,
  Blue, 32, 45, 88, 96, 109, 115, 202
  Green, 189, 200, 201, 217, 222,
    225, 228, 230, 231
  Western Scrub, 26, 32, 36, 40, 62,
    78, 80
  Stellar's, 25
Junco, Dark-eyed, 14, 37

K

Killdeer, 28, 55, 68, 89, 99
Kingbird,
  Cassin's, 14, 26
  Couch's, 45, 186, 201, 205, 213,
    217, 222, 228
  Eastern, 109, 117, 119, 134, 154,
    201, 209
  Western, 40, 47, 55, 84, 106, 109,
    117, 125, 153, 201
Kingfisher,
  Belted, 27, 32, 56, 66, 68, 70, 73,
    79, 94, 96, 99, 106, 107, 137,
    144, 205
  Green, 20, 66, 73, 79, 137, 151,
    205, 209, 213, 217, 225, 228,
    230
  Ringed, 217, 225, 230
Kinglet,
  Golden-crowned, 37, 75, 88, 99
  Ruby-crowned, 37, 75, 84, 88, 99,
    104
Kite,
  Hook-billed, 228
  Mississippi, 40, 84, 113, 121, 142
  White-tailed, 175, 217, 228
Knot, Red, 169, 193, 216, 217

L

Lark, Horned, 36, 42, 122, 125, 134
Loon,
  Common, 16, 88, 103, 117, 119,
    121, 177
  Pacific, 103

Longspur,
  Chestnut-collared, 14, 36, 59, 122,
    156
  Lapland, 36, 122
  McCown's, 14, 36, 59, 122, 156
  Smith's, 16, 36, 104, 122

M

Martin, Purple, 69, 134, 142, 154
Meadowlark,
  Eastern, 62, 84, 99, 115, 125, 132,
    208
  Lillian's, 16
Merganser,
  Common, 55
  Hooded, 55, 56, 122, 149
  Red-breasted, 68, 103, 141, 196
Merlin, 217
Mockingbird, Northern, 70, 109, 115
Moorhen, Common, 22, 89, 96, 168,
  190, 228

N

Nighthawk,
  Common, 44, 69, 84, 113, 115, 121,
    134, 203, 225
  Lesser, 203, 225
Night-Heron,
  Black-crowned, 42, 49, 88, 96, 196,
    200, 208, 217, 220
  Yellow-crowned, 42, 63, 88, 96, 109,
    113, 130, 137, 149, 173, 203,
    217
Nutcracker, Clark's, 45
Nuthatch,
  Brown-headed, 128, 137
  Pygmy, 25
  Red-breasted, 75, 115
  White-breasted, 94, 115

O

Oriole,
  Altamira, 225
  Audubon's, 225
  Baltimore, 109
  Bullock's, 20, 25, 36, 40, 55, 58, 208

Hooded, 217
Orchard, 19, 25, 36, 40, 55, 58, 62,
 165, 208, 222
Scott's, 18
Osprey, 97, 102, 104, 177, 217, 222
Oven Bird, 159
Owl,
 Barn, 22, 225
 Barred, 33, 75, 79, 88, 107, 151,
  203
 Burrowing, 28, 36, 40, 42, 45, 48,
  49, 186, 190
 Eastern Screech, 75, 78, 79, 80, 88,
  107, 151, 203, 225
 Elf, 18, 225
 Ferruginous Pygmy, 190, 230
 Long-eared, 200
 Great Horned, 22, 32, 44, 75, 78,
  80, 125, 200, 203, 225
 Short-eared, 36
Oystercatcher, American, 169, 177,
 182, 185, 196

P

Parakeet, Green, 217
Parrot,
 Red-headed, 217
 Yellow-headed, 217
Parula,
 Northern, 119, 137, 151, 203
 Tropical, 190, 222, 225
Pauraque, 195, 200, 203, 225
Phalarope, Wilson's, 43, 97, 177
Pelican,
 American White, 16, 33, 53, 88,
  103, 117, 119, 121, 125, 132,
  169, 185, 200, 208, 217, 222
 Brown, 169, 177, 217
Pheasant, Ring-necked, 36, 43, 44
Phoebe,
 Black, 14, 18, 20, 26, 27
 Eastern, 32, 70, 102, 104, 109, 222
 Say's, 21, 22, 26, 27, 29, 201
Pigeon,
 Band-tailed, 25
 Red-billed, 190, 230, 231

Pipit,
 American, 53, 122
 Sprague's, 122, 163, 190, 201
Plover,
 American Golden, 63
 Black-bellied, 33, 169
 Piping, 196
 Semipalmated, 33
 Snowy, 40, 44, 49, 182, 196
Poorwill, Common, 26, 44, 66, 79, 80,
 99, 226
Prairie Chicken, Greater, 148, 163
Pyrrhuloxia, 16, 18, 21, 29, 32, 186,
 200, 205, 213, 220, 225, 228, 230

Q

Quail,
 Gambel's, 21
 Montezuma, 25
 Scaled, 19, 21, 27, 28, 29, 35, 36,
  47, 49, 59, 200, 213, 230
 Green-tailed, 18

R

Raven,
 Chihuahuan, 28, 216, 222, 230
 Common, 79
Rail,
 Black, 177
 Clapper, 165, 167, 168, 177, 196
 King, 168
 Virginia, 35, 141, 156, 168
 Yellow, 56, 168
Redstart, American, 141
Roadrunner, Greater, 26, 29, 57, 59, 68,
 69, 70, 78, 99, 102, 155, 200, 203,
 222
Robin,
 American, 45, 115
 Clay-colored, 190, 225

S

Sanderling, 193
Sandpiper,
 Baird's, 169

Buff-breasted, 169
Least, 33, 205
Spotted, 55, 205
Upland, 63, 169
White-rumped, 33
Sapsucker, Yellow-bellied, 88, 115
Scaup, Lesser, 68, 75, 88, 113, 144, 153, 189, 205
Seedeater, White-collared, 230
Skimmer, Black, 158, 186, 196
Shrike, Loggerhead, 29, 109, 125, 132, 134, 142, 151, 213
Siskin, Pine, 45, 122
Solitaire, Townsend's, 37
Sora, 156, 168, 169, 190, 228
Snipe, Common, 16, 33, 141, 169
Sparrow,
    Baird's, 16
    Black-throated, 27, 29, 47, 53, 59, 68
    Botteri's, 216, 222
    Brewer's, 14, 22
    Cassin's, 49, 59, 222
    Chipping, 14, 22, 62, 73, 75, 80, 84, 106, 122
    Clay-colored, 14, 22
    Field, 73, 80, 84, 102, 104, 106, 113, 122, 125, 151, 154
    Fox, 70, 73, 80, 96, 99, 102, 106, 117, 122, 142, 151
    Grasshopper, 14, 49, 73, 104, 151, 163
    Harris's, 70, 73, 84, 96, 99, 123, 151
    Henslow's, 111
    Lark, 22, 28, 40, 49, 59, 68, 69, 102, 106, 106, 113, 151, 154, 185, 213, 222
    Leconte's, 99, 132, 141, 151, 163, 190
    Lincoln's, 22, 62, 70, 73, 96, 99, 102, 106, 117, 122
    Nelson's Sharp-tailed, 177
    Olive, 19, 185, 201, 203, 213, 217, 222, 225
    Rufous-crowned, 27, 29, 35, 40, 57, 59, 79, 80, 84
Savannah, 53, 70, 73, 99, 102, 106, 132
Seaside, 165, 167, 177, 196
Song, 56, 62, 70, 73, 84, 96, 99, 102, 106, 117, 122, 132, 142
Swamp, 56, 96, 102, 117, 142, 151
Vesper, 22, 70, 73, 75, 84, 96, 102, 106, 117, 141
White-crowned, 22, 62, 70, 73, 76, 80, 84, 96, 99, 102, 123, 142
White-throated, 62, 70, 73, 75, 80, 96, 99, 102, 122, 132
Spoonbill, Roseate, 96, 163, 165, 176, 184, 196, 208, 217, 222
Stilt, Black-necked, 16, 40, 44, 49, 89, 150, 169, 176, 182, 185, 208
Stork, Wood, 63, 96, 178, 185, 200, 208, 217
Swallow,
    Barn, 45, 70, 78, 115, 134, 142, 154, 213
    Cave, 18, 20, 45, 69, 203, 208, 213
    Cliff, 18, 20, 66, 69, 78, 154, 203, 213
    Northern Rough-winged, 18, 45, 109, 134
    Tree, 134
    Violet-green, 25
Swift,
    Chimney, 69, 134
    White-throated, 14, 20, 22, 25

T

Tanager,
    Hepatic, 25
    Summer, 73, 75, 77, 80, 86, 106, 107, 151, 159, 222
    Western, 159
Teal,
    Blue-winged, 32, 35, 56, 107, 185, 205, 222
    Cinnamon, 33, 35, 56
    Green-winged, 32, 49, 55, 75, 88, 89, 99, 102, 106, 125, 153, 222
Tern,
    Black, 119, 122

Caspian, 119
Forster's, 68, 97, 117, 119
Least, 94, 97, 119, 205
Sandwich, 192
Sooty, 192
Thrasher,
Brown, 109, 115
Crissal, 21, 27, 53
Curve-billed, 16, 18, 28, 35, 47,
    208, 220, 222
Long-billed, 18, 200, 201, 203, 208,
    213, 217, 225
Sage, 53
Thrush,
Gray-cheeked, 196
Hermit, 75, 99, 222
Wood, 137
Titmouse, Tufted, 32, 36, 62, 78, 84,
    86, 96, 101, 104, 106, 107, 137,
    144, 153
Towhee,
Canyon, 40, 47, 57, 69, 79, 80, 84
Eastern, 117, 137
Green-tailed, 18, 22, 53
Spotted, 22, 73, 99, 117
Turkey, Wild, 35, 59, 68, 70, 78, 96,
    102, 134, 155, 200, 203
Turnstone, Ruddy, 169, 185, 186

V

Verdin, 21, 22, 53, 68, 217, 222
Vireo,
Bell's, 58, 70, 99, 203
Black-capped, 77, 99, 101
Black-whiskered, 159
Hutton's, 25
Philadelphia, 196
Plumbeous, 25
Red-eyed, 62, 73, 79, 96
Warbling, 14
White-eyed, 68, 77, 79, 96, 99, 102,
    106, 109, 113, 137, 155, 225
Yellow-green, 222
Yellow-throated, 73
Vulture,
Black, 79, 208

Turkey, 79, 208

W

Warbler,
Black and White, 86, 119, 138
Colima, 18
Golden-cheeked, 62, 63, 66, 68, 73,
    77, 78, 79, 80, 99, 101, 106
Hooded, 138
Kentucky, 119, 151
Orange-crowned, 53, 222
Pine, 119, 138
Prothonotary, 94, 104, 151, 213
Swainson's, 138, 151
Yellow, 55
Yellow-rumped, 53, 122, 222
Yellow-throated, 119, 138
Waterthrush, Louisiana, 142
Waxwing,
Bohemian, 45
Cedar, 45, 84, 106, 115
Whip-poor-will, 226
Whistling Duck,
Black-bellied, 89, 96, 149, 156, 182,
    200, 201, 205, 208, 209, 222,
    228
Fulvous, 176, 182, 228
Willet, 97, 169
Whimbrel, 193
Woodpecker,
Acorn, 18, 25, 26
Downy, 37, 86, 88, 96, 106, 107,
    109, 112, 121, 137
Golden-fronted, 19, 27, 32, 40, 44,
    45, 66, 69, 70, 79, 102, 125,
    189, 203, 205, 208, 217
Hairy, 107, 134
Ladder-backed, 16, 32, 44, 68, 70,
    79, 86, 101, 106, 112, 125,
    205, 208, 217
Pileated, 119, 128, 134, 137, 150,
    151
Red-bellied, 62, 73, 86, 88, 96, 106,
    107, 109, 112, 121, 153, 202
Red-cockaded, 128, 133, 137
Red-headed, 128, 133, 173

Wood-Pewee, Eastern, 66, 80, 117, 119,
    137, 155
Woodcock, American, 128
Wren,
    Bewick's, 22, 26, 36, 40, 47, 53, 57,
        63, 78, 79, 80, 84, 112, 142,
        151, 213, 217, 222
    Cactus, 20, 21, 26, 27, 29, 32, 47,
        53, 68, 84, 203, 217, 222
    Canyon, 20, 21, 26, 68, 79, 80, 84
    Carolina, 45, 78, 80, 86, 112, 144,
        185, 217

House, 73, 122, 142, 208, 222
Marsh, 56, 156, 167, 168, 169, 178
Rock, 21, 26, 59, 79
Sedge, 141, 142, 163, 169, 208, 222
Winter, 88, 122, 141, 208

Y

Yellowlegs,
    Greater, 16, 33, 176, 208
    Lesser, 16, 33, 89, 97, 169
Yellowthroat, 165